USHER M

Lessons

FROM THE SET

A DIY GUIDE TO YOUR
FIRST FEATURE FILM
FROM SCRIPT TO THEATERS

Published by:
Library Tales Publishing
www.LibraryTalesPublishing.com
www.Facebook.com/LibraryTalesPublishing

Copyright © 2019 by Usher Morgan
All Rights Reserved
ISBN: 978-1732888814
Published in New York, New York.

For general information on our other products and services, please contact our Customer Care Department at 1-800-754-5016, or fax 917-463-0892. For technical support, please visit www.Library-TalesPublishing.com

Library Tales Publishing also publishes its books in a variety of electronic formats. Every content that appears in print is available in electronic books.

PRINTED IN THE UNITED STATES OF AMERICA

A DIY GUIDE TO YOUR FIRST FEATURE FILM FROM SCRIPT TO THEATERS

USHER MORGAN

About the Author

Usher Morgan is a filmmaker, entrepreneur and studio executive residing in New York City. He produced his first documentary film, *The Thought Exchange*, starring David Friedman and Lucie Arnaz in 2012, followed by his directorial debut, the award-winning short film *Prego*. His first feature film, *Pickings*, was released to critical acclaim and received a limited theatrical release via AMC Independent in March of 2018.

Table of Contents

"Pick up a camera. Shoot something. No matter how small, no matter how cheesy, no matter whether your friends and your sister star in it. Put your name on it as director. Now you're a director. Everything after that you're just negotiating your budget and your fee." ~ James Cameron

Introduction

It's Saturday night, and you find yourself inside your local movie theater. You take a seat in a dimly-lit room with a bucket of popcorn and an oversized cup of soda. The previews are kicking in – all the movies that are yet to come; the personal dreams of folks who have spent years of their lives making a single product that is now trying to grab your attention. You watch trailer after trailer for what seems like an eternity when, finally, the lights begin to dim and that infamous studio logo kicks in and everyone goes quiet – it's starting.

At that moment, you and everyone else around you are under the spell of the dominating voice inside that room – *that* is the voice of the filmmaker. You have willingly given your time and money to a deity whose sole purpose is to entertain you – and you *want* to be entertained; you want to feel, think, cry, laugh, and applaud as the story takes you into another time and place. You want to be enchanted, taken by the hand, and given a new experience (all within the course of 100 or so minutes), and every once in a while, you get your wish. Every once in a while, you leave the theater with a smile. The filmmaker to whom you've given your precious time and hard-earned cash delivered the goods; they succeeded in meeting your expectations and that *feels good*. That movie was "amazing!" It was worth the investment; it was something to remember, and more importantly to the filmmaker, it was something to talk about.

But every so often, the cards are not stacked in your favor. Every once in a while, you go into the theater with the same expectation but leave with a frown – the story wasn't funny or sad; it didn't make you "feel" anything; you didn't laugh, or cry, or applaud; it didn't take you anywhere or give you any new experiences, and, if anything, it left you with a feeling of annoyance or disappointment. In short, you were *not* entertained. The filmmakers had taken your hard-earned money, stolen your time, and failed to deliver on the promise they made. Your expectations were shattered, and you feel bad.

Most of the time, however, something else happens, and that something is... well, "nothing." Most of the time, you walk in, watch a movie, and walk back out when it's over, and the film you've just watched slips your mind by the following morning and rarely ever enters it again. This is where 50% of movies exist, in my opinion; they're good, but not great; they're entertaining, but not memorable. When someone approaches you in December and asks for a list of this year's "favorite films," these movies will never be on that list, mainly because you don't remember seeing them.

Enter the Filmmaker

Filmmakers actually have a lot in common with their audiences, mainly because they're both expecting to have a *good* experience; the filmmaker who made the movie you watched really wants you to have a good time. After all, no one wants to be a "disappointing filmmaker" and no legitimate filmmaker ever wants to make a bad movie. So as a filmmaker, much like the audience member entering the theater for the first time, you also find yourself surprised by how well (or how poorly) your movie is being received. If the audience loves it, you're happy and if they hate it, you're not and if they forget about it, you move on. Most filmmakers want to entertain people, to make them laugh, cry, applaud, and engage with their story – that is *why* they became filmmakers to begin with: to evoke emotion, to get people thinking, to get them talking. You've decided to become a part of a group of people who tell stories for a living, and your goal is, in most likelihood, to create memorable films that go on to make money, gain recognition, and be seen by audiences around the world.

So, How Did You Get Here?

Do yourself a favor. The next time you find yourself inside a movie theater, ask yourself the following question: "What was it, *specifically*, that convinced you to buy a ticket to this particular movie?" Can you track your decision to watch this film back to a single event? A "thing" that you were exposed to that made you go, "Oh yeah! I'm buying a ticket!" Did you watch a really cool trailer? Did you read about the film on Facebook? Get a recommendation from a friend? Understanding how you got into a movie theater in the first place will be of great use to you once you start designing your own marketing campaign in the not-so-distant future. It's something that I try to be conscious of every time I find myself inside a movie theater.

Now, a lifetime of industry statistics will say that the "thing" that drew you to the movie theater at that very moment was a combination of (a) **exposure** – meaning the movie is either notable enough to be featured in the media, or the distributor has enough of a budget to advertise and market it offline/online; (b) **brand/ name recognition** – the movie stars an actor or is directed by a filmmaker that you admire, it is based on a book that you've read, or is a part of a franchise that you love; (c) **content** – the content is appealing, the trailer evokes a reaction, TV spots are stirring an excitement and anticipation within you, the story seems really good, and the visuals are impressive; (d) **reviews** – the media talks about the film in a positive way, word of mouth and your inner circle are all saying that this is a movie that they either *want to* see, or that you *have to* see. These are the ABCs of marketing, and they apply to almost any and every product out there. There are many other elements at play, but they are fairly insignificant in comparison. If a movie meets any one of those criteria, it will draw an audience, and the more criteria it meets, the bigger the audience is going to be. So, if a movie gets a lot of press (**exposure**) but nothing else, it may still draw a significant number of viewers. On the other hand, if a movie has great content but no exposure, it will not draw a significant number of viewers and, unfortunately, there are many documented cases of amazing films with no-name talent and very little exposure that died at the box office and exist primarily in obscurity. On the other hand, I'm sure you can name a few box office smash hit films that were critical failures. Lastly, and this may not come as a shocker to you, if a small, independent film has **brand/name recognition** (like a recognizable cast or a celebrated filmmaker), it will *automatically* receive interest from the media (**exposure**). If the content is bad, it'll be destroyed by negative reviews, negative articles, and negative word of mouth, but if the content is good, it will be praised. All of that is *ammunition* that the distributor will use during their marketing campaign to try and convince you to drag your ass out of the house and visit the movie theater, and then, once you've done that, to sell you on the DVD, Blu-Ray, soundtrack, and watch the movie on-demand. That, in a nutshell, is how you got inside that theater and how you put food on the filmmaker's table.

> *"Talking about dreams is like talking about movies, since the cinema uses the language of dreams; years can pass in a second, and you can hop from one place to another. It's a language made of image. And in the real cinema, every object and every light means something, as in a dream." ~ Federico Fellini*

The Revenue Game

Making movies for a living is something that *a lot* of filmmakers aspire to. Being in a position where you can make films and release them to theaters or straight to video on a consistent basis is the ultimate dream for most, but it is also a cause of frustration and anxiety to many. I believe it to be the main reason why so many good people who venture into this business quit before their time. The cost associated with making films, along with the pressure and artistic skill demanded, and the obligation to adhere to budgets and generate revenue, can prove to be a challenging feat that many people assume is beyond their capabilities. There are plenty of people who proudly wear the "broke artist" tag and look with distaste upon those who go into this business for the dollar. The one thing that many "broke artist" types fail to keep in mind is that the movie business is a *business* and, like any other business, your job is to produce a great product, cost efficiently, sell it to consumers, and generate enough money so you can make more products. More products mean more revenue – that *is* the nature of any product-based business. The only way you can sustain your business is by making movies that generate revenue, and if you lose money on every film, you won't last long.

Now, as far as I know, there are two key ways by which you can derive your income from making and selling feature films: (a) you can make a movie and sell it to a distributor; or (b) make a movie and sell it on your own. That's it, really. However, when most independent filmmakers think about the prospect of getting their movie made and sold, they'll opt to go for option A. They'll send it to major film festivals in hopes that during their circuit, the movie will hit a cord with a capable distributor who would show an interest in buying it. If the distributor is *big*, they may get a theatrical release, and a good deal of money could follow. They'll be featured in the press, be courted by agents, and have an easier time getting funding for their next project – and life will be grand! And if the distributor is *small*, the movie will go straight to DVD/VOD/ Blu-Ray, and they'll make a little less money and maybe have to work a little harder to get their next movie lined up, and the next one – *it* will be the big break they've been waiting for.

Take any of those filmmakers and offer them the opportunity to distribute their own films and they'll snigger, "I'm not interested in doing marketing or handling sales; the business side of moviemaking is not something that I'm really interested in. I want to focus on making movies and let other people worry about selling them." There is nothing wrong with that approach, it is, as the name states, an *approach* – it's just one way of doing things. In fact, it's the go-to approach for a big chunk of the filmmaking population. However, what do you think will happen if you take that very same filmmaker and give them a failed festival circuit? Meaning their film got accepted into festivals, but no one bothered to buy it; no one licensed it or showed any interest in distributing it... Well, now these very same filmmakers are in "panic mode." They'll eventually make their way to signing a deal with an online film distribution company, and their movie will most likely die in obscurity. These online, independent film distributors are the kind that'll put your movie up on VOD and leave it there for seven years without doing a lick of marketing or promotion. They call themselves "film distribution companies," but in reality, they're more like vanity book publishers. They're "movie brokers" – meaning they take your movie, put it on iTunes, Amazon, Xbox, Google Play, and other VOD channels via an aggregator (to which you, as a filmmaker also have access), and maybe send a press release out via their website and social media channels, and that's it. The offer you get when you sign the contract is usually $0 in advance but 30% of the net, and you feel confident in the fact that you have a distributor and that your movie will finally see the light of day. A month later, the film comes out to VOD, and this "distributor" didn't put a dime into P&A (Print and Advertising). They didn't market the movie, they didn't *sell* it, they didn't build a marketing plan for it, and they don't intend to push it, promote it or sell it. It gets very few reviews from the indie-fans who might buy it online, and after two years of selling, you still haven't seen a dime – because the distributor had "marketing expenses" that kept you from actually seeing a profit. Believe it or not, that is the actual situation that many independent filmmakers find themselves in after spending years of their life pouring their hearts and souls into the making of their indie features. They hope and pray that it'll get picked up during the festival circuit and are willing to give up their rights to do so because the thought of leaving the festival circuit without a deal is terrifying.

Enter the DIY Film Distributor

This is where the current state of DIY film distribution comes into play. Some filmmakers who failed to sell their movie at a film festival and are not interested in giving away their rights to a vanity distributor would say "the hell with it." They'll bypass the broker and submit the movie to the aggregator on their own. If they can't afford the iTunes fees, then they'll send it straight to Amazon's Media on Demand and Video Central (free services that let you sell your movie on Amazon in both VOD and DVD/Blu-Ray formats), and other alternative services like Vimeo on Demand until they can afford the cost of selling on iTunes. That is all fine and dandy, but there is one major flaw in their strategy, which is: they don't have one. A big percentage of indie filmmakers who opt to self-distribute their films have no distribution or marketing plan in mind. They don't know what they're doing, so they'll either spend themselves to death trying to market the movie or put it up on Amazon with no marketing and get upset when the film fails to sell.

Independent filmmakers who are making a living via their art don't find themselves on one end of the spectrum or the other – it's wrong to say that if you want to make a living in movies then you must distribute your own content. It's also wrong to say that you should only focus on your art and leave the film distribution business to other people – and that is where this book comes into play. The purpose of this book is to prepare you for both scenarios: the best-case scenario, where you make a movie and sell it at Sundance, and the worst-case scenario – where you wrap your festival tour with no sales and are forced to distribute the film yourself.

This book is designed to give you real-world advice from someone who's *been there* and *done that*: made a movie and got it in theaters, did his own marketing, sold it, got reviews and earned enough money back to get to work on his next film.

It took a lot for me to make my first feature film, *Pickings*. We shot it for 35 days over the course of a year, and while I'll dig deeper into the making of it in later chapters, for now all you need to know is that after a year of tasking principal photography, peppered with all sorts of production problems and obstacles, our shoot was concluded (against all odds), and we had to go through an extensive post-production process to finish it. Long story short, it was picked up by AMC Independent, released to twelve theaters across six major cities and screened at several indie movie theaters in strategic locations. It received wide acclaim in periodicals such as the *Los Angeles Times, Hidden Remote, Film Journal International* and more. A few months after its theatrical release, the movie was sold to China and a couple of other territories. And as I am writing this book, it's making the rounds on VOD/DVD/Blu-Ray and has already recouped a big chunk of its cost. Since I didn't have any investors – every cent is coming back to my production company, which is now hard at work on my next feature (which I don't plan to fully fund myself, by the way) – you can say that I am now making movies "for a living." I earn 100% of my revenue, and I don't have to share it with a small, insignificant "vanity distributor" who would have let my movie die in VOD hell.

I guess the thing to keep in mind when deciding to enter the world of independent film is that you are, in fact, *independent*. Meaning, you are not tied to anyone or anything. You're not restricted to a singular strategy, you don't have a prior commitment to unions or guilds, and you're not expected to break box office records. You work independently; you are an *entrepreneur* working in the entertainment industry, and your products are motion pictures. So, if your goal is to make movies and sell them to a big film distributor at *Sundance*, this book will give you a lot of insight into the successful making of a feature film on a shoestring budget. And if you don't sell, then it's time to hit the Entrepreneur button and sell it yourself, in which case, this book will give you some life-saving tips on how to accomplish that successfully and turn a profit during your film's theatrical release. I wanted to write a book that I wish I could have read when I first took the plunge and dived into the independent filmmaking business, and this book does just that. It'll give you the tools you need to write, direct, produce, shoot, edit, market and sell your movie – independently.

The Job Description

When most people buy a movie ticket, they don't really think about the process of getting that movie made. They don't know what goes into the creation and distribution of a feature film and, to be frank, most people don't care, nor should they. They paid good money to be entertained, and if you've done your job well, they'll salute you; if you failed, they'll curse you; and if you did okay, they'll forget all about you. Their job is to watch your final product; your job is to make it, make it good, and make it on time and under budget, which is, of course, easier said than done.

In an interview for the *Los Angeles Times*, Alejandro Gonzalez Iñárritu (*The Revenant, Birdman, Babel*) was quoted as saying, "To make a film is easy, to make a good film is war. To make a very good film is a miracle." If you have had the pleasure of making a feature film from start to finish, you know exactly what Iñárritu was talking about. The process of writing, rewriting, budgeting, rewriting, casting, scheduling, planning, rehearsing, rewriting, shooting, solving problems, doing post, and handling the release of an independent feature film is a daunting one, and it can get especially rough for first-timers. I honestly think that the process is designed to test one's spirit and resolve, and it is in the difficult moments that we find out just how important film is to us. And if you *love* film, if you truly enjoy the process, then filmmaking becomes extraordinarily rewarding. The hard work pays off, and you find yourself addicted to the hustle.

When you are producing a low-budget indie film, you are expected to produce a piece of art in a financially responsible way

XV

and make decisions that reflect your business acumen, reflect your talent, and match your ambition at the same time – that to me, is an oxymoron, but it's also the job description. Your job is to express your artistic spirit while putting harsh limitations on yourself at the same time and finding creative ways around these limitations. It's to tell a story in an effective way without going over budget; it's to make an entertaining piece of art that people would want to pay money for and watch again and again and again. As an indie filmmaker, you can feel as if you're being torn apart between "business" and "art." The financial element limits you, and your creativity frees you. You have a million-dollar dream, but only $50,000 to work with. It's a delicate balance – mixing art and business, but it does get better with practice. The more movies you make, the more you learn how to handle yourself, the more confident you grow. And, if you keep your mental attitude in check and refuse to get discouraged when you fail, you can *only* grow. Soon enough, you'll find new ways of merging your business acumen with your artistic vision and use the two together in synergy to produce better pictures on schedule and under budget.

Get Experienced

In today's age, you don't need to be a sophisticated or particularly wealthy businessman/woman to produce and sell a commercial feature film, and there are countless books out there dedicated to teaching filmmakers the secrets to the craft of independent filmmaking. These are books that deal with the specific step-by-step processes involved in writing, planning, producing, fundraising, directing, marketing, and selling movies for a living. However, after reading many of these books myself and then making my own feature film from start to finish, I came to the realization that not many of them gave me the *education* I needed to survive my own experience. Not many of them delved into "days on set" and they mostly dealt with theory. The ones that were written by actual filmmakers never really covered "the DIY business" element and the commercial aspect of being an independent filmmaker.

This book is all about one thing: preparing you for the experience of making a movie and selling it, whether you sell it to a distributor at a festival or directly to the consumer. Ultimately, the only way to gain real-world experience is by working in the real world and gaining actual experience. But if you educate yourself about the process before jumping in the pool, you'll have a better chance of making it to the other side. Learning from the experience of others will give you a great deal of confidence, and it will save you money, time, and effort.

This book covers the most effective DIY approach to writing, directing, producing, and distributing your film to a wide audience, winning awards, getting reviews, getting press, and building the base for your next feature film. It offers valuable insight into the process of making and selling a feature film – from the very start (the idea) to the very end (distribution and foreign sales); from screenwriting to scheduling, pre-production to post-production; from writing checks to dealing with insurance companies, getting permits, solving problems, handling marketing and social media – basically, everything you'll ever need to know about the process, every lesson I learned along the way, and everything I wish I knew when I was first getting started in this business. If you want to venture into the world of low-budget, independent filmmaking, the information presented in this book will be a *life-saver!*

"When given an opportunity, deliver excellence and never quit." ~ *Robert Rodriguez*

What's Your Dream?

There are many ways to define "success" in this business. For some, it's money, fame, and recognition, and the more of it they have, the more successful they feel. For others, it's the ability to make movies for a living, to generate enough income from their films that they can live off it and use the revenue to make more films until they eventually die on set. For others, it's legacy – the thing they leave behind for future generations. For some, it's art, while for others it's just a business. Different people define it differently, and I'm sure you'll agree that none of those people are "wrong." There is no right or wrong when it comes to your own definition of success, but it is very important that you have one. Without knowing what constitutes success and aiming your efforts to achieve it, you could end up getting discouraged, even if you are closer to your goal than you realize. So, let me give you your first piece of "homework." I want you to write your *purpose* down on a piece of paper; write down your "dream," and be specific. Is it money in the bank? The ability to work alongside your favorite actors? Or it is that golden statue in your living room? Whatever your purpose in this business is, whatever your *ultimate goal* is, you should be conscious of it and take daily action towards achieving it.

Passion Wins the Game

Filmmaking is not the easiest endeavor in the world, nor is it fast, cheap, or passive. The process of writing, directing, producing, releasing, and marketing feature films is an ambitious one, and it takes time, practice, and dedication to succeed in this business. So it goes without saying that there are many who venture into this industry with hopes and dreams of succeeding, only to fall short and leave the game before they ever get a chance to win it. In other words, they see how hard it is, get frustrated by rejections, and quit – and I don't blame them. This is a hard business, but then again, the same can be said about *any* business. Any experienced filmmaker will tell you that the biggest difference between people who win and people who lose in this game is *passion*. Passion is obsession, it's energy, it's a sense of purpose. It's that thing that drives you to make a movie from the get-go, it's what gives you the power to persevere, it gives you a sense of excitement; it keeps you from getting discouraged and helps you sustain your vigor as you get rejected over and over and over again. Passion is the fuel that will keep you in this game long enough to win it and motivate you to improve your craft with every new project you work on. I think the ultimate question that every filmmaker should ask themselves is: "Do you really love movies?" And if the answer is yes, then you can't help but make a movie; the world can't stop you.

Strive for a Higher Standard

"Quality" is an interesting word because I don't think that it can be easily defined. It is, however, easily observable. You can spot bad picture quality from good picture quality; you can tell the difference between low-quality sound and high-quality sound. There are *standards of quality* that are easily observable by almost every person who knows what a movie is supposed to look and sound like. These are your **"Basic Standards,"** something that you can see and immediately judge without perspective or an understanding of the movie as a whole. And then there are standards of quality that are not easily observable, standards that require an investment of time, and these are your **"Analytical Standards."** So, if the picture and sound quality of a movie refer to the Basic Standard, then the quality of the story itself, the characters, and the narrative would be the Analytical Standard. At first glance, 95% of audiences will be able to decide if they want to watch your film (or not) if it meets or exceeds their Basic Standard. If the quality of your film isn't distractingly bad, if it's well-edited, well-acted, and well-directed, it could pique the interest of many people who could potentially pay their money and invest the time to watch it. The more your movie exceeds the average person's Basic Standard, the bigger the chances that audiences would be interested in watching it. The job of a film critic is to tell you whether a film adheres to their own Analytical

Standard, and these standards vary from person to person. Different people like different things, and while there is a degree of consent regarding what constitutes a good story, good plot, character, etc., there is always a variation there, and *that* is why it's fairly rare to have a 0% or a perfect 100% rating on Rotten Tomatoes. There will always be people who hate a film that other people love, and there are many films made today for hundreds of millions of dollars which have mastered and far surpassed your Basic Standard. They are beautiful to look at, the visuals are spectacular, and the technical side of the film borders on perfection; however, some of those same films do not adhere to most people's Analytical Standards. In other words, the story is crap. But even those films will have their admirers.

I have no problem with watching a movie that was shot on an iPhone, as long as the picture and sound aren't distractingly bad, but there is one condition to that tolerance (at least for me). To pique my interest and get me to pay money and spend two hours of my life watching a movie that was shot on an iPhone, it has to have really great content. In other words, it needs to adhere to my personal Analytical Standards, which are pretty high, and that's where movie critics come in. Movie critics are there to tell me if a movie is likely to adhere to my personal Analytical Standard, so I tend to view the Rotten Tomatoes score as "the chance I'll like this movie." And that is ultimately the message that I am trying to convey to you: in the film business, **content is king!** And your standard should be high and get higher with every film you make. So, if you lack access to the equipment that'll make your movie look and sound amazing, you'd better deliver on a really well-told story. And whether your film was shot on the Arri Alexa or the Apple iPhone, its quality will ultimately be defined by how all the different elements come together and mix into a single, coherent product – from beginning to end. Image quality, sound quality, writing quality, the quality of the edit, the acting, the pacing, directing, and lighting are all taken into account and judged by individuals and critics alike. Your aim should be to improve your craft with every new project you undertake; otherwise, you run the risk of standing still. There's nothing wrong with making B movies, low-budget guerilla films, and movies that lack a certain standard, especially if that's done on purpose. But if you're trying to move ahead to something bigger, or if you're trying to master the art of these B movies, you'll need to strive for a higher standard with each new picture. Be critical of yourself, be judgmental of your product, and give yourself the right amount of shit to motivate yourself into improvement (too little won't move you, and too much will kill your spirit). The ultimate goal is to keep this in mind: when you're finished with a script, criticize it, then improve it; when you're finished with a shot, criticize it, then improve it and reshoot it; when you're finished with a cut or an edit, criticize it, improve it, and keep going until it meets your standard. Once you get in the habit of being positively critical of your own work and setting a higher bar for yourself, the quality of your work will improve, and your films will get noticed. To be 100% frank, if you've made a masterpiece, like a *true* cinematic masterpiece, almost every film festival will accept it, every distributor would want it, and audiences will flock to watch it. But that rarely happens on your first low-budget indie film. So, raise your standards and strive to make your movies better.

Sign a Pledge

At the end of the day, the more you do something, the better you get at doing it, which is why you need to *practice.* I'm a big believer in the "just do it" strategy. Go out there, take an iPhone and an actor, and shoot something good, something entertaining, something that's worth watching. Learn to write, direct, move the camera, edit, and color grade your pictures. Take the time to improve your craft, combine theoretical knowledge with practical experience to produce higher quality products with every new project you make. There are people out there who *are* making it happen, and today almost anyone has access to a high-quality 4K camera. This is by far the most effective route if you choose to dedicate yourself to the craft and become a full-time filmmaker. Make a short film a month until you have the skills, connections, and confidence you need to proceed to the next step. Sign a pledge – it can be to make a no-budget short film per month, a feature a year, three hours of daily writing, an hour of learning, or whatever other commitment you'd like to make. The point is to *commit*, and once you commit to it, you *have to* make it happen. Just go out there and shoot, make movies, and repeat.

Keep a Journal

One of the reasons that I am able to write this book today is because I keep a detailed journal of everything I do right and everything I do wrong on every shoot I'm on. Every mess-up on set is recorded; every time I used creativity to solve a problem, and every move I made along the way is well-documented, and before I jump into a big project, I will usually review my notes from previous projects. I write lessons learned on working with actors and mistakes I made with exposing a certain type of camera; I note time-stealing mistakes and document everything that happens on my set. It's a practice that I can't recommend enough. Keeping a private filmmaking journal is a great tool that will help you improve your craft, and it's a foolproof way of making sure that you won't repeat the mistakes of the past. Reading it every once in a while puts you in a grateful state of mind and helps you maintain a sense of perspective on how far you've gone and how much fun you had on set. At the end of the day, the purpose of a journal is to remind you of the things you've done right and the things you've done wrong – it's the summary of your education, and it's worth writing in and reading every once in a while.

Be a Business Person

One of the reasons that many independent filmmakers "fail" in their efforts to make movies, build an audience, and gain notoriety is because they are looking at the world of filmmaking as an art form, which it absolutely is; however, even the best artists know that a beautiful painting does not exist unless there's someone out there who's willing to look at it. The moviemaking business is a business and, like any other business, it needs to be entered into with the understanding of how the business works. So the first thing to keep in mind is that you are about to venture into the "business" of making, marketing, and distributing movies, whether you sell your film to a distributor or distribute it yourself. The game is the same.

Directing the frame on the set of "Pickings" with Elyse Price

"If you can film an idea in your mind, follow that film idea shot for shot, scene for scene, that idea is worth making." ~ Craig Mapp

PART ONE
Screenwriting

Above All – Be a Writer

Movies are the amalgamation of artistic talents and technical know-how, coming together to tell a story through moving pictures, and, while technical know-how is readily available, it is the artistic talent that's a little harder to come by. And above all other talents, in my opinion, is the *ability to write* that will ultimately make the difference between success or failure in this business. Think about it: how many bad movies with big budgets are being made every year? And how many of those big-budget films are made by amazing technicians who've mastered the visual arts? Almost all of them, but it seems that the one thing that's missing from these films is the great script, and that's because good screenwriters are hard to come by.

It takes real courage to jump through a glass window while your whole body is on fire; it takes real patience to work with actors; it takes a lot of energy and creativity to light a scene and a really good eye to maintain it on camera; it takes a great ear to handle a mix and an amazing skill to masterfully paint a face. But above all else, the process of writing takes *everything* from you. It takes time, it's personal, and it can be very emotional, and without it nothing else really matters. Every single artist and technician who works on a movie set is working for the sole purpose of realizing the written word and putting it on the screen for the world to see. The script is the film's blueprint, it's the holy grail, it's the beginning of all things – and it's the art that I think you should spend the most time mastering. The better you get at writing, the better you get at making movies and the greater your chances of success in this industry. Now, there are many great directors who aren't writers, and that is an approach you can take, but I think that much like everything else in the DIY world, if you know how to do it yourself, you'll save yourself a lot of time, money, and resources. The journey you take to "prove yourself" as a competent director won't hinge on mere chance, personal connections, or the need to secure someone else's screenplay.

Ideas Are Not Stories

When I first got started in this business, I was obsessed with the "idea" of coming up with a "great idea." I thought that if I was ever to make my own movie, it had to be an "amazing idea," so I spent a good deal of time trying to come up with ideas that were "ground-breaking," only to learn one very important thing about ideas: *"Ideas are small parts of your story; they are not the story itself."* How many bad movies have you seen in your life that were based on really cool plot ideas? And how many great movies have you seen that are based on very plain, very simple ideas? Ideas get integrated into your plot, character, and visual style *as you write* the script, and they evolve alongside it. When a person tells me that they have "an amazing idea for a movie," it basically means that they have *"an amazing idea for a plot"* – which means absolutely nothing. You can have the best plot idea in the world, but that doesn't mean that the movie will be any good, or that it will ever get made. Also, having a "great idea" is of no value if you (the person pitching the idea) are not a capable screenwriter. If you don't know how to write a great script, you'll be relegated to hiring writers or trying to sell the idea to movie studios. If you can't write it yourself, of what worth is your "great idea?" If you want to be an independent filmmaker and make movies in the very near future, you'll need to sit your ass down and do some writing. The BIG difference here is between a *screenwriter* (someone who comes up with ideas and puts pen to paper) and an idea person (someone who's trying to profit from their ideas prematurely without doing any of the work).

> *"Screenwriting is the most prized of all the cinematic arts. Actually, it isn't, but it should be."*
> *~ Hugh Laurie*

How to Profit from Your "Great Ideas"

If you have great movie ideas in your head, but you don't know how to write, I suggest you take that as a sign from the universe that you should pick up a pen and put your great ideas down on paper and *learn* to write. Write a treatment, follow up with a 90-page script, then rewrite it, perfect it, register it, copyright it, and put it in front of people who can make it, or make it yourself. At that point, you no longer have a great idea; you have an actual screenplay that you can get made in the real world. The time and effort you put into your amazing idea will pay off big-time, and you'll be on your way to making something real happen. The sad thing is that many "idea people" don't really want to do the work; they just want to try and shop their ideas around. So I take the simple, practical approach that requires nothing more than hard work, hustle, and determination: take your movie idea and write it down, turn it into a great script, and only then will you have a shot at making something real happen.

Don't Let "The Great Idea" Get in Your Way

When I was writing *Prego* in 2015, my "idea" was to write a movie that shows what happens when a one-night stand results in a pregnancy with a simpleton. I immediately recognized, however, that my idea was far from original. In fact, it's been done a thousand times, a thought that lingered with me as I wrote, directed, produced, and ultimately released the film to festivals. At the time, I felt like I was making a mistake; I was kicking myself for not doing more to come up with an "original idea." I refused to watch it, grew resentful of the film, and was disappointed with myself for being an "unoriginal filmmaker." And then the festival circuit started, and *Prego* won almost every award it was nominated for, and I got bombarded with emails and screening requests. I released it online, and it quickly went viral, amassing more than a million views on YouTube and getting translated into five different languages. The relative "success" of this short sparked a debate inside my own head about the importance of the "original idea," and I soon came to realize what I should have known all along: *it's all about the quality of the script, not the originality of the idea!* Now, there is no doubt in my mind that an original idea can contribute greatly to the overall experience of watching a film, but not having one should not stop you from writing your film. You can work wonders with the simplest idea once you master the art of screenwriting.

The Best Ideas Come to You "While you Write,"
Not "Before you Start"

While it's true that *Prego* was not an original idea, and it's FAR from being a great film, there are *some* original ideas within it. For example, I decided to present the short from the female's point of view, something that I felt wasn't really done before. Some of the best jokes in the film came in later drafts, and the idea of having the room go dark as we dive into her point of view also came out during a final rewrite of the script. I can say with complete confidence that the best "ideas" came to me *while* I was rewriting my script (meaning while I was working/hustling/getting stuff done), not *before* I got started. Some people decide not to start writing until the great idea comes as a flash of inspiration, believing that they need to have the idea first before they ever put pen to paper. This is the biggest contributor to "writer's block," in my opinion, and I found that *hustle* tends to be the only cure.

The more I write, the more ideas I get, and the better my ability to distill the great ideas from the ones that don't really serve the story. And when you are immersed in the world you have created, ideas that pertain to the structure, characters, and visuals of the film would come popping into your mind throughout the day. Especially when you're not anywhere near a keyboard or a pen. This used to happen to me a lot while I was writing my first feature film, *Pickings*. I'd jot ideas down during the day and try to add them to my script during writing sessions.

Don't Try to Reinvent the Wheel

Take a look at the following synopsis: "A high school senior from the wrong side of the tracks longs for adventure, sophistication, and opportunity, but finds none of that in her Sacramento Catholic high school. Our film follows the character's senior year in high school, including her first romance, her participation in the school play, and, most importantly, applying for college." That is the official synopsis for the Oscar-winning film *Lady Bird* – and it should serve as a lesson to everyone who thinks that they need a "great idea" before they can start writing a movie. The great ideas in this film came out of the screenwriter's effort to produce an original piece of work, and they are integrated into the screenplay, but the core idea itself would be categorized by "idea pitchers" as "boring" at its worst or "simple" at its best. Movies like *Lady Bird, The Florida Project, Before Midnight, Reservoir Dogs, Friday, Dazed and Confused, Dark River, Beast,* and *Wild,* to name just a few, are the ultimate proof, in my opinion, that a great movie plot idea is nice to have, but it means nothing at the end of the day. The only thing that matters is "the screenplay" as a whole, the complete body of work. It's your ticket to making an amazing film, not the "great plot idea."

Ask the Right Question

Having said all of the above, you still need to know what your next movie is going to be about, if you don't already, and to do that, you need to have an "idea." So how do you conceptualize a film? How do you know what story justifies you sacrificing the next few years of your life making? There are two questions, when asked, that will give you the answer you seek: *(a) **What kind of story do I want to tell?** And (b) **why do I need to tell that particular story?*** This may seem like an oversimplification, but those two questions are the driving force that will keep you hustling for the next one-to-three years as you labor over your next feature film. A good movie comes from *within*, it's personal to the filmmaker. It means something to you. And, in my opinion, the only thing that matters when you're coming up with your next movie idea is that you have an emotional or personal connection it. You need to have a pretty good reason for making it. Making a movie for the sake of making a movie is a waste of everyone's time and money but making a movie that's *important* to you is something that will never go out of style. Those are the type of stories that linger on and make an impact on people. That connection, that "importance" is your mission statement – it is the reason for *why* you are choosing to make this particular film – and it will get you through countless production hardships. If you're an immigrant, write a story about an immigrant (literally or in the form of an allegory); if you lost a family member or have gone through a personal trauma, that's the story you should be telling next. Your next character should ideally be struggling with something that you are emotional about. That, in my opinion, is the master key to a good idea.

Plots Are Cool; Characters Are Cooler

If you make a list of your all-time favorite movies, I'm pretty sure that it will align with a list of your all-time favorite characters. Stories are driven by characters, not plots. Take the most boring character in the world and try to impose upon him the plotline of Neo in *The Matrix* and the movie wouldn't be half as good. Alternatively, take *Anchorman's* Ron Burgundy and throw him into the plot of *Fifty Shades of Grey*, and the movie would be a blast to watch. Characters are what make a movie tick; they are the fuel that drives the story – not the other way around. Focus your energies on writing characters. A good place to start would be to make a list of your all-time favorite characters; what is it about these characters that you find so appealing? What are the specific traits that make them interesting? And how did the filmmakers get you to empathize with these characters? I often dig into film analysis when I find myself attracted to a particular character; I try to study the reason within myself for liking, admiring, or being fascinated with a character.

7

Good Ideas Come from Research

The process of writing a screenplay always involves research, whether it's watching documentaries or other films, interviewing people, reading books, or just plain old self-discovery. When you research a topic, you get a lot of new information about it and about the characters that live within that world. It doesn't matter how well you think you know the subject matter – spend the time to research plotlines, characters in history, props, time periods, science, visual style, and other works of fiction. It costs almost nothing, and it pays off big time. In an interview for *Playback* with Kris Tapley, filmmaker Ryan Coogler said that much of what ended up in the *Black Panther* movie originated from his trip to Africa as part of his research, and while you don't have to go to Africa, you can access similar information by using the power of Google, reading, and conducting interviews. Do your research!

The Shower Principle

Have you ever wondered why the best ideas tend to come to you when you're in the shower? Or why it is that when you're a young child, your imagination is that much more active than when you're an adult? Well, the reason is quite simple: distractions and the lack thereof. When your mind is focused on an activity and when you are actively doing work that requires focus, your mind is focused on the job at hand, but when you do *nothing*, the brain allows itself to get distracted, to wander off and daydream. That's why kids are so much better at it than adults; they can take the time required to play and use their imagination. As adults, we have access to that precious time every once in a while: in the shower, when we play golf, when we're out for a morning walk, when we're stuck in traffic, and when we spend time doing tasks that don't require our brain to overwork. Sometimes that includes cleaning, doing dishes, etc. So when you lack the inspiration, put on your headphones and go out for a ten-minute walk. The purpose of this walk is to think actively about what it is you're currently writing (a scene, a character, a logline, etc.), then go back home and meditate, take a long shower, or just chill for a few minutes. Give yourself some time to play around in your mind, act out a scene, or visualize a sequence without pressure or restraints. This is what I do sometimes when I need inspiration, and it works for me! I hope it does the same for you.

Good Ideas Come from Reading

It sounds like a cliché, but it's true. The more books you read, the more you use your imagination, and the more you use your imagination, the easier it is to come up with new ideas. Books, whether in the form of novels, memoirs, or nonfiction, are a treasure trove of good ideas, and they can quickly get you thinking about and asking yourself questions about your own ideas. Keep a notepad handy and write notes, ideas, and thoughts as you're reading; you'll notice that notepad filling up pretty darn quickly. I find that whenever I need a creative boost, the best thing to do is go back to the basics – *reading*. It never fails. Books are also good tools to help you "visualize," and visualization is key for good writing and good directing. I keep a reading list for every new project I am working on. So if you're not writing about something, read books about writing. Out of all the advice in this chapter, this would be the one that'll make the biggest difference in your writing. The more books, scripts, and literary content you consume, the better writer you become.

"I spend most of my days pacing around, muttering that I have no ideas, feeling like I'm walking a plank." ~ Aaron Sorkin

Inspiration Comes from Music

I cannot tell you how many times I've walked down the street, headphones on, music blasting, and when a new song began to play, I instantly got an idea for a scene, a sequence, a shot, a character moment, or a storyline. I hate to think that I'm the only one experiencing this because, for me, it's just so darn effective. If you've never tried this before, I recommend you give it a shot. The next time you feel stuck or in need of inspiration, go out for a walk, put on your headphones, and listen to a *new* piece of music.

Write a Personal Story

One of the things that you are guaranteed to be an expert on is your own personal experience. The movie world is full of great movies that are extremely personal to the people who wrote them. From *Lady Bird* and *The Big Sick*, where the story is either inspired by or influenced by the filmmaker's personal experience, *to The Pursuit of Happyness, Hidden Figures,* and *The Wolf of Wall Street,* where the story is based on a book, written by the person who's gone through these experiences. The reason why these stories are so good is that the characters in these stories are generally the authors themselves. In many other cases, the story, subplots, and characters could be inspired by real life but also remain hidden under a cloud of fiction. A good example of these types of storytellers are the likes of J.K. Rowling, whose deep depression inspired the creation of the "dementors" in *Harry Potter*; Jerry Siegel, who created *Superman* as a result of being bullied in school; William Moulton Marston, who created *Wonder Woman* based on his own personal experience with powerful women; and as recently as Larry David and Jerry Seinfeld, creating a TV show where its characters and plots are based on the writers' actual life experiences. There are many, many more writers who created popular characters and stories based on their own life experiences and hid them well within the confines of fiction and genre so that they are not considered "based on true events." Try thinking of some life events, traumas, or catharses that you could write about, either literally or as allegories; every human being should have at least one of these in their arsenal.

"Borrow" from Real Life and Hide it Well

Continuing with the notion that great ideas, great plots, and characters are inspired by true events; the event itself doesn't need to have anything to do with you or your personal experience (in my opinion, it's better if it does, but it doesn't have to). You could easily decide to base your movie, your plot, and your characters on other real-life events, people, or circumstances that you're drawn to; the key is to hide it well. There are many characters in the world of fiction that are based on the likes of real-world people (Adolf Hitler, Vlad the Impaler, Al Capone, Winston Churchill, etc.). Stan Lee wrote *Ironman* as a fictionalized superhero version of Howard Hughes; *Batman* creators Bob Kane and Bill Finger based The Joker on Conrad Veidt's character, Gwynplaine, from Paul Leni's 1928 film, *The Man Who Laughs*. Alfred Hitchcock said that Norman Bates, the *Psycho* villain, was directly inspired by body snatcher Edward Gein; Don Draper from the TV show *Madmen*, was based on real-life ad man Draper Daniels; the beloved 1930s cartoon character Betty Boop was influenced by the mannerisms of singer/actress Helen Kane, and those are only a few examples. Many great characters, stories, and plots begin as personal obsessions of the writer – what happens if we tell a Romeo and Juliet story on the Titanic? Well, it's the movie *Titanic*! What happens if we take Bonnie and Clyde and turn them into mass murderers? *Natural Born Killers*. Take a real story that you're obsessed with, change the characters, and fictionalize it.

> *"When I'm writing something, I try not to get analytical about it as I'm doing it, as I'm writing it."*
> ~ Quentin Tarantino

The Power of Writing Exercises

I love writing exercises! They're designed to help you develop the skills you need to become a better writer. They challenge you to create great plots, characters, intentions, and obstacles and can often give birth to new movie ideas. I recommend doing at least a few of these "writing exercises" every month; you'll never know what kind of script or story they will inspire. I made a short film called *Fine Dining* based on a screenplay challenge in 2017; they are powerful tools that'll help you fine-tune your writing skills and, more importantly, get your imagination going on a consistent basis. Solving problems in writing is a life-saving skill. I recommend you get a copy of *150 Screenwriting Challenges* by Eric Heisserer, the writing exercises within it could change the way you write. In my opinion, writing exercises are the fastest route to becoming a better writer as well as being an immediate idea generator.

Write About Your Obsessions

Take a subject you're obsessed with – it can be anything from Nazis to computer hacking, sex dolls to bank robbers, fast cars to bird watchers – whatever it is, it must be something that you are obsessed with, something that you either love or hate, something that you either understand well or want to explore, something you find *fascinating* for any reason. For the sake of this example, we'll go with Sex Dolls. Next, pick an existing character you're either obsessed with or want to explore or understand well – let's say Dirty Harry... Now, keep in mind that when I write Dirty Harry, I'm not talking about Dirty Harry; I'm talking about a character that is inspired by Dirty Harry in one way or another. So are you getting a picture inside your head? A rough, tough lawman develops a relationship with a sex doll... (let that sink in). Okay, forget Harry and his doll; let's explore some ideas based on this formula of taking a subject and mixing it with an existing character you like:

Subject = Illegal Street Racing
Characters = Mad Hatter; Al Capone
Plot = An elusive, psychotic, illegal race car driver suffering from a Dissociative Identity Disorder steals the prized supercar of a notorious mobster and races it to the top.

Again

Subject = Computer Hacking
Characters = Sherlock Holmes; Zorro; Rapunzel
Plot = A private detective hires a selfless white horse hacker to track down his missing daughter after a recent picture of her is found circulating the web.

Again

Subject = New York City; Getting Stuck in Elevators
Characters = Santa Claus; Ebenezer Scrooge.
Plot = A reclusive, stingy billionaire with a bad reputation gets stuck in an elevator for two hours with a jolly old man on his way to give gifts to the poor and needy on Christmas Eve.

These are just off the cuff – they're not loglines or synopses – they're just ideas. You can use this formula to come up with new and creative ideas for plots that are based on cool characters or subject matter that *you* find interesting. Ultimately, it'll be your job to make sure that the "mashup" fits and that the story is worth telling, but if you write it down, you'll be surprised at how many ideas come into your mind as a result of this tool. Practice makes perfect; try using this approach to write a screenplay for a short film.

Reinvent History

Take any historical event you can think of. It could be ancient history, modern history, Greek history, or something that happened in your hometown six years ago. Mix it up in a pot, and you have yourself a plot (I didn't mean for that to rhyme, I guess that's just the magic of writing). Reinventing history is a popular writing trick that a lot of filmmakers turn to for creative ideas and inspiration; you can take a historical event and change it up in any way you'd like. From unsolved murders to the first black LAPD officer, any real-life event can be retold in any way you choose to tell it. You have creative license to write about the subjects that you want to write about, whether they're based on true stories, inspired by true stories, or *are* true stories buried behind an allegory. The universe and all the stories within it are yours for the writing. The only rule is… *"don't be boring!"* There are a lot of stories on Wikipedia, from pioneers to people you've never heard of, key events, murders, disappearances, government conspiracies, and much, much more. There is plenty of source material out there. You've just got to find it and have a good reason for writing it.

The "What If" Approach

This is my personal favorite approach to coming up with movie plot ideas. You take any circumstance, either real or fictional, and add a "What if…" to it. For example, what if Winston Churchill had an affair with his assistant? What if Gandalf had a wife and kids? What if human beings invaded earth as an alien species? What if a man and a woman who hate each other are forced to spend three days handcuffed to each other after a hostage situation leaves them stranded? What if the nerdiest man in the world was trying to get together with a supermodel? What if the coolest guy in school fell in love with a friendless loser? What if the best country singer in the south was a Pakistani immigrant with a beautiful singing voice and a love for American country music? What if a man was living inside your apartment walls? What if your neighbor was a sought-after serial killer, but he had a wife and kids and lived a normal life? What if a conservative man/woman learns that their husband/wife was born in the opposite sex? What if you woke up in the New York City Subway every night at 2:00 a.m., regardless of where you fell asleep the night before? The "What if" game works! Write down five to ten "What if" scenarios and see what kinds of ideas you come up with.

The Zero Dollars Idea

A big chunk of the no-budget/low-budget filmmaking community is always on the hunt for great ideas for movies they can produce for absolutely no money (or for very little money). There are some common approaches to making a $0 movie, and we cover them in later chapters. But, as far as story ideas are concerned, these can be a good jumping-off point:

1. Movies Shot on Free Location / Big City
Following; Before Midnight

2. One-Location Movies
Phone Booth; Friday, Buried; 127 Hours; Wreck

3. Movies Shot in Real Time
Silent House; Rope; Before Sunset

"Good ideas are common – what's uncommon are people who'll work hard enough to bring them about." ~ Ashleigh Brilliant

Pick Your Theme

Every good movie ever made has a strong theme, and that theme is the story's DNA; it's the overlaying idea that defines and drives your story, the characters, plot, and dialogue. You must be able to narrow your film down to a specific theme and stick with it from beginning to end. A theme can be a lesson, or the underlying moral of the story. For example, one of the key themes of *The Dark Knight* can be found buried within a specific line of dialogue: "Some men just want to watch the world burn;" the theme for *When Harry Met Sally* is "man and woman can never be friends; sex always gets in the way;" *Chinatown*, "You can get away with murder if you have enough money." Ideally, you should be aware of your movie's theme early on and keep it in mind as you write your characters, and the plot thickens.

Theme Categories

While the film's theme can be put into either a question (can money buy happiness?) or a statement (some things cannot be bought), at the end of the day, your theme will most likely stem from one of the following categories. These are some of the most common themes explored by novels, films, and short stories:

- Man vs. Nature – Stories that pin man against the powers of nature. *(Jaws, 127 Hours, Jurassic Park, Cast Away, The Grey, Wild)*

- Loss of Innocence – When a young protagonist is introduced to or thrown into the complexity of adulthood. *(To Kill a Mockingbird, Toy Story 3, Pickings, Empire of the Sun)*

- Man vs. Self – Stories that explore internal conflicts, illness, addiction, rites of passage, etc. Often, these films present the protagonist as his/her own worst enemy. *(Al-*

most Famous, A Beautiful Mind, Wall Street, Silver Linings Playbook, American Beauty)

- Revenge – Stories as old as humanity itself. *(Oldboy, Kill Bill, Death Wish, Hard Candy, True Grit, Once Upon a Time in the West)*

- Man vs. Death – Movies that explore the inevitability of death and the way in which human beings deal with it. *(The Bucket List; The Fault in Our Stars; Me, Earl, and the Dying Girl; The Lovely Bones)*

- Battle Movies – Stories that revolve around physical conflict and battle, either between two individuals, two nations, two worlds, or two galaxies. *(300, Saving Private Ryan, Avengers Infinity War, The Lord of the Rings, Pearl Harbor)*

- Man vs. Society- Stories where an individual is fighting against the injustices of society, social norms, or authority. *(Schindler's List, Fight Club, A Few Good Men)*

- Triumph over Adversity – When the human spirit fights to triumph, and when an exceptional character is stuck in a bad situation – you have yourself an inspirational story about the true power of the human spirit. *(Forrest Gump, The Shawshank Redemption, The Pursuit of Happyness, The Blind Side, Rocky)*

- Love Stories – It can be romantic, sad, or heart-wrenching, but stories about love will always tug at one's heartstrings. *(The Notebook, Titanic, Before Sunrise, Shakespeare in Love)*

- Good vs. Evil – By far the most used thematic category on this list; there's a bad guy doing bad things and a hero who stands up to stop him. It's the theme of almost any superhero film and the oldest one in the book. *(Harry Potter, Lord of the Rings, James Bond, Avatar, The Lion King, Shrek, Aladdin, Who Framed Roger Rabbit)*

Categories Meet Category

There is no rule that says that a story should adhere to a single category. For example – I'm sure you've noticed that *Lord of the Rings* appears twice on that list, once as a "Battle Movie" and then again as a "Good vs. Evil" movie. *Titanic* can be categorized as a "Man vs. Nature" meets "Love Story," etc. The purpose of this list is to help you better categorize your movie's theme; the theme and category will serve as your movie's DNA and will help guide the decisions you make along the way. It'll keep you in focus and give your film an overall *sense of purpose.*

Write Every Day

If you decide to plop down in front of the keyboard and write for 60 seconds without stopping – you've started. The only way to get started is to sit down and *write!* And to do it every day! Everyone has the same amount of available time in a day, and these days everyone has access to a computer, a tablet, or a piece of paper and can sit down for ten minutes, thirty minutes or an hour and write something down. I honestly feel as if that's the biggest hurdle for a lot of people - putting their asses down on the seat and writing the first two lines.

A good way to "force" yourself to write in the beginning is to make a ceremony out of it. Make a cup of coffee, take out a bottle of wine, prepare a playlist, and put on some music to get yourself "in the mood." Treat it like you would all your other favorite pastimes, and it'll quickly become one. And, while I understand that not everyone has the luxury of writing full-time, I do believe that you should make the commitment to write at least ten to thirty minutes per day, at a minimum.

Creating a daily writing routine is crucial if you ever plan to go beyond just "dreaming." This is the actual working part of things, and it can't be faked. If you write for a minimum of ten minutes every day, it is nearly guaranteed that those ten minutes will turn into an hour or more, because once you start writing and the creative juices start flowing, you can't bring yourself to stop. And if you do stop, that's okay too – you've gotten ten minutes in, which is a lot better than zero. Also, if you stay true to ten minutes of writing per day – that's a page (or more) a day. And the practice of writing a page a day will give you your first draft in about ninety days.

I'm a pretty busy guy, so to say that I have no free time to spare would be an understatement. However, I have the same regard to the habit of writing as I do to showering, shaving, and eating – *I have to do it*, and when you *have to* do something, you find time to do it. The act of sitting down and writing for ten minutes a day will keep you *in the zone* and keep your project fresh inside your head. It'll save you from becoming complacent, something that could ultimately lead to you abandoning your scripts and staying in a perpetual writer's block. So, write every day, make a habit of it, commit to it, and watch your stories come to life.

The Benefits of Writing Outside

Unless you live alone and have the discipline to tune out the distracting elements of your day-to-day living, I recommend you try this approach to writing. It's great to write at home when you can, but I found it helpful to experience my "writing focus" in various locations for inspiration. A few times a week, I'll head outside to write in coffee shops, restaurants, hotels, in the park, on the river, wherever I can turn an iPad on, really. I plug my headphones in and get to work; it's very therapeutic. It doesn't just "force you" to write for a prolonged period of time consecutively, but it is a known fact that merely being outside can induce creativity and help you think clearer. I have a pretty sweet setup with an iPad and a $20 keyboard case from Amazon; I just take that thing with me and can write anywhere, on any surface, at any time.

The Power of a Tape Recorder

In 2017, I found myself in a car with a young lady who couldn't stop talking! She wasn't talking to *me*, mind you, she was talking on the phone to a man she was clearly upset with, but her rhythm, her manner of speaking, her style and mannerisms reminded me of a really wacky Elmore Leonard novel. The lady was upset over the guy's lack of interest in her friends, but the way she was speaking was so compelling I couldn't keep myself from being hypnotized by that conversation. When I came back home, I tried to write that scene from memory but couldn't quite find the rhythm, mannerisms, and vocabulary that she used. Ever since then, I always keep a recorder app on my phone. When I have writing sessions with friends or when I find myself at an unexpected place, I quickly hit the "record" button. Whenever I hear great lines of dialogue spoken in the real world, they're a click away from being on my phone. The habit of recording and writing real-world conversations will help you become a better writer, in my opinion. And even though characters don't converse like regular people, sometimes, every once in a while, you'll meet a real-life person who talks like a really cool movie character, and that's worth studying!

"You love all your characters, even the ridiculous ones. You have to on some level; they're your weird creations in some kind of way. I don't even know how you approach the process of conceiving the characters if in a sense you hated them. It's just absurd." ~ Joel Coen

Write and Shoot a Silent Movie

"Character speaks louder than words" is something I heard over and over again from acting teachers and screenwriting gurus, but I never gave it too much thought until I started watching silent films and reading about the filmmakers who made them. One book that comes to mind is *Hitchcock Truffaut* by Francois Truffaut. In it, Alfred Hitchcock was talking about the power of silent cinema and how it taught him to "direct the camera and the actor without relying on verbal information."

Silent films have the power to reveal a character's true intentions, their malice, kindness, hopes and dreams, fears and pet peeves, without ever uttering a word. The marriage between the actor, their actions, and the camera is all you really need to tell a story in an *efficient* way. And say what you will about Alfred Hitchcock, he was nothing if not efficient. I am currently working on a short silent film called *Rekindle Not*. The experience is teaching me a lot about effective storytelling. You don't really need any resources, just take an actor and give him/her a strong need and put something in their way. You can shoot it on an iPhone; the quality doesn't matter because its purpose is purely educational.

Watch Silent Films

Before you make a silent film, I suggest you sit down and watch some. What you'll learn is that you don't need much to tell a compelling story; all you need is a character with a *strong desire* and something in his/her way. Using blocking to tell a story nonverbally is a treasured skill that few directors possess, and it's something I wish I'd done before I shot my first feature film. While it's true that dialogue serves a very important purpose – you should also be able to tell an emotionally moving story without relying on it. Watching and making silent films will ultimately improve your craft as a filmmaker. If you don't believe me, try watching the opening scene to the movie *Up!*; it's a masterclass in how to make someone cry in five minutes or less without saying a word.

Be Economical

Whether you plan to write, direct, and produce your script, sell it to a production company, or pitch it to your mom and dad for funding – at the end of the day, someone other than yourself is going to be reading it, and you have to keep that person in mind as you go about your writing, especially when it comes to action lines and scene description. When you write a script for a movie you plan to shoot with your friends in a warehouse somewhere, the rules are different than when you write something you plan to pitch to an agent or present to an investor, so please bear that in mind as I ramble. I used to have the need to write *long* action lines and fill the page with rich descriptions of sets, characters, and situations before writing a single word of dialogue. That habit was abandoned after I ran through the first table read for my very first feature film and noticed that it took a little over four hours to read a movie that was supposed to be two hours long. My need to "overly describe" everything was stealing valuable time from people who were there to help me get my movie made.

Scene description and stage direction should be short and to the point (Read the screenplay for the movie, *"Up!"* and the movie *"Gone Girl"* - to see what economical writing looks like). Another error I made was to write very long dialogue scenes. I had a scene that lasted thirteen minutes on paper where the key antagonist was being introduced. It wasn't really necessary; I was just falling in love with the sound of my own voice. I could have told the very same story and got the same results in four minutes. And at the end of the day, that's exactly what happened. We ended up spending a lot of time on set trying to shoot lines of dialogue that never made it into the final cut; that's time and money wasted. Take a lesson and learn to be *economical*. Another big problem with writing long, sprawling scenes is that your actors are supposed to memorize them. This is hard enough during plays, where the actors have several weeks to rehearse on a daily basis, but it'll be very difficult during the production of a low-budget indie feature that doesn't have the budget for a long rehearsal period.

Remember the Rules of "Intention and Obstacle"

The source of all drama is *conflict*, and conflict is created when "A" needs to achieve something very important, but "B" is getting in his/her way. Dave needs his job to pay the bills, but Bob is trying to get him fired; Amy is in love with Dan, but he's about to get married to Rachel; John needs to diffuse the bomb before the time runs out, but he doesn't know where it's hidden, etc. It is your job to ensure that every scene, every character, and every story abides by the rules of intention and obstacle. The heart of the story is the path our protagonist takes to overcome that obstacle and ultimately get what they want (or not). The higher the stakes, the more powerful the force that drives your character. So, whether you make a movie like *Friday*, where the characters want to defeat a neighborhood bully and get enough money to pay back a dangerous drug dealer; or if you make a movie like *Before Sunrise*, where two people fall in love despite the fact that it may be their one and only night together, there is *always* an obstacle. That obstacle should have its presence felt throughout the film until it is either defeated or not. Of course, you can always take the *No Country for Old Men* approach to narrative storytelling and just wrap the story before it is res...

Read Scripts (with a Twist)

"Read scripts" is something that I'm sure you've heard before; it is the screenwriter's guru mantra given to anyone who aspires to become a screenwriter. It's been the common cure for amateur writing for many years, and for good reason. Reading screenplays will give you a *standard* – it'll paint you a picture of what a screenplay is *supposed* to look like. Most gurus and teachers suggest that you start by reading some well-written classic films, and you'll find these in almost any screenwriting book: *Tootsie, When Harry Met Sally, The Social Network, The American President, Glengarry Glen Ross,* etc. However, while I am a big proponent of the practice, I also believe that there's a missing piece to that puzzle. I don't think you should just read well-written scripts (you absolutely should), but I also believe that you should add screenplays of movies that *you* love to that list. If "reading scripts" paints you a picture of a standard, then "reading scripts of movies that you love" will paint you a picture of your *personal* standard and your own *unique voice*. Reading screenplays of movies that you love (and other people may hate) will still better serve you than to read scripts for movies that you, personally, may not have enjoyed watching, or movies that don't speak to you but are on the "must read" lists. I say that if you *love* that movie, and you love that script – then that's *your* voice!" and most likely that will be the kind of script that you consider a masterpiece. So, if you think that *Austin Powers* is a cinematic masterpiece, that's the script you should be reading! I recommend making a list of ten movies that you absolutely *love*! Go online and read them, dissect them, and try to figure out why you love them so much.

Find Your Voice

Screenwriting guru Syd Field used to implore his students not to share their rough drafts with anyone, but to be their own harshest critic instead. If you want to find your own voice as a writer, you need to earn your own approval and build confidence within your own mind before sharing your work with other people. Everyone has different taste, and not everyone is going to like your writing, even if it's amazing. You could have been born with the magical dialogue-writing powers of Quentin Tarantino or Aaron Sorkin, but if you share your rough draft with a person who hates Tarantino and Sorkin or who just doesn't like a lot of dialogue, they'll brush it off as "too wordy" and destroy your confidence. Your natural instinct, if you respect this person's opinion, would be to revise your script to match their taste. *Big mistake!* That's the fastest way to kill your voice and become just as bland as any other filmmaker you've never heard of or get frustrated with the process and get stuck in writer's block. I made that mistake myself when I first got started, and you can bet I'll never do it again. However, having said that, I do have a select group of people with which I often share my drafts, but it's not because I lack confidence in my writing, but rather because I want to hear them *speak* my dialogue in their voice and judge its quality for myself. I am, however, fortunate in that regard because I've been working for quite some time and have built relationships with some wonderful actors whom I admire and respect. But again, if I love a piece of dialogue that they don't, it'll most likely have no bearing on my decision to keep it or cut it out, *especially* if it's there for a good reason. There's a trend of people sharing their scripts on social media groups via Facebook and the internet in general, not a trend that I'm a fan of. When you share a logline, a rough draft, or a treatment with someone who doesn't have your best interest in mind, their negativity can destroy your creativity, and their apathetic positivity can be worse.

The *big question* that you should be asking yourself is this: How will you ever find your voice if you are looking for the approval of strangers? If you've read enough scripts, if you've practiced and mastered your craft – you'll be at a point where you only need one person's feedback on your draft – yourself. Any additional feedback should only be sought from people who are going to be a part of your project, or people you know have the film's best interest in mind – the actors, the director, the producer, etc. Be careful who you choose to share your script with and how you dissect other people's feedback.

"Boys, you must strive to find your own voice. Because the longer you wait to begin, the less likely you are to find it at all." ~ Robin Williams, Dead Poets Society

Write a Movie or a TV show You Know

This is one of the oldest tricks in the book but one that I recommend wholeheartedly. Pick an episode from your favorite TV show and watch it at the end of the day before you go to sleep. Then, the next morning – sit down and write a scene from memory. Unless you've seen that episode two million times already, there will be lines of dialogue that'll slip your mind. A lot of times, you'll end up "inventing" scenes and lines of dialogue to fit the story in your mind, and some of them can be pretty good. I did the same thing with *Everybody Loves Raymond*, and the result was a silly, quirky short film about a husband and wife arguing about the validity of their emotions. The good thing about this exercise is that it lets you work with a stock character you know well and understand.

I created a script that ended up being produced as a short film, based on the opening scene to *Pulp Fiction*. The screenplay was inspired by the Honey Bunny scene with a little twist; instead of two robbers calling it quits on high-stake jobs and deciding to rob restaurants, I wrote Vlad Dracul and his wife Lisa into the scene, calling it quits on drinking blood out of hospital blood bags and deciding to kill and eat people again. You can check out *Fine Dining* on YouTube when you get a chance; it's amusing, to say the least. The visuals took about four to five months to complete, but the script was the result of a writing challenge much like this one.

Elyse Price and Joel Bernard in Fine Dining

Don't Be Afraid of the Rough Draft

There's a big difference between a rough draft and a first draft. Your rough draft, in my opinion, is the draft that no one is ever going to see but you; it's the version of the scene, or story, or line of dialogue that just goes straight from your head to the page without any filter, thought or edit. A first draft, however, is the first draft you *send out*, after taking the time to analyze your story and do some editing.

Some people think they can't write because they start writing a scene, and it sounds and looks like poop, so they throw away the page and say, "The hell with it! I can't write!" That's how many people end up in writer's block, with thirty scripts in development and not a single one that they think has any merit. The only thing standing between you and your first draft is your willingness to resist the urge to throw away the crummy rough draft. The key here is to *just write*. Even though it's bad, cheesy, idiotic, and doesn't make any sense – write the damn thing first, then read it and see what you're doing wrong, and fix it, read it again and fix it again; it's called "editing," and it's an inevitable part of the process. If you keep writing and deleting and writing and deleting, you'll end up in a loop – which will ultimately lead to you getting stuck and giving up.

"Writing the first draft of a new story is incredibly difficult for me. I will happily do revisions, because once I can see the words on the page, I can go about ripping them up and moving scenes around. A blank page, though? Terrifying. I'm always angsty when I'm working my way through a first draft." ~
Marie Lu

27

Actors – A Writer's Best Friend

If you have no actor friends, do whatever you can to find some, then add them to your group of collaborators and start sharing your work with them; make friends with them and surround yourself with them. I can promise you one thing – they are on the lookout for you just as much as you are on the lookout for them. My advice to you is to take some acting classes or attend an indie theater and hand out business cards that say "filmmaker, screenwriter, or director." Believe me – you'll be the most popular kid in school. Listening to an actor reading your lines out loud is the only way you can *really* know how good or bad your dialogue is, how clear your stage directions are, and what your movie will actually *feel* like when an actor plays the role you wrote for them. Another great benefit to having actor friends is that you get to write parts for *specific* people, which will make the quality of your work all the better. It will appear as though you are "getting more" out of your actors, because you wrote the part specifically with them in mind.

Forget the "Gift" of Dialogue

Dialogue is one of those screenwriting topics that many screenwriters drool over, either with awe or aggravation over their inability to master it. The consensus seems to be, for many indie filmmakers, that writing great dialogue is a "gift," reserved to a limited few. The very mention of the word "dialogue" brings to mind filmmakers who write captivating conversations that stands out from the rest; their characters often deliver clever dialogue that borders on the brilliant. A little research will show that every filmmaker who is known for their "gift" spent years inundated in the art and craft of writing dialogue and improved their skill over time. From Quentin Tarantino, who wrote four scripts before making *Reservoir Dogs* and spent a big chunk of his youth working at a video rental store, to Aaron Sorkin, who grew up as a theater kid, watching *Who's Afraid of Virginia Woolf?* at age nine and falling in love with the sound of dialogue. Sorkin wrote several plays before taking *A Few Good Men* to Broadway, where it piqued the interest of TriStar and became his first feature film. The same goes for David Mamet, who wrote several Broadway shows and served as a drama teacher at Yale before going into the movie business.

So, I suggest you make a conscious effort to erase the word "gift" from your mind because it implies exclusivity to which you have no access. Instead – try to understand that most of the movies you watch and love are not made by these gifted few – but rather, they are created by filmmakers like you, who practiced the craft on a consistent basis and developed their skill with every new project they made. I won't deny that there are people who appear to have an easier time learning, but all that means to me is that the people who don't will need to work harder to get to where they want to go... that's it. If you spend the time trying to improve your dialogue game, you will improve it; it's that simple. There are some great books about dialogue that you should definitely check out, books such as *How to Write Dazzling Dialogue: The Fastest Way to Improve Any Manuscript* by James Scott Bell, and *Dialogue: The Art of Verbal Action for Page, Stage, and Screen* by Robert McKee. However, at the end of the day, the best way to master dialogue is to write it, hear it, fix it, and write it again. Practice makes perfect.

Kill the Cat

One of the many reasons that *Game of Thrones* was such a remarkable book/show is because it wasn't afraid to kill its leading characters, or at the very least, severely injure them. That strategy was used by storytellers for ages as a means of "setting the stakes," and it's one of the reasons why many film critics look down on movies that present unbeatable characters who jump into dangerous fights and emerge victorious without a scratch – they're *boring!* As time goes by and audiences become more and more sophisticated, the demand for higher stakes is rising, and even superhero movies like *Avengers: Infinity War* recognize that the stakes must be higher for people to remain engaged. The characters they love can get hurt or lose the fight; in other words – *the cat could die!* Someone could lose an eye (*Thor*), be severely injured (*War Machine*), lose their best friends (*Guardians of the Galaxy*), and our hero could end up dying altogether, forever (*Logan*).

So, what Kill the Cat is actually saying is that you shouldn't be afraid to be mean to your characters. Establish the unimaginable (losing a child, a job, the car, a best friend) and then deliver the worst. Show us how your characters deal with that loss, how they grieve, bounce back (or not), and emerge victorious (or not). Don't be afraid to kill the girl they love (*The Dark Knight*), or show the cruelty of the world they're in (*Inglorious Bastards*), or force them to cut off their arm (*127 Hours*), or regret the things they didn't say (*Lady Bird*), or kill their cat, literally (*The Grand Budapest Hotel*).

The Treatment Scene Breakdown

There is a cool trick I picked up when I was writing *Pickings* that has changed the way I write and contributed greatly to the quality of my work, and that is the Treatment Scene Breakdown. While writing the treatment for a film, I'll create a simple table (see next page) and break down my script, scene by scene, beat by beat. This method will help you maximize the efficiency of your film's structure and give you an actual picture of how your movie is progressing. It's a great analytical tool that'll help you keep track of pacing and character development; it allows you to analyze your story structure and make the most out of every scene. For me, it's a substitute for putting a bunch of cards on the wall because there's more space to write stuff in, it's more fluid, and I can still reorganize the scenes in any way I want, at any stage, without missing a beat.

Scene	Short Scene Description	Scene Breakdown	Purpose of Scene / Plot Points / Character Arc
S01	Opening scene, introducing The Truman Show and its main character, our protagonist, Truman.	1. A documentary-style interview with CHRISTOF, introducing Truman; MERYL (Truman's wife) and MARLON (best friends), all speaking to the camera in a documentary style interview. During these interviews, we cut in and out of a bathroom, where TRUMAN (our protagonist) is speaking to a mirror, doubling as the lens. — **CREDITS: THE TRUMAN SHOW.** 2. Truman, still speaking to himself in the mirror, is being interrupted; he's late. Steps out.	1. Introducing the protagonist, Truman - a man unaware that his daily life is recorded and broadcasted around the world. 2. Introducing our key characters, Christoph (the creator/director), Meryl (the wife), and Marlon (the best friend). 3. A glimpse into Christoph's motivations into making the show: He wanted to create something real, unfabricated, something honest.
S02	Truman – Driving to Work	1. Day 10,909 – Truman steps out of his home, greets his neighbors (all wearing cameras, we see things via their POV); greeted by SPENCER and his DOG. We're spying on Truman from cameras placed in various locations and scenes throughout the film. 2. A huge metal spotlight drops from the sky, crashing a few feet away from where Truman is standing, right as he's about to get into his car. He picks it up and looks up in wonder. 3. Driving to work, Truman hears a news story on the radio about an aircraft shedding parts; the announcer asks his audiences to remember the "dangers of flying." Truman nods in agreement. As Truman drives to work, we reveal THE TOWN.	1. Establish Truman's daily routine; we'll come back to this later. 2. Inciting incident #1 – Truman finds the spotlight. Unsuspecting. 3. Establish how the show "manipulates" his reality; the fallen spotlight leads to a reiterated lie about how dangerous airplanes are, a motif we'll come back to. 4. The show created an entire town; various characters all know his name and interact with him.

Every decision you make in your movie should be made to achieve a *result* and have a *purpose*. This way of breaking down your treatment allows you to establish the *purpose* of each scene and understand what your character's *motivations* are for the scene in question. This will become super-handy once you start working with actors, and the dreaded "what's my motivation in this scene?" question arises. Another cool tool I use is the "key emotion table." Once I have my scene breakdown, I'll go through it, scene by scene, and for every scene and every beat, I ask myself a very important question: "What is the key emotion here?" As an audience member, what am I supposed to be feeling in this moment? Is it sadness? Happiness? Dread? Tension? Am I supposed to feel bad for a character? The response could help you visualize your shot list down the line, and maximize the scene's potential for evoking emotion (which is what a good scene is supposed to do anyway).

Analyze Your Drafts

Those of you who are experienced in film analysis may have asked the question: "Do most low-budget indie filmmakers conduct a thorough analysis of their screenplay before diving into pre-production?" The answer should be "yes!" or, at the very least, "they should." Regretfully, there are far too many who choose to dive into the making of their first film after the first draft is complete, believing that their enthusiasm alone will make their picture worth watching. You may think I'm joking – but I'm not; as a person who owns and runs his own film production and distribution company, I can't tell you how many first/rough drafts I have waiting for a response in my inbox – people who send me a rough draft of a screenplay, hoping to get it made on the merit that it was "written" or that it's done. I can't tell you how many friends I had to refuse after learning that the script they wanted me to direct was lacking and that they never took the time to edit it, polish it, and make it better. So, take a film analysis or film theory course, and if you don't want to spend the money, you can find plenty of film analysis tools on the internet (YouTube is a haven for that kind of thing).

Conducting a narrative structure analysis of your draft will make the difference between a great end product and a bad one. For me, taking film analysis courses and studying my own movies was a big source of inspiration and a great source of personal development. Analyze each draft when it's finished, take notes, and apply them to your next draft.

Show, Don't Tell

When discussing the essence of exposition with a group of screenwriters in 2018, I learned and understood *why* so many amateur writers rely so heavily on it to convey information. What is it about the nature of expositional dialogue that makes it the #1 choice of bad screenplays? The answer is – it's effective. The purpose of exposition is to give your audience an overview of a situation, introduce characters, past events, and reveal critical information about your story. However, it also has the potential to be *very boring* and could destroy your film if not handled carefully. Exposition can convey information via cleverly written dialogue that buries it within its style (*Pulp Fiction, Get Shorty*), via narration in the first two minutes of your film (*Coco, Lord of the Rings*), in a single scene (*Chinatown, The Godfather*), in text or animation format (*Star Wars, Jurassic Park*), during an intense action sequence (*Terminator, The Matrix*), or via characters that are so vivid and entertaining that they're able to mask that exposition behind a cloud of charm and whimsy (*Back to the Future, Amélie, The Life Aquatic with Steve Zissou*). Because exposition is so effective in relaying information, it is often misused by writers who lack the sophistication to use subtext. Writers who rely on exposition to tell the audience how a character thinks, feels, or what the character is about to do are by far the worst offenders, and I am greatly disappointed whenever I see small and big movies alike rely on that type of exposition to deliver information to the audience; this approach assumes that the viewer is not intelligent enough to think on their own. The key lies within the "2+2 approach" to storytelling. Pixar's Andrew Stanton talked about his "2+2 approach" to storytelling at a TED Talk in

2012. If you want to give information to your audience, the first thing to keep in mind is the *show, don't tell* approach. The second thing to keep in mind is that you don't need to give your audience an important piece of information right off the bat; you want to show them the pieces that, when put together, will give them the information they need to understand the plot. Here is a great *show, don't tell* example from one of my all-time favorite films. See if you can spot the places where a bad writer could have easily just had the characters say what they're feeling:

* * *

Sam picks up one of the books. It is called *The Girl from Jupiter*. There is an illustration on the cover of a young, alien princess with glittering tears on her cheeks. Sam examines the other books in the suitcase. He looks slightly puzzled.

SAM
These are all library books. In my school, you're only allowed to check-out one at a time. Some of these are going to be overdue.

Sam hesitates. He suddenly realizes something. He asks bluntly:

SAM
Do you steal?

Silence. Suzy nods reluctantly. Sam looks confused.

SAM
Why? You're not poor.

34

Suzy stares at the books. She absently brushes some dust off them. She rearranges them slightly. She says finally:

> SUZY
>
> I might turn some of them back in one day. I haven't decided yet. I know it's bad. I think I just took them to have a secret to keep. Anyway, for some reason, it makes me feel in a better mood sometimes.

Sam thinks about this. He leans his chin against his fist. He says seriously:

> SAM
>
> Are you depressed?

Suzy bites her fingernails. She shrugs.

> SAM
>
> How come?

Pause. Suzy says philosophically:

> SUZY
>
> Well, I can show you an example, if you want -- but it doesn't make me feel very good. I found this on top of our refrigerator.

Suzy looks into her leather folder and shuffles through some pages. She withdraws a small pamphlet.

```
INSERT:

The cover of the pamphlet. There is a
drawing of a broken teacup and the title
"Coping with the Very Troubled Child."
Sam frowns. His eyes widen.
```

Moonrise Kingdom
WES ANDERSON

* * *

The Cure to Expositional Dialogue

Subtext is the underlying meaning of the words that are coming out of your character's mouth; everything your character says should have some meaning or carry some weight that either gives us an insight into the way the character thinks, feels, or in some way helps to advance the plot without relying on exposition. In other words, *writers resort to expositional dialogue when they don't have a real understanding of the character's motivations.* Usually, when a character in a well-written screenplay dives into exposition, it's to relay important information to another character who doesn't already have it. Poorly written screenplays, on the other hand, use exposition to relay the character's thoughts, opinions, and to state facts that the characters are already aware of, but which must be repeated out loud for the sake of informing the audience. This is where the chart I illustrated in the treatment breakdown comes into play. When you know the character's motivations in a scene, when you truly understand your character, you can write their dialogue in a way that expresses what they feel and think without actually saying it. For example:

* * *

CHARACTER A
Were you leading them on?

CHARACTER B
No. I wasn't.

CHARACTER A
Well, then. Why hadn't you raised
any of these concerns before?

CHARACTER B
Because this whole thing is
ridiculous, and frankly – a big
waste of my time! How much longer
are you going to force me to sit
here and listen to your clients
lie about me? I shouldn't even
be here right now; I should be
at my office where I make more
money and do more than you and
your clients put together.
    (beat)
I'm smarter than you are. I'm
better than you are.
    (beat)
I'm changing the world, and it's
something that these blood-
sucking parasites will never
understand. So, fuck you.

* * *

This is a scene with zero subtext. The character has a thought in his head about the situation at hand, and so he goes out and says it in an unfiltered, unimaginative way – in other words – *it's boring!* Let's give it another go:

* * *

                    GAGE
    Were you leading them on?

                    MARK
    No.

                    GAGE
    Why hadn't you raised any of
    these concerns before?

                    MARK
                (quietly)
    It's raining.

                    GAGE
    I'm sorry?

                    MARK
    It just started raining.

                    GAGE
    Mr. Zuckerberg, do I have your
    full attention?

                    MARK
    No.
                    GAGE
    (beat)
    Do you think I deserve it?

                    MARK
What.

                    GAGE
Do you think I deserve your full
attention?

                    MARK
I had to swear an oath before
we began this deposition and I
don't want to perjure myself,
so I have a legal obligation to
say no.

                    GAGE
Okay. "No" you don't think I deserve your attention.

                    MARK
I think if your clients want
to sit on my shoulders and
call themselves tall they have
a right to give it a try. But
there's no requirement that I
enjoy sitting here listening to
people lie. You have part of my
attention - you have the minimum
amount. The rest of my attention
is back at the offices of Facebook
where my colleagues and I are
doing things that no one in this
room, including and especially
your clients, are intellectu-
ally or creatively capable of
doing. Did I adequately answer
your condescending question?

                    39

```
GAGE just looks casually at MARK. MARK
doesn't meet his gaze, or the looks from
DIVYA, TYLER and CAMERON...
```

The Social Network
Aaron Sorkin

* * *

I hear a lot of people ask the question, "How do I learn to write great dialogue?" Well – *that's* your answer. Reading well-written screenplays by talented screenwriters will help you sharpen your dialogue writing skills, but *understanding subtext* is what makes for great dialogue writing.

Take Great Dialogue and Ruin It

A cool trick I learned from a screenwriting teacher is actually practiced in the previous example. Take a really good scene, with really clever dialogue, and rewrite it – with lots of exposition. The goal is to take what the characters are saying, but instead of being clever and hiding their true meaning behind subtext, it serves you to write the scene unfiltered, much like the previous example from *The Social Network*. This exercise will give you a window into the mind of a character and is the quickest teacher to show you the difference between what a character means and what a character says.

> *"I admire writers such as Elmore Leonard who can nail a character in three or four lines of dialogue, so he doesn't need pages of back story or clumsy exposition." ~ Mark Billingham*

The Exposition Test – A Line by Line Review

As we established before, there are several degrees of offenders in the expositional dialogue game. The biggest offenders are the ones narrating information that is clearly visible on screen or that can be presented inside the frame. This is usually the first indication of a first-time writer who didn't take the time to write a second draft. These will go something along the lines of, "Oh, my God! Look! There's a car heading our way, and we're about to crash into it!" It may sound dumb, but I'm sure you've seen a few of these offenders before, which only proves my point – people are still making movies in 2019 with characters who speak this way. The second worst offenders are by far more common; they are the ones narrating information that the characters already know (but the audience doesn't) for the sole purpose of informing the audience of a new piece of information. A famous example of this type of expositional dialogue can be found in the Disney animated film *Big Hero 6* (surprisingly, because the rest of the movie is actually pretty good):

* * *

TADASHI
What would Mom and Dad say?

HIRO
I don't know. They're gone.
They died when I was three, re-
member?

* * *

This sort of exposition won't kill your film, but it shows a serious lack of creativity and, in my opinion, is just lazy. Ask yourself this question: How would you write the very same scene? Or would you come up with another creative way of translating the same information to the audience?

* * *

TADASHI
What would Mom and Dad say?

Hiro says nothing, his eyes drops to the
floor. Silence. CUT TO: a shot of an old
family photo in black and white; it meets
Tadashi's gaze.

* * *

Do yourself a favor: sit down and write a scene where two siblings
are having a discussion, and the death of the parent comes up.

Character is Defined by Choices

Many first-time screenwriters try to establish characters by giving
them lots of dialogue (I'm guilty of that as well). But true character is revealed when a character *does* something, not just when
they *say* something. It is revealed by the choices they make, in how
they handle *external conflicts* (struggle between the character and
an outside force) as well as their *internal conflicts* (characters and
self). How does your character handle obstacles and challenges in
the story? What kind of person are they? Do they steal? Use vio-
lence? Try to rationalize their way out of trouble? Do they hustle,
scheme, blame themselves, other people? Do they turn to drink?
Drugs? Run away? Or face their problems head-on? Try giving
your character a small challenge before your movie actually starts
to see what route they take to meet it. Their choices will *define*
them, making it easier for you to write dialogue for them and making them more interesting to watch. Also, keep in mind that your
characters are *your* characters; they are created from your imagination, they carry your DNA, and they should evoke some strong
emotion within you, much like a real person would.

My Two Cents on Script Doctors

Script doctors are an interesting phenomenon in my opinion. While it is clear that script doctoring can be a lifesaver, and many notable script doctors are doing amazing work in Hollywood, they are often far beyond the reach of low-budget, indie filmmakers. In reality, when low-budget indie filmmakers are on the lookout for script doctors, what they'll get is someone who is not qualified in the slightest to give them any sort of advice about their script, not to mention the quality of their writing. Many of them never wrote, revised, or sold a script, and in some cases – they have no interest in reading the materials you send them. In my opinion, most "affordable script doctors" are not worth the investment. If you are, however, on the lookout for a script doctor you can afford, I suggest you take a screenwriting class, and more often than not, other students and teachers at those classes would be willing to read your script and give you their honest opinion on its strengths and weaknesses.

Screenwriting Contests

Once you have finished a few drafts of a script and have the confidence to allow other people to read it and critique it, try submitting it to screenwriting contests. There are some amazing programs out there and some really great competitions that reward winners handsomely via money and exposure. I recommend you check out the Austin Film Festival Teleplay & Screenplay Contest; The Blue Cat Screenwriting Contest; The Big Break Screenwriting Contest; the Page Awards Screenwriting Contest; Slamdance; Sundance Screenwriters' Lab; and the Creative World Awards, among others. If your script gets in, the exposure can give you the tools you need to get your movie made faster. And if it doesn't – look at the bright side, you wrote a script which you can now produce and turn into a real film.

Write to YOUR Budget

If your goal is to write, direct, and produce your own films, then there's no point in writing something you can't afford to do or something that could require a hefty fundraising effort. This, obviously, depends on your skill-set, experience, and your ultimate ambition. If you are a VFX master, then you could and should definitely make a VFX-heavy film, but if you don't know a thing about VFX, then what's the point of writing a movie that *depends* on it? Writing a movie that you can afford to make *tomorrow* will make your life a whole lot easier today and will increase the likelihood of your movie actually being made once the script is complete (even if you only have $300 in the bank).

Write With What You Have

Sticking to the point of writing to budget, filmmaker Robert Rodriguez (*Sin City, Desperado*) suggests that you write a script that incorporates locations and props that you already have free access to. All you have is an apartment? Great! Write a story that takes place in your apartment (*Hard Candy, Friday, Rope*). Got a car? Awesome! Why not write a story about a man who picks up a psychotic hitchhiker? Shoot the whole thing in the car (see Tom Hardy in *Locke*). Do you live in NYC? Great – you have access to the biggest movie set in the world, as long as you don't block the sidewalk and keep things minimal – optional permits are *free*! Shoot a film that takes place in the streets of New York, Las Vegas, Chicago, etc. The opportunities are endless. Take what you have access to and write it into your movie.

> *"This industry is all about work, and just because*
> *Sundance exposed me to the world, it is my job to*
> *stay deserving in that world. The work never ends;*
> *the hustle just get harder, and you get stronger!"*
> ~ Gina Rodriguez

No Movie is Written, It's Rewritten

The main reason for the existence of bad scripts, in my opinion, is the unwillingness of the writer to poke holes in their own work and rewrite the draft until it works. A bad script can be full of bad dialogue, a flawed premise, or a sloppy plot. All are things that can and should be improved with a rewrite, sometimes two, three, four, ten drafts, or more. The purpose of a rewrite is to *edit* your own work, to rewrite the dialogue where it doesn't work, to fix plot-holes, enhance the plot, breathe more life into your characters, and make every moment as important as it possibly can be. Basically, make the darn thing better. Don't be one of those screenwriters who send out rough drafts to people with the idea that "it's ready!" Rewrite it, then edit it again and again and again until it *meets your standard*, until you can read it and "feel" something. If it's anything short of amazing in your mind, then it's probably not worth greenlighting yet.

Write Some Shorts

Almost every person living in the free world today has access to a camera, whether it's your iPhone, Galaxy, or your dad's crummy home-video camera. So, if it's your goal to write, direct, and produce a feature film – you'll *need* to make a couple of short ones first. Sit down and write a script you can afford to film tomorrow – don't worry about distribution or who might see it, or what people are going to think about it, just write it! Writing, directing, and producing a short film will prepare you for the real thing, it is the finest filmmaking masterclass in existence, and the teacher is God himself. Ultimately, it is the *only way* to get real-world experience and become a legitimate filmmaker. It is the only way of getting intimate with the process. No book will ever teach you what a short film could—that's the bottom line. The more movies you make, the better you become at making movies, and a short film is a mini movie, isn't it? So, why wait? Who's stopping you? Make a commitment *right now* to write, direct, and produce your first short film before the end of the month. Also, while you're at it, try signing up for weekend filmmaking challenges, they're free, and they're amazing!

There is Only ONE Rule

I attend the NY Book Expo every year, and every year I get to sit for a few hours and listen to famous authors talk about their process, and every time I come back home with a different point of view. Recently, I attended a breakfast panel where writer Barbara King-solver was discussing her process, the way by which she comes about new ideas and how she approaches writing in a nutshell. She'll have a *remarkable* personal experience (positive or negative) and decide to write about it. She has a lot of ideas floating in her head on a daily basis, and she finds the need to force herself to focus on one idea at a time as to not get lost in the writing process. About five minutes later, Nicholas Sparks takes the microphone and admits to the contrary – he only has one idea, and when he's done writing, he thinks that *it* will be his final book, and then – another idea comes into his head; when he's done with a new book, he has no idea what the next one is going to be. Similarly – Stephen King is a very disciplined writer who has a daily writing routine. Aaron Sorkin, on the other hand, does not. He admittedly spends a big chunk of his day watching ESPN and searching for inspiration; every writer works differently. It doesn't matter what your process is, all that matters is that at the end of the day, when you greenlight a script – that script had better adhere to one rule, and one rule only: *"don't be boring."* That's the only rule you are not allowed to break. Everything else – your approach, your methods, your style, etc. is flexible. There is no right or wrong approach to screenwriting, but there are many ways to go about it, and everyone will approach the craft in a different way. The cool thing about writing is that you learn about yourself and your craft with every new piece of material you work on. If you want to know what kind of writer you are, you need to write – and make a habit of writing every day and rewrite it until you deem it worthy.

Writing Software

This is a highly debated topic and one that has no right or wrong answer. But because I've been repeatedly asked, "What kind of software do you write on?", I'll take this opportunity to respond. For me – the app that gives me the most bang for my buck is Celtx, mainly because I can write everywhere and resume anywhere, and it gives me the tools to break down the script, input my shot list, create a schedule, etc. It's an easy-enough, although flawed solution. Most professionals write on Final Draft – and so did I for a long time, and I might switch back once they upgrade their iPad app (I do a lot of my writing on the iPad). So, the answer to that question is irrelevant – if I couldn't use Celtx or Final Draft, I'd write my stuff on a Word Document. As long as I'm writing, I'm happy.

Writer is King

There is no doubt in my mind that *the script* is by far the most important asset you can have in the film industry today. If you have no money, no experience, and no connections but you have a 120-page masterpiece on a PDF, then you have something that Hollywood wants and is willing to pay a lot of money for. You will, therefore, have an easier time getting agents, producers, and directors to read your script and help you get your movie made. *Life is made easier by an amazing screenplay.* It is why I encourage people to focus their energies on gaining as much theoretical knowledge and practical experience in writing, *above all else.* This is why I also think that you should make a daily, conscious effort to improve the quality of your writing. Read scripts, read novels, listen to podcasts and sign up for newsletters and blogs that dissect the art of writing. *Write every day,* work to become a master of the craft. It's a difficult goal to achieve, but it's the *pursuit of the goal itself* that makes the quality of your current work better than the quality of your last. And it'll be the *thing* that determines the quality of your script, and as a result, the quality of your film.

Write with Distribution and Marketing in Mind

The artist within you may be tempted to think that creating a script with the word "marketing" in mind is a despicable sell-out, but I can pretty much promise you that every studio movie ever made was made with marketability in mind. Every time a film studio (big or small) makes a movie, they do so because they want to have a product to sell; the decision to make a movie is a business decision, not an artistic one. And sometimes these movies suck, while other times – they rock! The difference between suck and rock has nothing to do with the studio's marketing plan or the decision to make a marketable movie, but it has everything to do with the script – the film's *blueprint*. The point is this – you can make a business decision to create a marketable movie, but every decision that follows must be an artistic one, and that is where your movie is made. Don't shy away from making films about subjects that are easily marketable. In fact, I'd encourage you to keep your film's marketability in mind while you write it. The earlier you can think about how your film is going to be sold and marketed when it's complete, the better. And once you make a business decision to create a marketable film, tell the businessman within you to buzz off for a few months while the artist within you writes the script.

Your First Table Read

When I first got into this game, I was under the impression that table reads are reserved for big-budget films and TV shows, studio movies, or theatrical plays, but that's only because I didn't understand their true purpose. In principle, you should conduct two key table readings: one after completing the second or third draft of your script and the other during pre-production. Your first table read serves a very important purpose – it opens the table (literally) for discussion about your screenplay. It answers questions you may have and allows people (whose opinions you value) to give you honest feedback about the quality of your work. Are your characters relatable? Did the plot make sense? Is it exciting? Boring? Too slow? Too fast? What are some of its flaws? What did people like or dislike about it? Are there any plot-holes? Was there something that didn't make sense? These questions and more should be answered by the end of your first table read. So, after finishing your second or third draft, invite a group of friends, colleagues, actors, and directors, and ask them to donate two hours of their time to sit with you and your friends at your home, drinking wine, eating cake, and reading a script that goes into production a few months from now. All you ask is that people give you *honest feedback*, a fact that should be reiterated before the reading starts. Hand out feedback forms, have snacks, and show your appreciation for the friends and colleagues who came through for you (they didn't have to show up, so the fact that they did is amazing!).

Once the reading is over, you should take the time to have an honest discussion about your script. That discussion is going to open your eyes to new ideas and get your brain storming with fresh thoughts and interesting prospects; it'll answer questions and give you a real picture of opportunities missed and/or goals accomplished. I'm telling you – it's worth doing. The best part about these table reads for me is that people tend to give you feedback even if they're not writing it down. If the scene you wrote is hilarious, people will laugh out loud; if the scene is sad, the room will instantly go quiet; if the scene is tense, you'll be able to *feel* it in the room. A table read really gives you insight into what it will *feel* like to screen the best version of your film to a group of people you care about and whose opinions you value.

Both Pixar and Marvel are known for running "Brain Trust meetings," in which filmmakers who worked on the company's other films contribute feedback and offer support throughout the process. Read the book *Creativity, Inc.* for a fascinating look into what a "Brain Trust" really is; it will change the way you approach the business of making art.

Final Word on Writing

Just like any other skill, your ability to write well will improve over time with practice. The more you read, the more you write, and the more "writing" you absorb, the better writer you become. Read scripts, read novels, read articles, read blogs, and watch YouTube videos about the subject of writing; become *obsessed* with writing, and the world will show you the way.

"People say, 'What advice do you have for people who want to be writers?' I say, they don't really need advice, they know they want to be writers, and they're gonna do it. Those people who know that they really want to do this and are cut out for it, they know it." ~ R.L. Stine

Tips for Non-Writers

The reason I rant and rave about the importance of mastering the craft of screenwriting is that I think that it opens all the right doors for independent filmmakers. However, some people have a great directorial vision with absolutely no writing ability or lack the desire to write; while this portion of the book is targeted towards indie filmmakers who write their own scripts, I thought I would take a minute to give you my two cents on how to get a great script without actually writing it yourself.

Adapt a Play

In 2018, an actor friend of mine introduced me to a play that he used to be in when he was in school. The fella who wrote the play suggested that I take a look at it and perhaps be interested in adapting it to screen and shooting it as a short film. I read the script and immediately saw its cinematic potential. I shared my ideas and thoughts with a group of close friends (all of whom are actors who were in the original play), got the writer's blessing to shoot the film for no charge, and shot it on-location in Queens. Currently, *Dual Action* is in post-production and will be making its way to film festivals in 2019, and it cost less than $700 to make.

Joe Trombino in Dual Action

Film a Monologue

Over the past few years, I've been working to improve my compos- iting skills via VFX apps like Adobe After Effects, so in 2018, my close collaborator, Katie Vincent, and I decided to shoot a short VFX film which was shot entirely on green-screen. The short film is basically a five-minute monologue about the end of times, de- livered by a white snow queen of sorts, a beautiful yet dangerous creature who is now awakened to bring an end to mankind by cov- ering the land in snow and ice. It's an allegory for how we torment and abuse Mother Earth, and the inevitable consequences of that abuse that will ultimately come back to bite us. We shot the thing for less than $500 (the cost of makeup and an LED light I wanted to buy for myself), and the results are amazing. I can't wait to share this with the world. *The Last Frost* will hit the festival circuits in 2020.

Shoot a Silent Film

I mentioned the importance of silent films in earlier chapters, but I want to take this opportunity to again remind you that there can be a lot of power in a silent picture. You can make an actual silent short or just a short film about a character who can't speak. The ability to shoot silent pictures will greatly enhance your directorial skill and give you a greater understanding of how cinema works, like how to move the camera, how to move the actor, and how to block the scene. No dialogue writing abilities needed.

Try Public Domain

There is a vast wealth of true stories, fiction novels, films, and plays circulating around the world-wide-web that are currently in the public domain, and a quick Google search will reveal them to you. You can take any piece of work that's in the public domain and remake it, retell it, and shoot it. It's not only a great way to get experience, but it's also the best way of creating branded content without spending a whole lot of money in the process. Want to make a movie about Zorro? Go ahead, he's in the public domain. How about Dracula? Sherlock Holmes, Alice (from *Alice in Wonderland*), Ebenezer Scrooge, Frankenstein, etc. These are all characters in the public domain, and anyone can write a story about them.

Now, just because I said the word "Zorro," you shouldn't automatically calculate the 20 million dollars you think it'll cost to make a Zorro western epic. Who said that you should be restricted by *any* production standard? For example, let's say you decide to make a feature film about Rapunzel. Could it not be shot in a Poconos cabin for $20,000? Could it not be filmed on a limited budget with a limited cast and a limited crew? The way in which you opt to tell these stories can vary, but rest assured that a low-budget version of Zorro can still utilize the name "Zorro" in its script and in its marketing. All you need is a mask and a sword, everything else is creativity.

"Filmmaking is like any kind of art form. You have to try to figure it out, and you're going to do that by trying." ~ Nicolas Winding Refn

Writing Resources

<u>Favorite Screenwriting Books</u>

- *Screenplay* by Syd Field
- *The Art of Dramatic Writing* by Lajos Egri
- *Making a Good Script Great – Linda Seger*
- *Story* by Robert McKee
- *The Writer's Journey* by Christopher Vogler
- *Into the Woods* by John Yorke
- *The Anatomy of Story: 22 Steps to Becoming a Master Storyteller* by John Truby
- *Screenwriting: The Art, Craft, and Business of Film and Television Writing* by Richard Walter
- *The 21st Century Screenplay* by Linda Aronson
- *Save the Cat* by Blake Snyder

<u>Favorite YouTube Channels for Writers</u>

- *Now You See It*
- *Nerdwriter*
- *Lessons from the Screenplay*
- *Every Frame a Painting*
- *The Closer Look*
- *Channel Criswell*
- *CinemaSins*
- *Films&Stuff*

PART TWO
Strategy

The Game Plan

So, you have your script. You wrote it, read it, tested it, got feed-back on it, and, in your eyes, it's *perfect*. You are now ready to roll, right? Well, not so fast. There's a big mountain you have to climb to get from where you are today to yelling "Action!" This is the *game plan* phase. The game plan covers *everything* you need to make your movie in a clean and organized fashion. It's your business plan, your "to do list." It's the path that will lead you from a printed PDF to a motion picture on the screen. This is where stuff gets real.

The DIY Strategy

This book is designed specifically for the low-budget, indie film-maker – and if you are one, you are most likely an expert in one or more fields of filmmaking. This is key if you're going to make a movie on a non-existing budget and with a minimal crew, but even the most prolific DIY filmmakers can't master every element of filmmaking on their own and will need to hire outside help to have their movie made. However, your job, before you ever step foot on set, is to *be prepared*. You need to know how to write, produce, direct, edit, and release a movie if you're going to be a true DIY filmmaker. This knowledge will only serve you in the long run, and as you go on to make bigger and better films it'll be the con-fidence builder that helps you through a lot of hurdles and gives you the technical know-how you need to finish your movie under any and every circumstance. If you can *master* several elements of DIY filmmaking, you'll save thousands of dollars on pre-pro-duction, post-production, and everything in between. Having the right knowledge in this game will mean the difference between winning and losing.

Embrace the DIY Spirit

When I used to hear the term "low-budget, DIY filmmaker," I'd cringe because in my mind I was thinking, "Why would I want to learn about DIY low-budget filmmaking? That title doesn't correspond with my ultimate goals. I don't want to make low-budget movies, I want to make *big-budget* movies! I want to work with famous actors and produce real content." The honest truth is that most filmmakers working in Hollywood today *are* in fact DIY low-budget filmmakers. Anyone from Tarantino to Scorsese, Robert Rodriguez, and Christopher Nolan use and utilize DIY, low-budget filmmaking techniques in their current work, despite the humongous budgets they appear to be working under. In addition, most of them started from nothing and had to prove themselves with a DIY low-budget film before ever getting a chance to work for a major studio. And, even after getting hired by bigger companies, they are still required to adhere to budgets.

Christopher Nolan made three short films before making *Following* for a mere $6,000. Robert Rodriguez had a lifetime of practice as a DIY filmmaker before making *El Mariachi* for $7,000. Quentin Tarantino made a low-budget DIY indie feature called *My Best Friend's Birthday* for under $500. Even someone as celebrated as Steven Spielberg made three low-budget shorts before making his first feature, *Firelight,* for a mere $400.

Anyone and everyone who is doing something meaningful in this industry today started as a low-budget, DIY filmmaker – and the skills they developed over that period of time are ingrained in the way they make their movies today. It's the ultimate prerequisite to being successful in this business, and it's something that you need to embrace.

The Big Benefit of DIY Filmmaking

Knowing how to "do stuff" in the world of film is a valuable asset that could end up saving you a lot of money, give you an edge when raising funds, and make you more likely to succeed in the long haul. If you've taken the time to study screenwriting and understand story structure, your first movie will be better. The same goes for cinematography, editing, VFX, etc. The more you know – the *safer* you are in this business, the smaller your footprint, and the better your end product will be. When you have a budget, you can hire experts, but when you don't – your movie relies on *your* ability to do a lot of the work yourself. Dov Simens used to say that if you want to make a $1,000,000 film, you first need to make a $100,000 film, and if you want to make a $100,000 film, you need to have completed a $10,000 film. And the only way to guarantee the quality of that $10,000 film is to take the time to learn the basics of DIY filmmaking (writing, producing, directing, editing, post, and release). Being a master of all trades is actually useful for those engaging in the art of low-budget DIY filmmaking.

Understanding Your Funding Strategy

Before you start breaking down your script and build a budget – you need to know what kind of movie you are making and *how* you plan to fund it. And in this department, there are really only two possible choices: one is to make a movie that you *can* afford, and the other is to make a movie you *can't* afford. If you decided to write a movie that you can shoot tomorrow, then allow me to congratulate you – you are officially in pre-production. However, if you've written a movie that you cannot afford, then you need to decide what your funding strategy is going to be. Meaning, how are you going to fund it? Bank loans? Donations from friends and family? Crowdfunding? Private investors? Or are you taking the Executive Producer route? Etc. We'll cover funding shortly.

The Shooting Strategy

Your shooting strategy is a short game plan that is based upon the complexities of your script, and it's something that you need to be aware of before you jump into pre-production. You can narrow it down to a single-sentence summary of your entire production process in CAST, CREW, DAYS, LOCATION, and BUDGET. For example, if you have a story taking place inside a car (one location) with three actors, your shooting strategy is going to be: *A one-location, 3 cast, 4 crew, 10-day shoot under a $10,000 budget.* Having that shooting strategy in mind will simplify your pre-production process and will give you and your production team a better understanding of the road ahead. So, if I tell a vendor that I'm working on a one-location, 3-cast, 4-crew, 10-day shoot, under a $5,000 budget, they don't need to ask me whether I'm shooting on film or digital. They already know if I can afford squibs, 4K HMIs, an Alexa mini or super-speed lenses. They will have a way better understanding of how this shoot is going to unfold. A $10,000 shoot will probably consist of a DSLR or a Mini Cinema camera, two rented lenses, one AC, a makeup artist, a gaffer, and a sound person (and maybe some free PAs) – again, that's a *probably.*

The Distribution Strategy

Having a clear idea of how you plan to get people to watch your movie is something that you should have as soon as you figure out what your budget is since it will dictate the manner by which you finance, produce, and shoot the film. The fact is that most low-budget indie films with no-name actors in them rely heavily on festivals and word-of-mouth marketing to succeed. Distribution is a *major* challenge, and even if a distributor picks up the film, the filmmaker and his investors are unlikely to see any profits at the end of the day. Which is why this book digs deep into DIY distribution, and it is my goal to make sure that you're not being jibbed by small-time, unknown distributors who will take your movie and give you nothing in return. More on that later, but for now, you need to know if you are going to be distributing this movie yourself, or if you plan on selling it to a distributor. In most likelihood, you would want to have a plan A (selling to a distributor at a film festival) and a Plan B (if it doesn't sell – distribute it yourself).

The No Budget Film School

One of the greatest weaknesses of first-time, low-budget indie filmmakers also happens to be one of their biggest strengths – *enthusiasm*. That enthusiasm is hunger. It's motivation, it's energy, it's the desire "to do," the desire to tell stories, to entertain people, make them laugh, think, cry, and "feel." And if you are reading this book, you're probably overwhelmed by that desire. It has infiltrated your very being and has occupied your mind for a very long time. That enthusiasm makes you want to jump out into the world and make your first feature film *tomorrow!* And that's great! However, that very same passion can hurt you, let you down, and ultimately lead to disappointment if not managed and filtered properly. Just because you have everything you need to make a feature film tomorrow, that doesn't mean you need to start working without preparation, especially if you've never made a movie before. All you need to do is follow the path which every filmmaker should take on their way to their first feature. And that is the no-budget real world film school – making a movie (short or feature) for no money.

Theoretical Knowledge

The first time I ever spent money on "film education" was when I took the Dov Simens course in 2014. As a high school dropout who went to school overseas, I couldn't get into US-based film schools because I didn't have a GED (and frankly, wasn't very interested in getting one). So, I took it upon myself to "self-educate." I watched tutorials on YouTube, read blogs, and took online courses - and to this day, my film education continues, it became something of a never-ending journey for me. The good news is that the cost associated with this kind of education is always *dwarfed* when compared with the "traditional" film school experience.

If you choose to follow the standard path of making a few shorts before undertaking your first feature, I think that self-educating would be the best way to get started. Make a conscious effort to spend X number of hours each week on gathering theoretical knowledge. Watch videos, read articles, read books, etc. Teach yourself to write, produce, direct and edit movies and then go out and make one for $0.

Putting Theory into Practice

Commit yourself to learn anything and everything you can about the process, and then go out there and implement what you've learned in the real world, the result is *a movie*. A sequence of shots, a story, a character, something real that has your name on it. Something you can take to festivals, a product you can screen and get feedback on. This is the process of materializing your vision. The key is not to drown in theory, not to read book after book about the craft without having the courage to go out there and shoot something on your own. A decent balance would be one book, one film. For every book you read, you make a short (or two, or a feature). Putting your theoretical knowledge to the test is the best way to learn what works, and what doesn't.

Mastering the Basics

Your job at this moment in time is to train, to make yourself a master in every element of filmmaking so that you can jump into your first movie – *experienced*. You need to be a really good writer, a really competent producer, and a very efficient director. You need to understand editing, sound mixing, marketing, promotion, and distribution – and you can't get that from textbooks alone. The only way to get this kind of experience is by making short films and making them often. Sure, you can go for the "trial and error" approach on your first feature, but consider the fact that your first feature film is actually going to be used as your calling card – it's your first *real* work of art, and if you're planning on charging people money to see it, you're going to have to deliver the goods. So the goal should be to make a great short film before you spend the money on a feature. Master your basics *before* you get started.

Film School

The question of whether it's wise to spend all that time and money on film school could be answered by a simple question: *What's your strategy?* If your strategy is to follow the path of some of the filmmakers I mentioned earlier – to build yourself up from nothing, make small, no-budget shorts that lead up to your first feature and then take it from there – then the answer is no, you don't really need film school. The money you'll spend on film school could be used to make a pretty sizable feature film, and you might be able to squeeze a name actor in there as well. If your strategy is to be hired in the industry, i.e., work in television, or as a cinematographer, makeup artist or gaffer, and you have the money to spare – sure, go for it. Film school is an excellent place to meet people and make connections. In fact, I think that's one of its biggest benefits. At the end of the day, the only way to learn to make a movie is by making a movie. Theoretical knowledge is great, but it's not going to turn you into a filmmaker. If you want to be a filmmaker you'll need to make some films. It's as simple as that.

"All You need to make a movie is a gun and a girl."
~ Jean-Luc Godard

Mastering Adobe

Whether you're going to be working with an editor, or even if you go solo, understanding how to edit is something that should be high on your list of priorities. I handled all elements of post-production on every single one of my films, and while I did work with assistant editors when I had the budget, the ultimate power to edit the movie was mine. That's a power that I think you should have. Considering the fact that an average editor charges anywhere from $100 to $200 a day, a two-week, two-pass-cut would run you anywhere from $1,400 to $2,800 (not including the trailer, promo clips, and others). That's money that you could be spending somewhere else. In addition, if you master the editing skill, you could generate revenue with it during off-time and while you're in between projects. I also believe that if you master the craft of editing films, you'll automatically become a better filmmaker because you'll be better equipped, you'll make decisions on set that correlate to editing choices, and your use of the camera will become more effective because you'll have a solid idea of how you're going to cut a shot with the next. You'll have a better understanding of cross-cutting, long cuts, and camera movements. Editing is a skill that you must possess if you plan to become a successful DIY filmmaker.

After Effects

I don't think that you need to become a compositing master before deciding to embark on your first feature film shoot, but I would recommend that you take a week or two to learn what you can about the subject via Adobe After Effects. From making movie titles to creating visual effects, color grading, adding on-screen graphics, removing objects or keying green screen - having control over a software like Adobe After Effects is a skill that's worth investing in, and it's something that'll stay with you forever. And again, the education is free of charge.

Photoshop

One item that will save you a lot of money in pre-production, during production, in post-production, and during the film's distribution is Adobe Photoshop. Designing a movie's logo, credits, titles, posters, and artwork is something that generally can be appraised in the tens of thousands, and that's money better spent elsewhere. The Adobe package costs around $50 a month, and it comes with everything you need to shoot, edit, and release a movie. They even have their own free tutorial library @ tv.adobe.com. A lot of editors are switching to Premiere, and most artwork is done in Photoshop, so I recommend you get in on that action. You'll see more examples of just how useful it can be in later chapters.

Working for Free

Before you make the jump into making feature films, I highly recommend you lend yourself as a helping hand on a legitimate movie set. Go online and search for film shoots on the prowl for PAs, interns, and assistants. Offer your services for no charge and make it your goal to spend X number of hours on a set before going into production on your own movie. This experience will truly teach you how to handle yourself on a movie set. Watching another director work with actors can also be a valuable insight into the effectiveness of their methods.

"What Joe and I love about the film industry, it's like the wild West. We're two guys who grew up a million miles away from the film business; it doesn't matter where you come from or where you go to school. All that matters is, can you find a way to practice the craft and express yourself in a way that people respond to." ~ Anthony Russo

Learn by Networking

I cannot stress this enough: one of the best things you can do for yourself is to get out there and network, network, network. Introduce yourself to actors, directors, producers, cinematographers, anyone and everyone who is working in your industry, in your city, or in your town. Surrounding yourself with like-minded people who are as ambitious and hard-working as you are is the fastest way of reaching your goals. Other people can teach you a lot and give you access to their genius and resources. You'll find that you get to meet a lot of the same people during festival circuits. Don't be afraid to ask them out for a drink and see if they're open to collaboration. You can also meet other filmmakers by searching for networking groups in your city or town, as well as by attending acting classes, writing classes, improv classes, and cinematography classes.

Take a Day to Study Web-Building

A professional-looking website will go a long way in selling your brand and give the people you work with *confidence* in your ability to deliver the goods. Your film's official site can be its strongest marketing platform, so I recommend you take some time to learn the basics. Now, if I were to give you this advice four years ago, you would have dismissed it as being "too complicated." But in 2019, building a website is one of the easiest things you can do. Site builders like Wix and Squarespace allow you to design a beautiful-looking website in less than an hour. Utilizing your newly found skills in Photoshop will give you the tools you need to design assets, graphics and artwork (see? I told you it would come in handy).

"Every day's a hustle."
~ Richard Linklater

Making a $0 Short Film – Checklist

You can read all the books in the world and watch every filmmaking course ever made, but at the end of the day, nothing beats real-world experience. If you've never made a movie before, I suggest you start with a short film or a small, one-location feature. Write a short film that you can afford to shoot *tomorrow* by using gear, props, and locations that are *free* to you. Here is what you need to make a $0 budget short film:

(1) **A *great* screenplay** – Make sure you go through a few rounds of rewrites and that the script adheres to the quality for which *you* would like to be known. Follow the tips in the writing section and do your homework. Rewrite it until you think it's amazing!! Anything less is not acceptable.

(2) **Script breakdown** – List all the props, locations, actors, etc. in your script. I use Celtx, but you can use a simple Excel sheet as well. Find what works for you.

(3) **Free location** – Most no-budget shorts are shot outside, in the filmmaker's apartment, or in a location to which they have free access.

(4) **Free props** – If you have access to a free prop that could make your movie look more expensive than it actually is, then you must figure out a way to use it in the script. That could be a car, a computer, a fancy sword, a rocket launcher, whatever you can get your hands on for $0.

(5) **Free crew** – You should do what you can to make sure that you have more than one person behind the camera. If you have friends or know people who need the experience, you can bring them on board as first

AC, sound mixer, makeup, etc. Don't be afraid to ask for favors, it's a skill that'll save you a lot of money down the road. If you don't know anyone, you can advertise on Craigslist or on some other social media group. There are plenty of students looking for work, and while I'm sure your ad will get some hate mail ("how dare you advertise an unpaid position?"), you'll be surprised at how many people will actually respond positively. Those people want *experience*, and as long as you're willing to give them a good work environment, they'll work hard for you.

(6) Food – Take the time to make some sandwiches for people before the shoot. Don't ask people to work for you for more than four hours without food, even if you're shooting in the park.

(7) Free camera – These days, any person who owns a smartphone has access to a 4K camera. And if you have no choice but to shoot on the iPhone, it's better than to not shoot at all. There are several apps you can use as well to give you more control over your image, such as Filmic Pro (an app that allows you to rack focus, control aperture, save high-res MOV files, shoot in high-quality 4K mode, and more). If you have a couple of bucks to spare, rent yourself a DSLR camera and a 35mm lens. You can rent these online at sites like KitSplit and Share-Grid. (On the day I wrote this chapter, I did a quick search on KitSplit and found a Sony A7s II package with lenses and everything for $60 a day, a C100 with a Lens + Tripod for $135 a day, and an Ursa Mini kit with all the bells and whistles for $200 a day).

(8) Free permits – If you're filming in *some* big cities, and you are not blocking the sidewalk, you can get an optional permit for free.

All you need to do is call the Mayor's Office and ask for an Optional Permit. If you live in New York City, you can visit their website, fill out the form online, and fax it. While Free Permits are not required by law in New York, they are going to give you a sense of legitimacy, and if anyone comes by and asks you to move – you will have the support of the city. A permit can take anywhere from a day to a few days to get, depending on how busy the city is – so you want to make the request at least a week in advance.

(9) Use available light – If you're working on a $0 budget, you're going to have to utilize a lot of natural light, lamps, and practical lights. You can light a scene with a street lamp, or any $10 flood light when shooting indoors. Making a short film for no money serves as a great cinematography learning opportunity for anyone who aspires to be a filmmaker. There are countless videos on YouTube that will teach you how to beautifully light a scene with standard lights that can be found in any home. Get a silk or a collapsible diffuser to soften sunlight when shooting outdoors. You can use a sheet or buy a decent portable diffuser for $13 on Amazon.

(10) Make it FUN! – Keeping a fun work environment for everyone can be a challenge when you have to manage 85 people on a set, but when you're dealing with a minimal cast and crew of under 10 people, the task becomes way more manageable. Keep a positive attitude, play music, crack a smile, and make a conscious effort to ensure that the people who are giving you their time and effort are having fun! This will guarantee a positive experience and a better made end-product at the end of the day.

Create an IMDB Page

Now that you've actually made something, it's a good idea to create an account with IMDB that has at least one credit in its contribution portfolio – so take this opportunity to create that contribution by making an IMDB page for your $0 budget movie. It's free; you just have to visit contribute.imdb.com/updates?update=title – and make sure that you have a website set up and that you have that announcement on social media because they'll ask for it. List the actors, the director, producer, editor, and set an arbitrary release date; you can change it later.

Distributing Your $0 Short Film

There are not too many outlets where you can profit from short films these days, and with your first $0 budget short film, that's most likely not the reason you made it. The basic channels out there are YouTube, Instagram, Facebook, Twitter, and Vimeo. But there are other channels you can utilize to market and promote your short film (if you have no money for festivals, that is). Some of them include Short of the Week; Film Shortage; Films Short; Fandor; Filmdoo; Viddsee; NoBudge; Whatashort; to name a few. You can also put it up on Amazon and either sell it there or offer it for free on Amazon Prime by going to videocentral.amazon.com.

"Don't just be seduced by the same old, same old.
There are interesting things you can explore that
may get your film out there to audiences better
than the traditional distribution mechanisms."
~ Alex Gibney

Getting Reviews

Yes, your short film can be reviewed online by professional film critics. Some of them will charge a fee while others will do it for free. The list includes Screencritix; The Independent Critic; Indie Shorts Mag; FilmSnobbery; UK Film Review; Pretty Clever Films; DIRTfilms; Gorilla Film Online; Film Quarterly; etc. If you happened to have made a horror film, then you're in luck. There are hundreds of websites and blogs dedicated to reviewing, featuring, and promoting short horror films, and they are just *begging* for good content. I'll dig into the specifics of getting reviews in the chapter on Distribution.

Consider Film Festivals

Yes, most film festivals are NOT free, but they do offer one thing that is worth its weight in gold – *exposure*. Festivals are *the place to be* for anyone who wants to network and socialize with other aspiring filmmakers, it's the place to win awards, handle sales, get reviewed, make deals, and hand out your business card. It's where you *need* to be if you want to socialize with like-minded professionals who are on the same path as you are. Film festivals will give you and your film a great deal of exposure for a fairly low investment. The key to a successful film festival tour is to be strategic, be smart, and be *early* – the earlier you submit your film to a festival, the less money it's going to cost. You can find free submission festivals by going to websites like FilmFreeway and searching for festival submissions under $10 - there are quite a few of them. Now, keep in mind that once a film has been released online, it will most likely not get accepted into most film festivals. Also, you need to plan your festivals in accordance with your desired release date, meaning that if your film is ready to be submitted to festivals in March, and you've decided to release it online in October, only submit to film festivals that are running between March and October, otherwise they might overlap with your film's release. Make sure to read the festival rules before submitting.

Setting Up an LLC

Unless you are making a feature film for less than $2,000, then spending $200 on setting up an LLC is a *requirement* for several reasons. For one, it gives you a layer of personal legal protection in case anything goes wrong. If something horrible happens, you and your personal assets are safe and protected. Second, it gives you a clear financial advantage, both from a budgeting perspective and from a taxation perspective. As the owner of an LLC, you are saving thousands of dollars in taxes and are able to deduct all sorts of different expenses that are related to your movie or to movie-making in general. And third – it protects you from surging insurance prices on future projects if anything does go wrong and you become the subject of a claim. This is the equivalent of paying higher rates on health insurance because you have a pre-existing condition. Setting up an LLC should be one of the first things you do once you decide to greenlight your film. It also gives you the power to set up a separate bank account, which makes you more budget conscious, responsible, and transparent with your funds.

Copyright Your Script

Copyrighting a screenplay is fast, easy, and cheap. You can opt to use the services of a website like LegalZoom, where it costs around $50, or do it yourself via the U.S Copyright Office (around $30) at www.copyright.gov/registration.

Send Your Script to WGA

If you want to have an added layer of protection, you may submit your screenplay or treatment to the WGA (The Writer's Guild Association). You don't have to be a member of the Writer's Guild to register with them; all you have to do is go to www.wgawregistry.org/registration.asp (West Coast) or www.wgaeast.org/script_registration (East Coast) and pay the $25 fee. This gives you the option of listing your WGA registration number on the copyright section at the bottom of your screenplay's first page. It'll give you some peace of mind as you start sending it out to people.

Get a Website

One of the first things you need to do in pre-production is to buy a domain name and create a website for your upcoming movie. I usually do this fairly early on in the pre-production process. It costs less than $15 to register a domain name with a company like GoDaddy, and if you opt to use a website building service like Wix, it'll run you an extra $14 a month to maintain it. Alternatively, you can build a Wix website and keep it around for free, but you'll need to be okay with having the Wix logo displayed at the bottom of your page. And of course, you can always opt to use Wordpress, which costs nothing.

Building an official-looking website before announcing your upcoming film for the first time is important. You want to be able to direct people to an online hub where they can learn everything there is to know about your upcoming project, and that hub can be easily created via a paid web-building app like Wix, or a free web-builder like Wordpress. I built all of my websites on Wix, and they look pretty good (check out the website for my film, *Pickings* @ www.pickingsfilm.com). It's encouraged that you add a newsletter registration option on the first page and include links to your film's social media pages so that people can stay in touch and get updates on your progress.

"Look yourself in the mirror and ask yourself, what do I want to do everyday for the rest of my life...do that." ~ Gary Vaynerchuk

Social Media

Use your Facebook page as an outlet to announce your movie, and once the announcement is made – leave it alone. Don't touch that page until you have a social media strategy in place and the film's marketing is underway. Here's why: If you end up hiring a publicist or selling the movie to a distributor, social media marketing is going to become a major part of their P&A campaign, and you can run the risk of *spoiling it* by posting content on social media prematurely, before the film develops an audience. When I was getting ready to release *Pickings*, my PR strategist requested that we delete every social media post we'd posted up to that point since, apparently, you can't announce old content to the press and make it newsworthy. So, much like any other piece of the marketing and distribution strategy, social media must be timed and managed in accordance to the film's release. My advice to you is to build a social media presence and post teasers strategically, don't post content before you have a social media plan in place. I'll dive into the specifics of social media planning in the Distribution chapter.

Create a Business Plan

Making and selling movies is a business and, like any other business, it needs planning. The purpose of a movie business plan is to figure out your strategy for making it, funding it, releasing it, marketing it, and distributing it. A business plan should be part of your production from the very beginning. It'll give your investors (even if that's just you) a look into your movie, the story, the strategy for raising the funds, and how you're planning on using these funds to make the movie. In addition, the marketing plan (which is often included within the business plan) covers the way in which you are going to sell and market the film to your audience; it presents the step-by-step strategy for marketing, selling, and profiting from your film. There's no way around it; go online and look at movie business plans and marketing plans, download them, and use them as a template for your own film. It's not the sexiest thing in the world, but you *need* it. Your business plan shouldn't be 100 pages long; the good ones are short and to the point (the one I made for *Pickings* was thirty pages long) and should include a confidentiality agreement to the reader; an executive summary (a synopsis of the film, why you are making it, and how much money you need to make it); a team wish list (list of actors, artists, and technicians you want to work with, or already have agreements with); a production plan (shooting dates, dates of production, post-production, festival touring, etc.); financials (budget, tax credits, rebates, investor's repayments, etc.); marketing strategy and publicity; distribution strategy (are you planning to sell to a distributor? Or distribute it yourself? If so, how?). Be as thorough as you can.

Script Breakdown / Budget

There are countless books out there that will teach you how to create a detailed budget, and some of them try to make it seem more complicated than it actually is. Software like Celtx and StudioBinder will do it for you, or you can visit the many websites that offer free downloadable breakdown sheets online. The process is simple enough, you go through the script, scene by scene, page by page and take note of every item you're going to need for the scene you're reading. Location, cast, extras, props, wardrobe, lights, effects, etc. This gives you an *overview* of every scene you plan to shoot, it is the first step you take in pre-production once your script is ready to go. There is a panoply of classes, online courses, and articles that dive into the specifics of how to break down a script, but if you use a software like Celtx or StudioBinder then the process is pretty self-explanatory. The reason I like writing with Celtx, specifically, is that once you're done writing, the process of breaking the script down is integrated into the software. Once you have the breakdown, you can get to work on the budget. You can also opt to create an Excel sheet and skip the monthly charge of a dedicated software. Whatever you do, make sure you keep everything organized as your production team will need access to those breakdowns later on. Organization is always a lifesaver.

74

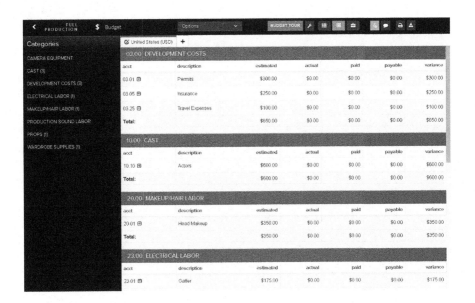

"I like to think I'm making films in the film business where movies are making enough numbers for the studios to let me keep working, but you also want those films to have content that makes you proud you made the film. That's not easy, but it's a fun puzzle to figure out." ~ Wes Craven

PART THREE
Funding

Hiring an Executive Producer

Unless you plan to fund the film yourself, you will have to go hunting for an Executive Producer, preferably one who loves your script, likes you (as a person), and wants to help you get your movie made, but, most importantly, you want to find someone to whom you can sell your vision of the film. Fundraising is a lonely process; it is by far the loneliest place in filmmaking land, and it's where a lot of dreams go to die – you have a script, you have a vision, you have everything you need to move to the next step, but you don't have the money yet. This is why partnering with an Executive Producer is so crucial; they'll help you navigate through the lonely land of fundraising and get you one step closer to getting your movie made. The interesting thing about Executive Producers is that they feed off confidence, so, unless you have 100% confidence in your abilities to not only raise the money but make this movie happen and make it profitable, your chances of hiring a good Executive Producer are slim. This is where it helps to have made a movie in the past. If you're trying to get an Executive Producer on your first film, you're facing an uphill battle, but if you've already made a movie before (especially a successful one), you are miles ahead of the competition.

Showcase Your Talents

Generally speaking, one of the first questions you'll have to answer when dealing with a serious Executive Producer or when trying to solicit an investment from an investor is: "What have you done? And can we see it?" This is when experience pays off. I would even argue that this is one of the biggest purposes of short films – to showcase your ability to tell a compelling story and evoke an emotion in ten minutes or less, and with very little money. It's the best "you" selling tool there is, and it's an asset that your Executive Producer will appreciate and should capitalize on. If you are an experienced indie filmmaker, that's half the battle won. Investors will feel more confident putting their money in your hands, especially if they think you have what it takes to get good reviews and get your film into one of the big festivals.

Create a Kickass Film Proposal

The purpose of a film proposal is to showcase the details of your project to potential investors and to convince serious producers to partner up with you and help you get your movie funded. Financiers want to see that you have your stuff together and, most importantly, they want a quick and effective introduction to your project without having to read through an entire business plan – this is where a film proposal comes into play. A film proposal should ideally include your film synopsis, your biography (along with any awards you've won), the film's logline/elevator pitch, a cast wish list, a list of your team (who have you assembled thus far? Any interest from actors, cinematographers, and other people attached to the project), a mood board (a visual representation of your film that showcases the potential look of the film), budget top-sheet, and wrap it up with a quick sales pitch and your directorial vision in a nutshell. This is where knowledge and experience in the Photoshop application can come in handy. I've seen my fair share of film proposals, and I can tell you that I only read the professional-looking ones. You can't put a bunch of boring text on a white piece of paper via Microsoft Word and expect to wow anyone. If you invest the time and energy in creating a professional-looking film proposal, you'll come off like a pro, which is exactly what you want. In the funding game, impression is everything.

Getting *Early Interest from Established Actors*

As previously established – if you can add a recognizable face to your feature film, your movie is more likely to stand out, get into bigger festivals, and succeed in the long run. The bigger the star, the greater the exposure and the more likely you are to raise funds and reach an audience. Most filmmakers will seek to attach a well-known actor to their film early on, and there are several reasons for doing so. Of course, you want to manage your expectations here. Chances are you won't land Ryan Gosling or Emma Stone on your first, low-budget indie film (unless you're working with a significant budget or have a masterpiece for a script), but you could land a great working indie actor. There are many actors who consistently work on low-budget indie films, many with first-time filmmakers. These include Dave Franco, Emily Browning, Casey Affleck, Rooney Mara, Kristen Stewart, Jason Schwartzman, Danny Trejo, Michael Madsen, Elijah Wood, and more. Recognizable actors will often invest their time in low-budget indie films if the quality of the script is amazing! So, if you have a *fantastic* screenplay, you can nab a recognizable name.

Getting a commitment from an actor early on will pique the interest of studios and executive producers, it'll make it easier to get your film funded. In addition – and this may sound like a joke – but getting a recognizable actor to be in your indie film will actually help you *save money* in the long run. That's right, you'll have some added costs, but you'll be surprised at how many vendors are willing to work for less if you give them the opportunity to work alongside a recognizable face. Commercial locations (such as bars, stores, etc.) would be willing to offer discounts, and you'll now have the option of raising funds via product placements. Additionally - makeup artists, wardrobe fitters, cinematographers, and other professionals could potentially agree to a lower rate for the chance to work alongside a face that they can put on their reel. Overall, your movie will become more appealing, and more people would be willing to get involved. In addition, getting a recognizable actor early on also means that you'll have an easier time once casting officially begins. Actors want to work with other actors they admire, and if you've managed to secure a working indie actor, your casting agent will use that as a *sales pitch* to other actors.

"Be so good they can't ignore you."
~ *Steve Martin*

Can You Afford an Established Actor?

Many low-budget indie filmmakers are under the impression that a recognizable name is beyond their reach and that they don't have the money to hire one, so they never bother checking. Well, while I didn't have a name actor in my first feature film, I've had the pleasure of negotiating with their agents, because for a long time *Pickings* was going to be a union SAG shoot with a name actor attached. However, because of the cost and logistics involved in SAG production, and the fact that I was working on a non-existing budget, I made the decision to hire actors who were experienced, but not necessarily well-known, and to go non-union. And while a few of our actors were working on TV shows like *Orange is the New Black* and *Gotham,* none of them were "recognizable," and that proved to be a big challenge as we were marketing the film, a challenge that I should have seen coming.

So how much will it cost to get a recognizable actor attached to your film? That depends on three major factors: (a) and I can't stress this enough – *the script.* If an actor loves your script, they will agree to be in your film and might also be willing to take a pay decrease if they believe it'll serve them artistically. The second factor is (b) schedule – if the actor has to make room for your film in their schedule and it's an inconvenience, you bet the rate is going to be higher. If you book an actor in between jobs, and they don't have a scheduling conflict (and that happens more than you'd think), then they might be more willing to negotiate their rate (after all, even actors have bills to pay). If an actor is super-busy, their rate goes up. If they just finished a TV show or a film and have nothing on the horizon, you have some wiggle room. The last factor will be irrelevant to most of you but may apply to a few of you, and that is (c) the filmmaker. If the film director has made a critically successful film (well-reviewed), that could be a ticket to landing a name actor in the early funding stages.

Getting a Letter of Intent

What you're looking to get from your potential celebrity is the Letter of Intent – basically a letter from the actor or his/her agent, saying that they are available to shoot your film on certain dates and that they are interested in working on your project. This Letter of Intent will be the gold key that gets you the capital you need to make your movie if you choose to hire a recognizable name, and it's not that complicated to get. All you need to do is call agents who represent the actors you want to work with (they're all listed on IMDB Pro), and say that you're working on an upcoming feature film and would like to hire X. The first phone call always ends the same: "send me an email," so you compile an email with a copy of the film's One Sheet or Film Proposal and follow up the next day. Once the actor's schedule is confirmed with their agent, they'll ask for a copy of the script. Once an actor is confirmed, they may request a deposit or a contract – so be ready for that.

Negotiate!

You won't have to look hard to find a film investor who wholeheartedly believes in the idea that "he who makes the gold, makes the rules" and the fact of the matter is that as you pitch your film to potential investors, you'll receive some ridiculous offers and proposals among the ones that make sense. You should have the wits to say "no" to the ones who want the entire pie and are unwilling to negotiate. There are many ways to structure film financing, and if you're working with an experienced Executive Producer, they should be able to guide you, but on many low-budget indie films the investors will ask to get a "first paid" clause (meaning their investment is paid out of the gross, and it's the first thing that comes out of the film's revenue), and they would also expect to have ownership of the film. In the indie world, most investors won't ask for creative control but could request the right to veto your final cut. You need to be able to say, "forget it" if the terms are not to your liking. It may sound like an obvious statement, but you'll be surprised at how many filmmakers give away 95% of their share of the film's profits for a chance to prove themselves, when in fact they don't have to. They cling to the first deal that comes their way in fear of losing the money and become slaves to it. Don't be one of those people – be willing to say "no" if the deal isn't in your favor.

Sell Yourself, Not Your Film

The people who choose to invest their money in movie-making ventures are people who have some sort of appreciation for film (they're not dummies). Some of them think it's cool, some of them think it's a good investment, and some of them are straight-up cinephiles, and the one thing they all have in common is their shared appreciation for the craft of film and the people who make them. *That* is something that you should be ready to take advantage of when pitching to investors. When you're meeting with investors, when signing, working, and dealing with investors – you must put your love and affection for the movies on display and play the part of the enthusiastic filmmaker who's ready to take over the world.

When an investor chooses an investment, he or she will take into account two major factors: (a) the film, and (b) the filmmaker. People tend to forget about the latter piece of the puzzle and focus all their attention on trying to sell their film and present it as the best investment in the world. The problem with that approach is that you neglect to sell yourself – the partner, the *person* with whom they'll be in business. Present yourself as a man/woman who is deeply in love with their craft, your *passion* is the bestselling tool you have, and I can guarantee that it will make your fundraising process a whole lot easier. As the writer, director, and producer of this exciting new project, it is your job to articulate your vision and get the people around you super-pumped and excited about it! You want them to be your cheerleaders, because if they are, you'll have their trust and their faith, and they won't try to mess with your vision. Picking the right partners is crucial, and it is up to you (or your Executive Producer, if you have one) to do your homework and make sure that you are partnering with someone who's got the movie's best interest in mind, and someone who likes you as a person. Keep in mind that a financier today could be your financier tomorrow, and that every connection you make could last a lifetime.

The Acting Daughter Motif

There is one recurring motif of which many filmmakers are painfully aware, and that is the "acting daughter" motif, and it goes a little something like this: You're out location scouting, you see a house you really want to film in, and then the owner comes to you, shakes your hand and says, "You know, my daughter is an actress," or "If you need a guy to show up as a mobster, I was in the mob, and I've been taking acting lessons." Then, a few days later, you're meeting an investor, and they'll throw the same pitch your way: "You know, my daughter/wife/son/whatever would be perfect for this role." Get ready for this to happen with every new person you meet, and I'm not kidding. One out of ten people you interact with will throw this pitch your way. The question is: can you and should you take advantage of these situations? Can you promise someone a role in a film in order to save money on a location rental, or to solicit an investment from an investor? Can you promise someone a role in exchange for a free accountant, or some free props? The answer – absofuckinglutly you should!! I'm sure you'll be glad to hear that this sort of bartering happens all the time. Now, artistically, you don't want to promise a major role to a person if you don't even know if they can act, but walk-in roles are a different story. You can accommodate twenty seconds of screen-time to a character who has one line or interacts with your lead character for a brief moment, or just sits in the background with a drink in his hand.

I attended a Q&A with David Lowrey at the AMC near my house upon the release of his film, *A Ghost Story*. And I remember him telling the story of how they landed their primary location for that film. They promised the location owner (an air conditioning contractor) that they'd feature his granddaughter in the film, and they did. Originally, she was supposed to play an extra, but Lowrey was impressed by her abilities and gave her a speaking role instead. Meanwhile, in Usher-land, I managed to save a big chunk of money on PR for *Pickings* after hiring a publicist to play the role of a waitress in the film. She had one line – and that one line saved me a couple of grand in the long run. So, get ready for that "acting daughter motif" and be prepared to take advantage of it.

Don't Sign What You Don't Understand

If you're working with a good Executive Producer, they'll sometimes be willing to cover your legal costs while investor negotiations are underway, especially if they're well-established. Most people just download film funding agreements from the internet and tweak them, but when you're dealing with professional movie studios, investors, or people who've done this before – they'll usually send you their own funding contract. At this point, it is *crucial* that you take that agreement to a lawyer for review before agreeing to the terms. If the contract is easy and simple enough to understand, that's fine, but if you're looking at text and have no idea what it means, don't sign it! It's better to spend the money and get a lawyer to flesh it out for you than to sign something that you don't understand.

> "Success stems from the producer creating the optimal conditions for the filmmaker's own creative process. Not from steering the filmmaker through a one-size-fits-all approach." ~ Jason Blum

Shoot the Film in Rehearsal

One cool trick that I've seen used by DIY filmmakers during the funding process is the use of animatics or rehearsal screenings. What the filmmaker would do is bring a couple of friends over and shoot the film on an iPhone or a DSLR in one session, beginning to end, like a play, either on a stage or in their home. This allows you to (a) visualize your film and understand your shot list better; (b) show your cast/crew/investors/producers what the movie is going to look like; (c) get exposed to new problems that you were not aware of that you can now fix in pre-production and be better prepared for when you shoot it for real. When I made *Pickings*, I rehearsed the film with my cast for about a week, and then I shot the entire thing as a play. That allowed me to figure out different blocking for different scenes and gave me a better understanding of pacing.

Shoot a Pitch Trailer

Another cool thing you can do to attract potential investors is to shoot a pitch trailer (also known as a proof of concept trailer). Instead of filming your entire script with your friends and screening it to investors, you could opt to produce a high-quality trailer that will serve to replicate your "dream trailer" for this film. This approach can be useful for investor and studio pitches, or when you're trying to land a name actor but have no prior experience. It's also used by plenty of folks in the industry as part of their crowd-funding campaigns. We did the same thing for *Pickings* during our Indiegogo campaign in 2016 (more on that later).

> "*Time goes on. So whatever you're going to do, do it. Do it now. Don't wait.*" ~ *Robert De Niro*

Behind the Scenes, The "Pickings" Pitch Trailer Shoot

Schedule Investor Screenings

Investor screenings are where deals get made. You rent a screening room, bring potential investors in, and give them all copies of a nicely designed, beautifully printed brochure (the Film Proposal). You then screen your presentation to a room full of people capable of handing you a check on the spot. If you have a pitch trailer or a rehearsal film – that'll be the place to show it, otherwise, you can screen a short film or a feature you've worked on.

Crowdfunding

The one piece of advice that I am not qualified to give would be in the crowdfunding arena since the only crowdfunding campaign I ever did failed to reach its goal. What I can do is talk about my own experience with crowdfunding and what I think I did wrong. I'll start by saying that many people get their movies funded via crowdfunding and that it is, by far, one of the most approachable methods of movie funding available to indie filmmakers today. I couldn't approve of it more. My mistakes with crowdfunding had more to do with the producer I trusted to run the campaign than anything else. When the script for *Pickings* was complete, I recruited an "Executive Producer" who had no prior experience but had a lot of heart and a lot of passion for my film. She believed that she could raise upwards of $350,000 to make the movie. I trusted her word and asked her to sign an Executive Producer contract. She'd raise the money and get a percentage of everything she brought to the table, and if she were to raise more than $500K, she'd get a 5% stake in the movie itself. It seemed like a fair deal to me, so I gave her the "go ahead." She worked tirelessly for a few days, setting up the Indiegogo campaign; we produced a two-minute pitch trailer for the movie (which kicked ass, by the way, and you can watch it on www.pickingsfilm.com), and we were all ready to go. Less than four days after the campaign had launched online, my producer decided to leave the country, stranding myself and my entire production with an Indiegogo campaign we couldn't market or make changes to. The fundraising effort died, and the movie almost died with it. I guess there are plenty of lessons to be learned from this situation, but for me, the most important lesson should be to hire an Executive Producer with a track record. Had I hired someone serious, had I not accepted the first offer that came my way by a willing, yet inexperienced producer, it would have been a completely different story.

The Self-Funding Approach

There are many filmmakers who are scared or worried about their ability to write, direct, and produce a feature-length film, especially when at risk of losing someone else's money – and this is where the self-funding strategy works best. The idea is to write a feature film that you can afford to shoot tomorrow, regardless of how much money you may have access to today. Funding your own film is, by far, the best approach for many first-time filmmakers, and it's the same approach that I took. It's the one I endorse the most, and it's what this book is about. Had I not had the money to make *Pickings,* then I would have made it anyway, but for less money. I refused to allow anything or anyone to discourage me from making the movie that I wanted to make, and so I did it anyway.

So, if you don't have the money to make your dream film, and you're worried about the funding process – don't make your dream film! Put it aside, keep it in a drawer, and know that you'll return to it once you have gained the experience needed to make it *the right way!* For now, focus all of your efforts on writing, directing, and producing your *first* feature film on a budget that you can afford with no producers or equity partners – just you and your team, whoever that may be. It's not going to be easy, but it can be done, and it should be done, and you are the only person who can do it. No one is going to make your movie for you.

"You can take a handful of dollars, a good story, and people with passion and make a movie that will stand up against any $70 million movie."
~ *Jason Patric*

"I have a strongly visual mind. I visualize a picture right down to the final cuts. I write all this out in the greatest detail in the script, and then I don't look at the script while I'm shooting. I know it off by heart, just as an orchestra conductor needs not look at the score... When you finish the script, the film is perfect. But in shooting it you lose perhaps 40 percent of your original conception." ~ Alfred Hitchcock

PART FOUR
Pre-Production

Connect with Talented People

I can say without a doubt that my movie wouldn't have been half as good as it is if it weren't for the talented people that I partnered with along the way. Specifically, a cinematographer who had an eye for quality, actors who were not only kind enough to give me their time but who also had no qualms about giving me 110% of their talent and effort, PAs and interns who didn't mind doing more than they had to because they knew that this was a small, low-budget indie film and that they contributed as much to the production as anyone else did. The key when it comes to finding and managing talent is perseverance, combined with a strong sense of vision and an unwillingness to settle for low quality. Lots of folks hire their actor friends just because they know them, and they know that they could get them for $0. Lots of folks settle for the person offering the cheapest rate as opposed to finding other ways of working with more talented (and more expensive) people by offering them credits, pro-bono work, and other forms of compensation. What I'm saying here is that there is more than one way to skin a cat, and just because someone appears to be out of your reach, that doesn't mean that they actually are.

You can hire people by offering all sorts of incentives, and in my opinion, it's better to try and do that than to settle for a person who has a low standard for quality. Settling for something because it's cheap when there is a clearly better alternative is lazy and, in my opinion, the quickest way to kill your vision and butcher what otherwise could have been a better film.

> *"When I was a kid, there was no collaboration; it's you with a camera bossing your friends around. But as an adult, filmmaking is all about appreciating the talents of the people you surround yourself with and knowing you could never have made any of these films by yourself." ~ Steven Spielberg*

The Producer

Most of you reading this book are probably planning to produce your first feature film on your own. After all, you produced a short film (or a few), so how different is a feature? Well, the answer to that depends entirely on both your *confidence* and *experience* levels. At the end of the day, if you're a low-budget indie filmmaker, then you *are* your own film producer (be default) because you are in charge of *everything* from pre-production to distribution, from hiring the crew to managing the release schedule. A producer is responsible for making sure that the film gets delivered on time and under budget, and for every short film you've ever made, that role was most likely handled by you. So, if you've worked on enough sets, and you are confident in your ability to do the work yourself, then you probably don't need to hire a producer, but that doesn't mean that you don't actually *need* a producer – all you need to do is get creative with credits and offer a Producer's credit to friends, family or team-members for doing some extra work behind the scenes.

A producer credit, and the responsibilities that come with it, should only be given to someone who has a vested interest in the success of your picture, someone who is *as* invested in it as you are, and someone who is willing to put in the work and save you money, time, and resources. Lots of younger filmmakers recruit their mom or dad as producers because they are less likely to interfere with their creative process, but I have a much more lenient approach to giving producer's credits to those who actually deserve it (especially when it comes to your *first* feature film). During the making of my first film, I agreed to give a certain vendor a producer's credit because he gave me free access to lots of high-end gear that otherwise would have cost me thousands of dollars. On another project, I gave an actress I trusted (emphasis on *trusted*) a producer's credit and a producer's role when it seemed like the movie wasn't going to happen without the extra hand. Her stepping in as a producer and taking on some of those responsibilities (without compensation) helped to ultimately make the movie we wanted, together. When shooting a super-low-budget short, I gave my swing a producer's credit in return for a day of helping me organize and obtain shooting permits in New York City. You can use the Producer, Co-Producer, or Associate Producer credit to reward people who have a vested interest in the success of your film and convince them to come aboard and offer a helping hand.

The Cinematographer

If you're shooting a film on a shoestring budget, you may not be able to afford a Director of Photography (DP) who knows what he/she is doing, but if you *can* afford it – do it! Your DP is basically your number 1 creative partner on set. At times, he/she might be your only friend, and their advice and support throughout the process are critical. Especially when you feel like you're uncertain about a decision, or if you have visual ideas that you'd like to explore further but lack the *technical* know-how. A good DP will understand and share your vision. He/she will be invested in your film, and it's extremely important that they are on your side. A bad relationship with your DP can mean the end of your picture, and so a shared degree of respect for one another is consequential, to say the least. I can honestly say that my first feature film, *Pickings*, wouldn't and couldn't have been made the way that it was if it weren't for my cinematographer, Louis Obioha. I relied heavily on his experience and expertise throughout the shoot, and his know-how not only made the movie look gorgeous (which it does) but it gave me the education I *needed* to finally go off on my own and DP my next project.

If you don't have the budget to hire a cinematographer, you should take the time needed to learn anything and everything you can about cinematography before finding yourself on set with your cast and crew (who are going to be looking at *you* for answers). You don't want to run the risk of appearing as if you don't know what you're doing. This is the main reason why DP'ing your own short films is such a valuable asset. It gives you the tools you need to run the set as a director/DP when the time comes to shoot your feature.

The Line Producer

When I made *Pickings*, I opted to save the $3,700 it would have cost to hire a Line Producer and decided *not* to hire one, but instead to be my own Line Producer; it was probably one of the biggest mistakes I made on that shoot. That decision ended up costing me a lot more money and wasted *a lot* of time. For starters, a Line Producer is your "event coordinator;" it's their job to make sure that the project stays on budget, on schedule, and that the film isn't being derailed due to unforeseen events. And if it does, a good Line Producer can put you back on track ASAP and take a lot of pressure off you. Now, will I hire a Line Producer when shooting a one-location, $20K romantic comedy? Maybe not; the logistics aren't that complicated, and the budget is pretty straightforward, but when you're filming a movie like *Pickings* for $350,000 with six locations, 115 cast and crew members combined, thirty-five days of shooting, stunts, effects, prop guns, cars, squibs, visual effects, police presence, and complicated permits, then yeah... maybe find room in the budget for a good Line Producer.

Many low-budget indie filmmakers will end up hiring their Line Producers as Unit Production Managers as well (UPM). The UPM title itself is actually reserved for DGA-approved films, but their duties remain the same. In a nutshell, a Unit Production Manager is responsible for organizing the business and finance ends of things; it's their job to keep the production under budget and to make sure that everything is running smoothly. They'll draw up the shooting schedule, oversee the budget, hire crew, negotiate rates, book vendors, suppliers and equipment, oversee location bookings and arrange for permits, and make sure that your film keeps up with union rules and regulations. They are some of the hardest-working people on a movie set and will often be credited first during the film's end title credit sequence.

The Assistant Director

Directing a feature film is very similar to playing a strategy war game; you need to know what each player on your team can or can't do. You must be able to clearly explain your vision, give orders, and trust that they'll be executed. At the same time, you also need to keep your eyes on the ball and make sure that the job is done *well*. Filmmaking requires organization, discipline, and the ability to manage people, and no one does that better than the Assistant Director. The Assistant Director (AD) can sometimes appear to be your best friend or your worst enemy on set, sometimes both at the same time. It's her/his job to make sure that the production stays on schedule by tracking daily progress, checking time, calling lunch, prepping call sheets, and keeping the peace on set. It's the "keeping track of the schedule" part that can sometimes cause friction between the AD and the director (for example, when the art gets in the way, and the director wants to squeeze in new shots that weren't on the shot list, or when your artistic style conflicts with their time management). So, if you picked an amazing AD who you get along with fine, that's great; otherwise, you might want to think consciously about how you are going to maintain a healthy relationship with your AD on set. Buy him/her a drink before the shoot starts and spend the hour talking about your overall game plan.

Ultimately, you are the boss on set, and what you say goes, but running a set like a dictator is the fastest way to get a mutiny on your hands and have people revolt against you. So, the best way to handle an AD is to consider yourself their *partner*; the magic word is "compromise." If you decide to spend an extra thirty minutes on shooting something that's not in the script, not on the call sheet, and not on the shot list, then you need to either (a) sell your vision to stop them from calling time every five minutes, or (b) compromise, remove a less important shot for the sake of making time. Because at the end of the day, the AD wants to do a good job, and doing a good job means that they may, at times, have to keep the director in check as well.

Another possible source of friction on set could be the pairing between the AD and the Cinematographer. Depending on the personalities you have on set, these fellas may sometimes be a source of conflict on set, and those conflicts are a real energy drain. The main reason for AD/DP conflicts arises from a virus that plagues every artist working on a movie set, the one that impacts the DP the most – it's called being a perfectionist. When a DP with an eye for detail says that it'll take ten minutes to set up the light for a shot, he can count on the AD calling time after nine minutes, but most of the time, a DP's ten minutes turn into thirty, or more, if not kept in check. So give your AD the respect she/he deserves and be willing to compromise; don't piss your vision away, but don't be a dictator either; find the balance.

PAs – Lifesavers Supreme

Production Assistants do everything that *has to be done* on a movie set, from getting coffee to making script copies, carrying C-Stands, holding flags, carrying equipment, driving, running errands, and helping cast, crew, or makeup when they need it. The great thing about PAs is, that in the low-budget indie world, they can be found for free, or very cheap, and the really good ones will stick around. They want to gain experience and are willing to put in the work to prove themselves. They also count on getting paid or being promoted when you call them back for another project, so try not to take advantage. The only problem that you should be aware of with enthusiastic PAs is that they don't like saying "no," especially if the director makes a request directly. So, be careful not to ask too much of your PAs because they could easily get worn out, and when PAs get super tired, that's when mistakes are made. Give them the respect they deserve, don't overwork them, feed them, and you'll be fine!

SAG Proficiency

If you choose to work with SAG, you need to be aware of and follow their rules and regulations to the letter. There isn't much flexibility when it comes to SAG contracts, and so hiring a producer or AD who knows his/her way around a SAG contract will save you a lot of time and energy. The first time I ever hired a producer on a project was when I needed to work with SAG actors for the first time. I didn't know much about SAG contracts or SAG rules and regulations, and I needed someone who could file the paperwork and represent our film with the union because that wasn't something I knew how to do, and I didn't want to mess it up. Breaking SAG rules will get you fined, and understanding SAG rules will help you get accustomed faster to their way of working, so it's something that I recommend wholeheartedly. Your alternative would be to make an ultra-low SAG short film on your own before taking the plunge into the world of feature filmmaking, thereby gaining some experience and getting yourself familiar with their rules.

No One Tells You Anything

One of the most important things I learned about people management on the set of my film was that people generally are afraid of "bothering" the director/producer when small problems arise; people's frustrations are kept to themselves and are "whispered" among the team because no one wants to bother the filmmaker. People are afraid of being "that person," the person who complains, so they keep their problems quiet until they eventually implode and become *big*. This problem exists in every hierarchy, and you'd better keep an eye out for it and address it early on, especially if you're heading into a long shoot with a group of people you don't know personally. Encouraging people to bring their questions and problems to you *personally* will help alleviate tension and improve the efficiency with which problems are resolved on set.

Get to Know Your Crew

I'm of the belief that when you have to spend a long period of time with someone, it had better be someone you *like*. And so, when we started hiring crew for the making of *Pickings,* my cinematographer and I invited them all to have a drink at a local bar. That night, we all bonded and grew to really like each other. I did the same and more with my cast, and that's something that I plan on doing on every feature I work on. Filmmaking is a collaborative effort, and if you get to know and grow to like the people you work with, that alone can eliminate lots of drama, headaches, and bad blood – when everybody loves everybody, making movies becomes a pleasure. Crew people are a breed that very much follows the "bro" mentality, and many of them respond very well to confident leadership. Many of them want to eventually do what you're doing now, so keep that in mind when you're on set. Show confidence (fake it if you have to), have fun, and treat everyone with respect, and your crew will love you. *Respect* is the name of the game, and getting to know your crew makes that game easier to win.

Keep Morale High!

When things get rough, when problems arise, and people get tired, when you're going through thirteen-hour days, shooting overnights, messing up people's sleep schedules, and keeping an airtight ship – cast and crew will get anxious, tired, and grumpy. So the one thing I always try to do now is to keep my people happy. I picked up a quick tip from Kevin Smith on how to keep morale high on set. Kevin buys hamburgers for his crew in between meals; he gives his cast members treats and knick-knacks and various souvenirs throughout the day, fun things to keep the atmosphere light – these aren't very expensive but can be lifesavers when you're shooting for a long period of time. Tarantino plays music on set and keeps his cast and crew members from falling asleep by taking pictures of sleeping team members with a purple dildo called "Big Jerry." He then hangs those pictures on a big wall that travels with the production wherever it goes; some directors play cards, throw a football, play basketball, and find other ways of keeping the atmosphere light during downtime. When I made my first feature film *Pickings*, I didn't really know that it was something that I was supposed to do, but I ended up doing some of it by default. We celebrated the end of the day by having a drink; we went to the beach, played pool, and overall had a good time during downtime. Later on, I learned that I was really saved by my lead actors – who were all a big source of positivity and, unbeknownst to me, helped keep people from giving into despair when things got really rough. My cinematographer used to go to Dunkin Donuts every morning to pick up treats for his crew before the craft services table was set up in the morning, and my cast and I used to play the Mafia party game during the course of shooting. We had some really high highs and some really low lows – but at the end of the day, we pulled through it, and I couldn't have done it without my team. I realize that not every shoot is going to be that hard, or that easy, and that there's always potential for morale to drop and for people to get discouraged, but I am smarter, I am better, and I am more experienced, and now – whenever I'm on set – I always take a proactive role to keep my cast and crew in a good mood!

Anything Short of Enthusiasm is NOT ACCEPTED

One of the biggest mistakes that I made with my first feature film was to "convince" certain people to take on their responsibilities. It's a mistake that ended up costing me a lot of time and money and nearly derailed the entire production. Our movie was very close to being shut down because of a couple of "bad hires." Early in the process, about a week before we started shooting, I had to ask a very important member of my team who had control over our schedule "not to quit" because I felt like she was going to leave the project and I didn't want it to delay our starting date. Big mistake! I convinced her to stay and gave her a raise – and then, a week into the shoot, she couldn't take the pressure and decided to quit anyway, leaving the project in shambles and our schedule "up in the air." Similarly, I had to convince an actor to stay – the actor, less than a week before principal photography commenced, decided to take on another, better-paying project and break his commitment to me because it was a "better career opportunity." I convinced him to stay and even moved my schedule around to accommodate him. Big mistake! That actor didn't show up on time and, when he did, he wasn't ready to do his job. He was rude, unprofessional, and basically an asshole to everyone on set, myself included. And while he only shot for five days on-set, his character was very important to the movie and ended up being cut from the entire film, not out of revenge, mind you, but because he couldn't read his lines without stumbling over himself. Something happened to him between rehearsal and shooting that made him freeze up and not remember any of his lines. That experience taught me a very important lesson: if someone isn't 600% sure that they want the job, don't hire them – they'll end up screwing you over.

Attend Film Festivals

I attend a lot of film festivals and not just the ones that my films are screening in, but rather film festivals of all shapes and sizes, and that habit has already paid off tremendously. Carrying a business card that says "Writer, Director, Producer" at any film festival serves as a handshake introduction that says, "Let's collaborate." From meeting actors to cinematographers, ADs, publicists, agents, etc., attending small, big, and medium-sized film festivals is the ultimate networking opportunity, and it's where I met actors who acted in my films, as well as DPs and filmmakers that I developed friendships with. The habit of attending film festivals is a valuable one, so make a commitment to attend at least a few film festivals every year, and when your projects get in, go! It's your career; it's your chance to introduce yourself, get exposure, and meet other professionals who are playing the same game as you.

Keep a Journal

When you make a movie, you're doing 10,000 things at once: from planning to executing, hiring, auditioning, communicating, and handling various tasks on a daily basis. So it stands to reason that you're not going to remember everything you do right or wrong. Sometimes, mistakes will be repeated, good deeds will go unnoticed, and you could say the wrong thing at the wrong time and experience the effect of those actions later. Keeping a journal is something that I can't recommend enough. It's a compilation of life lessons by *you*; it's book material; it's a great source of reflection, a list of all the good and bad compressed into lessons that will educate you with every new project you work on and prepare you for the next. Every time I finish a phase, whether its pre-production, on-set, or in post, I write something in my journal. I write every single thing I did wrong and every single thing I did right. And every time I approach a new project, I look over my notes from previous films. That is one practice that I cannot recommend enough.

Your Second Table Read

Your second table read serves a very important purpose: to meet with your team, read the script, answer questions, and brainstorm. It's really more of a production meeting than anything else, and it is the moment of truth where your key makeup artist, wardrobe, DP, stunt super, and other department heads get to read the script with you and write down all of their questions. Once the reading is over, you'll be confronted with questions concerning your vision, and you will take this opportunity to ask some questions of your own. "In this scene, what do you envision in terms of makeup?"; "How many cameras will we have for this crash?"; "Do you need to see him jump through the window in a single take? Or can we cut into it?" Generally speaking, you will have a vision board/look sheet and will need to take the time to hold independent production meetings with every key department head. Some department heads will ask to do a test (camera tests, makeup tests, stunt rehearsal, etc.), and it is you and your producer's job to see that it gets done. But the reason why it is important to hold one table read with everyone is that the collaborative nature of filmmaking allows people from various departments to suggest ideas and vocalize thoughts that will ultimately influence other department heads. The DP could give color suggestions and feedback to your set and wardrobe designer; your VFX supervisor can suggest ideas to your key makeup head; all are ideas and contributions that will help influence the ultimate vision presented to you by your key department heads. Filmmaking is a collaborative effort, and while you are the boss, it is crucial that you open the stage for collaborations and allow the artists that you work with to contribute their ideas and suggestions, and then judge for yourself. The truth, in most cases, is that the film director of a low-budget indie feature is generally the least experienced person there. Everyone around you has been on way more sets then you have, so hiring amazing people and listening to what they have to say is *key* if you want to be successful in this business.

Casting

Casting, without a doubt, is one of the most important filmmaking decisions you'll ever make. You can have the best dialogue ever written, but if you cast the wrong actor, all of that hard work will go to waste, and your movie will die before it even started. And I'm talking from experience, as someone who made *horrible* casting choices in the past and paid dearly for them. I implore you to take this process *seriously*. You need to be as meticulous with casting as you are with writing or choosing the right type of camera.

*"Casting sometimes is fate and destiny more than
skill and talent, from a director's point of view."
~ Steven Spielberg*

Breakdown Services

There are more than a few resources out there for filmmakers who handle their own casting. Many of these services are cheap, some are free, and all are accessible online. You're most likely going to use Breakdown Express (www.breakdownexpress.com), which doesn't cost anything up front and gives you access to some really talented actors. Or you might try a website like Backstage (www.backstage.com), which costs about $25 per ad. You might also try your luck with Central Casting, NY Casting, and LA Casting. Here's a good piece of advice: never, ever put your personal email or phone number in the breakdown service ad. Your mailbox will be overflowing with headshots, and people will be calling you every two minutes with a request that you "take a look" at their reel. So be very careful with what information you choose to reveal in the breakdown ad. What I do is set-up a Gmail address like Casting(filmname)@gmail.com or a personal email address via GoDaddy for each new production I'm involved in. That way, once the casting is complete, you can shut it down and not have to worry about your inbox being bombarded with emails.

Video Auditions Serve a Purpose

Most working actors these days are more than willing to submit a video audition before getting called in for a physical audition. Big and small production companies alike are now taking advantage of the fact that every person living in the US has a high-quality camera in their pocket, and that camera (their phone) can be used to record and send a video audition to the filmmaker, exposing them to potential actors without having to rent a space and spend hours going through amateur actors who are clearly wrong for the role. However, there is a dangerous trend that involves casting decisions being made on the merits of a video audition alone, and that is where casting mistakes are often being made. The true purpose of a video audition is to give you an idea of a person's ability to perform – it doesn't tell you if the actor is right for the role. That decision should only be made in a face-to-face audition, and for a good reason. A good actor is a person who responds well to direction, and as a director, if you're not in the room directing them, then you have no idea how good of an actor that person really is. Also, much like crew, you want to hire actors that you like and actors that you have a good rapport with, and that's something you can never get in a video audition. So, by all means, ask your actors to submit a video audition, but make sure you hold real-world, physical callbacks where you get to meet and interact with your actors, where you get to ask them questions, give feedback and watch them respond to it. That's the importance of the actor/director dynamic, and it's what's going to make the difference between a successful film and a failed one.

Casting is Terrifying

When you're sitting on the other side of that table, you rarely ever think about the state of mind that the actor is in when they walk into a room. During my first casting session ever I had no idea how terrifying the process was to the people coming in and out of the room. But when an actor friend came to visit me at the end of the day, she told me that she sat next to a lady who was waiting outside and that the lady was *terrified*. She was shaking, nervous, and wasn't ashamed about vocalizing her doubts in her ability to pull off that audition. I was oblivious because most people who walked in the room that day *delivered*, at least in their presentation; they seemed relaxed, confident, and had their stuff under control. The following day, I altered my approach and made a conscious effort to produce a relaxing casting environment for the actor. I took off my hat, so that they could see my eyes, I smiled more, was courteous and kind – in other words, I wanted to make sure that they were at ease. I don't know if it had any effect on their delivery, but two years later, I met an actress who auditioned for me at a film festival, and she remarked that she remembered my audition because I took my time with her; I was nice, friendly, and left a really good impression. The fact that she remembered me two years later and had cared to comment about the audition made me realize that kindness does indeed have an effect, and it goes a long way to ensure that people remember your name and associate with it positively.

Be Nice

Not to harp on the subject, but I do want to reiterate the value of kindness in this game because I think that it's important. I'm mortified by filmmakers who treat their actors (in the audition room and on set) with any degree of disrespect, dismissal, or abuse. When you're in charge, when you're "the boss," you have to make a conscious effort to abide by that old Spiderman rule "with great power comes great responsibility." Abuse your power, and you run the risk of scarring people, hurting them, and hurting your own brand in the process. There is absolutely no excuse to be anything other than kind in this business, and I recommend that you make a conscious effort to keep your ego in check, and handle disputes, disagreements, and conflict with kindness and respect. Other people are watching, and everything you do and say on set will go around and spread like wildfire. So, adopt the mentality of being kind to people – it will go a long way. However, you absolutely must draw a clear line in the sand and let no one cross it. Ever. Just because you're nice doesn't mean that you should allow people to take advantage of you, abuse you, or mistreat you or anyone else in your cast and crew, ever. Never be a pushover and always stand up for yourself, or else you run the risk of losing people's respect. But never resort to a loss of temper; be calculative and strategic about your responses.

"Genuine kindness is the ultimate strength."
~ Gary Vaynerchuk

The Casting PA

I cannot tell you how important it is to have a PA present during the casting session; the casting PA will make your life easier in more ways than one. In addition to doing their actual job (calling people in, operating the camera, running errands, and keeping track of time), they also serve a deeper, psychological purpose for the people auditioning, especially if they are a member of the opposite sex. This might not be the most politically correct thing to say, but it's true; it's a part of human nature, and in the real world (and especially in 2019), people in this industry are painfully aware of the power dynamics involved in male directors interviewing female actors, and male actors trying to impress their female counterparts in ways that go beyond their qualifications as an actor. This isn't just about gender; having two people in the room makes the production look more serious than just having one person sitting at a small table all by himself/herself. It's also a well-known fact that children and their parents are more likely to be at ease when the child goes in to audition in a room that has a representation of both genders, especially if the parent is requested to stay out of the room during the audition. So, whether you agree with these opinions or not, you should consider the benefits of having a PA or a friend present. At the very least, they'll save you a lot of time, and at the very best, they'll eliminate any uneasy feeling that may be associated with the audition process and help you leave a good impression.

Chemistry Tests

If you strive to present an authentic relationship between characters, especially siblings or couples, it would be in your best interest to see how these actors interact in real life. One of the things I did for *Pickings* was call in the child actors and put them in a room with actors that I'd already cast as their family members. I wanted to put them in a room and let them talk, converse, interact with one another; we did some games and questions and answers – it was fun for everyone involved. I had the kids tell sad and happy stories to their sibling and got a good glimpse of how comfortable they were with one another. And I'm glad I did. The relationship on screen looks authentic because the actors weren't acting. That same energy, that same chemistry was taking place in the rehearsal space as well, and I think that everyone agreed that it was a great practice. At the end of the day, the decision to cast an actor is entirely up to you – and miscasting can lead to trouble, so my approach is to take any steps you can to resolve potential hurdles in pre-production, and that includes the practice of chemistry tests.

Be an "Actor's Director"

When I first got started in this game, an "experienced" filmmaker took it upon himself to inform me that dealing with actors was going to be the most unpleasant part of my job as a director and, regretfully, there are many amateur film directors who believe that. The truth of the matter is, that after completing my first feature film, I can honestly say that working with actors is the most rewarding and enjoyable part of my job. I honestly love it. Actors, by their nature, are ultra-creative people who want to please – they want to do a good job, which is why the relationship between myself and my actors is *sacred* in my mind. I decided early on that I was going to be an "actor's director," meaning a director who understands actors and does whatever it takes to give them the tools they need to succeed. One of the ways I did that was to take acting lessons after I had already completed a feature film, and that experience opened my eyes to the true nature of the actor. I also became a better screenwriter as a result (learning to always keep motivation in mind when writing is a powerful acting tool that translates to screenwriting perfectly). And so, I wholeheartedly recommend you start focusing your attention on the craft of acting if you are to improve your skills as a director. At the end of the day, there is one thing that you are trying to establish with your actors early on, and that is *trust*. And if you cast an actor, that means that you must put your trust in their ability to portray the character. They need direction sure, but that direction will come easily if they trust you and respect you, and that trust and respect has to start with you.

Avoid the Line Reading

If you've had the pleasure of working with actors for a prolonged period of time, you might have come across the term "line reading." A line reading is when a director tells an actor how to specifically say a line. In a nutshell, if you wrote the line, "You'll never be my father" and have a very specific way in which you want the actor to say it, you can't be blamed for wanting to tell the actor *exactly* how you want them to say it. However, in the mind of the actor, that represents a lack of trust in their ability to portray the role and embody the character that you have given to them. It would be the biggest indication that a film director has no idea how to direct or work with actors.

The relationship between a director and their actor is a sacred one, in my opinion, and it is why I tend to refer to my actors as "collaborative partners," because experienced directors know that acting is an incredibly vulnerable experience. And establishing trust between the actor and the director is the most important thing you can do for that relationship. After all, if you think you can do a better job playing the role than the actor you hired for the role, then go ahead and do that. Plenty of directors do. But if you sharpen your communication skills and learn to work *with* actors, you will ultimately improve your directorial game and make your movies all the better.

Take Your Time

You've seen it in films before: an actor goes on an audition stage, says two lines, and the person on the other side of the table yells, "Next!" Now, I'm not a professional casting agent, but even I know how horrible that experience must be for an actor, and how much of a disservice that casting agent is causing him/herself when they either rush the actor or dismiss the actor before they ever get a chance to *act*. Directing actors, at its essence, is a collaborative process. The actor gives, and you take, then you give back, and the actor takes, and together you craft a scene and a character, and you create a feeling that translates through the screen and induces an emotion. That's the magic of acting, and that magic cannot be rushed, and you cannot expect to conjure it in thirty-five seconds or less. So my advice is to take your time.

Next time you find yourself in the audition room - smile, be kind, ask them to take a seat, relax. This isn't a job interview (although it is, you don't say it), it's just me and you – getting to know each other. Ask them about their day, their trip, their wild weekend, how long have they been acting? What kind of roles do they generally find appealing? What are some of their other hobbies? etc. I like to talk to the actor for at least two minutes before I ask them to read anything – it gives them a chance to relax, and it removes any sense of intimidation they otherwise would have felt towards me (keep in mind, when you audition, the person on the other side of the table is, more often than not, intimidating, especially when it comes to inexperienced actors).

Once I get to know the PERSON and the ACTOR, I then ask them to read the script. They'll generally ask me if I have any notes, questions, or if I want it read in a certain way – my response is always the same, "Do it your way first; I want to see what you bring to the table." Giving the actor this kind of freedom does two things: (a) it shows that you have confidence in your abilities as a writer/director, and (b) it shows that you have trust in them – that's important.

Be patient with them, let them read the sides all the way, and when they're done – you only give *positive* feedback, but with a twist. "It was great, I love how you did X. Now, let's try it *this way*" – that "this way" is direction, not a line read. You're not reading the line, you're giving them an emotion, or you put the text in context. So, instead of "be more scared," you say "try shriller" or "try it quieter, look around, you're scared." The key is to eliminate the word "be more..." and replace it with "try..."

Pick the Right Sides

As someone who has actor friends, I spend my fair share of time helping them get ready for auditions, and I've noticed, time after time, that there are filmmakers out there who send out the strangest sides to leading/supporting characters. They'll either send a part of a scene that has one very unimaginative line of dialogue, or one where the character has to say something random that doesn't feel like it carries any meaning in the story. The true purpose of sides is to give the director a glimpse into how an actor portrays a character; in other words, it tells you if the actor is a good fit for the role. And if that's the case, then why on earth would you send the actor a scene where the character asks a waiter for the check, when there's a big, very important scene only a few pages later? There is no point in watching an actor read a non-important scene that doesn't serve the story. With the exception of day players and actors who have only a handful of lines, the only sides that you should be sending to actors are those that show you the embodiment of the character. You need to send them something challenging, something that, if mastered, will tell you how good of a fit this person is to play that role.

Legal & Insurance

Yes, you are planning to shoot a feature film on a limited budget, but here are my thoughts about insurance – *you need it!* The purpose of film production insurance is to protect you from harm, and I can say with absolute certainty that it has saved my ass on more than a few occasions. Most locations, gear rental places, cinematographers, and gaffers are going to ask for a COI (Certificate of Insurance) before letting you rent or use their stuff. I keep coming back to Hiscox (for gear) and the Philadelphia Insurance Company (for shoots) because I had a good experience with them. Hiscox allows for low monthly payments which are way preferable to the higher cost of other insurance providers. Now – if you are filming a $20,000 feature film in one location (most likely your home or neighborhood) and you are using your own equipment – then use at your own risk. If anything happens, you won't sue yourself, but if you're going to be renting out expensive equipment or using locations where anything can get damaged, you'll need to get that insurance. Hiscox tends to be the cheapest option, they'll give you a general liability protection and cover your gear for around $50 a month, which is pretty cheap considering that you can print Certificates of Insurance online and that the deductibles are pretty low.

Guerilla Doesn't Mean "No Permits"

So, what if you can't afford it? What if insurance is out of your budget? Then make the film without it, but keep in mind that if anything goes wrong – it's your ass. To be totally honest, I shot plenty of projects without getting insured and on every one of them, I knew the risk. They were mostly contained to an indoor setting or shot on a free location and a guerilla team of two to four people (cast included). However, there is only one circumstance under which I will never, ever shoot a guerilla film without insurance or permits – and that's when prop guns or stunts are involved. There are plenty of horror stories about filmmakers who played around with prop guns without a permit, and when the cops showed up, someone got shot. That is a real life or death situation. To shoot with a prop gun (firing or replica), you must obtain a mandatory permit from the city (unless you're shooting indoors), and to get a permit from the city, you'll need a liability insurance policy. Without the permit and the insurance, I'll never bring a gun to set, even if it's a toy. However, whenever a permit is not needed or cannot be obtained by the local film office, I'll personally call the local precinct and let them know that we're filming inside and that there's a prop gun on set. And I was told on several occasions that it was a "good call" to do so. You can never be too safe.

Get LegalShield

For $50 a month, you can have access to a group of lawyers who are there to consult you on legal matters pertaining to your shoot. They can give you sound advice on contracts, handle disputes, and guide you through the legal thicket. They are worth the cost.

Keep Records

Make sure you keep accurate records of every agreement signed. My method is to scan signed docs using the "Tinyscan" app on my iPhone – it allows me to upload documents directly to Dropbox.

Remise, Release and Forever Discharge

When interviewing insurance companies, always ask if they settle claims with "Remise, Release and Forever Discharge" papers. If you shoot a scene inside a bar, and someone accidentally breaks something very expensive, the bar owner will settle the claim with the insurance company. A Remise, Release and Forever Discharge basically guarantees that the bar owner can't sue you after the fact for lost revenue or any other damages that arise from the accident. It's basically an added layer of protection that you'll be very happy you have when and if the time comes. It doesn't cost any extra money, but the insurance company should be able to offer it as a part of your policy.

Worker's Comp – Hire a Payroll Company

If you're making your first, ultra-low-budget, indie feature film, I would highly recommend that you seek the services of a payroll company. The logistics involved with hiring W4 employees on your own requires a lot of professional knowledge and understanding of your federal and state tax laws, including Worker's Comp and Liability Insurance. It requires that you register with the state and file quarterly reports, and – in a nutshell – will make your life very complicated. Your best option would be to hire an entertainment payroll company (emphasis on the word "entertainment"). The main difference between an entertainment payroll company and a traditional payroll company (like Paychex, for example) is that with a traditional payroll company, *your* LLC company is hiring the actor/crew member as a W4 employee. The payroll company reports it to the state on your behalf and does all the filings for you, as opposed to an entertainment payroll company, where your cast and crew are hired under *their* EIN, the company hires, pays the taxes, handles the state and charges you a fee in return. *They are the employer, not you.* They deal with SAG, the state, and everyone else, and the tax liability is on them if they mess anything up. They take away your need to fill out tax forms, calculate taxes, and file with all of the various governmental agencies, as well as having to issue checks and deal with payments at the end of the week. To save you time, here are some of the best options out there for indie filmmakers making movies in the United States today:

> **Media Services.** My choice when working on low-budget SAG films and short films.
> www.media-services.com

> **ABS**. An industry standard company; does a lot of business with indie filmmakers.
> www.abspayroll.com

> **Cast & Crew**: They handle big projects, $2m and up.
> www.castandcrew.com

* Disclaimer – I am not getting paid or being endorsed in any way by these companies. This list is based on my own personal experience. I'm sure there are other companies out there offering better services, but I have no experience with them.

Auto Liability

Keep this in mind if you have a car in any of your scenes, or if you're driving your cast to location at any point during the shoot. Payroll companies will ask you to send them a COI with Auto Liability Protection. This will add an extra $200-500 to your insurance cost, and some (not all) payroll companies will ask that you add that in as a requirement. So before you sign with a payroll company, make sure you ask them if they require an Auto Liability on the Certificate of Insurance.

Traditional Payroll

So, keeping in mind the part where I say that you should absolutely *avoid* hiring your cast and crew as W4 employees under your own LLC, there are a few cases where it might not be the worst idea to do your own payroll. The most obvious one is if you are shooting a movie non-union, non-SAG, and you have absolutely no money to spend on payroll. You can opt to do your own payroll with a non-entertainment payroll company (for example, Intuit or Paychex offer services at around $35 a week. They'll help you file with the state and handle the reporting on your behalf). You'll be considered a temporary employer, but you will need to make sure that they close your account with the state when the production is over, and you are no longer hiring. Established companies like Paychex and ADP will guide you through the process of hiring your employees and eventually terminating them and closing your account with the state. Other reasons for using non-entertainment payroll can be (a) if you're an immigrant under a business visa, and hiring employees is part of your Green Card requirement; (b) if you have an existing business and already have an account with the state; (c) if you're applying for certain grants and film tax credits that require your LLC to be the employer; (d) if you are funding the film via an SBA loan that requires your company to hire local people; etc.

1099 MISC

In addition to issuing paychecks, your LLC will need to pay certain individuals as W9 contractors. Any member of your crew who owns and operates their own business or operates as "self-employed" will most likely ask you to pay them as a 1099 contractor, as opposed to a W4 employee. In addition, any payments made to non-employees will need to be paid under the Contractor category. Payments made to location owners and private vendors will also be made under 1099, and as far as crew members are concerned, it's not uncommon for gaffers, cinematographers, makeup artists, costume designers, and set designers to request 1099s as well. The benefits of 1099s are numerous, and the topic is way too complicated for this book to cover, but one known fact about 1099 is that it's cheaper and easier than a W4. You pay less money in taxes, and there is no need for Worker's Comp because the person getting paid is working as an independent contractor, and they are responsible for their own taxes at the end of the year.

Some no-budget, non-union indie filmmakers opt to hire their entire cast and crew as 1099 contractors and make all payments on their film under "contractors for hire." It's cheaper, requires very little paperwork, and eliminates the need to hire a payroll company. However, you should definitely check your state's laws regarding "employees" vs. "independent contractors" before making a decision in that regard. It's not my job to advise you on which course of action you need to take, but I will say that if you choose to pay everyone under 1099 MISC – it's still better and safer than paying your cast and crew in cash or under the table. Either way, you should consult an accountant before making a decision to find out the best course of action for you. Just keep in mind that the 1099 approach to cast members won't fly with SAG. If you opt for a SAG contract, then you have no choice but to handle salaries as W4s.

Rate Sheets

Every payroll company is going to offer different rates. I recommend you call a few of them and ask for rate sheets to get prices before settling for any specific payroll provider. Generally, you can expect to pay around 16-19% of your salaries to the stuff you can't avoid, such as Social Security, Medicare, Worker's Comp, etc., and the payroll provider will generally charge anywhere from 0.5-1.5% as a fee; that's on top of a check-mailing fee, ACH fee, Wire fee and Stop Payment fee. Generally, the cheapest way to deal with payroll companies is via checks; they tend to charge less for checks than they do for ECHs. Again, this varies – it's your job to do your homework and find the best rates; make some phone calls and get prices before committing to anyone. If by any chance, you have the budget to hire a Production Accountant or a Line Producer who doubles as a Production Accountant, they will usually have their own way of handling payroll, and they'll take it off your hands completely.

Guilds and Unions

There are four primary industry guilds/unions that you need to be aware of:

- Writers Guild (WGA)
- Screen Actors Guild (SAG)
- Producers Guild (PGA)
- Directors Guild (DGA)

Each of these guilds will offer various benefits and protections to their members, but as someone who's making their first-time, low-budget indie feature film, there is only one union in here that you need to concern yourself with, and that is the Screen Actors Guild (SAG). If you want to work with real actors, and you have the budget – SAG is the way to go.

Becoming a SAG Signatory

Before you can hire a SAG actor to be in your film, you need to become a signatory. Basically, your company and your film need to get approved by SAG, and the process of going about it is not that complicated. All you need to do is go online to the SAG website (www.sagindie.org/signatory/) and apply. They offer phone support as well and are generally pretty accommodating when it comes to answering questions by indie filmmakers. Make sure you submit all the required paperwork at least five weeks before you start shooting, and be sure to read their rules and regulations carefully and take extra measures to adhere to them. This is also where it pays off to establish an LLC company before you start production since it makes the process of hiring, making payments, and dealing with SAG a lot less complex. Keep in mind that working with SAG can be a pain. There's a lot of paperwork, lots of regulations, reports, and things to keep in mind to the point that it makes sense why so many amateurs choose to work outside the system. However, if you plan on hiring professional actors and eventually make progress in this business, you need to become a SAG signatory and learn to work with SAG contracts. Also, keep in mind that as a SAG signatory, you can work with non-SAG actors by issuing waivers, but that doesn't work the other way around. You can't hire SAG actors without becoming a signatory first.

SAG Budgets

The type of SAG contract you get and the rules you must abide by will depend to a large extent on your film's budget. The bigger your budget, the higher your actor's day rate, and the greater the cost of making your film. As of 2019, the minimum day rate for a SAG actor under their low-budget agreement is $125 a day. A typical SAG contract defines the actor's day rate, compensation for overtime, legal work hours, rest periods, meal times, exhibition rules, nudity rules, etc.

There are six basic SAG agreements that you need to be aware of:

- Short Project Agreement
- Student Film Agreement
- Short Film Agreement
- Ultra-Low Budget Agreement ($250K or less)
- Modified Low Budget Agreement ($250K-700K)
- Low Budget Agreement ($700K-2.5M)

If you have no prior experience with these contracts, I strongly suggest that you look into hiring a SAG producer—someone who has experience with SAG and knows how to file the paperwork, represent your production with the union, and make sure that you are in compliance—or make a low-budget SAG short film to see what you're going to be dealing with on your upcoming feature.

Deferments

One of the more popular options that SAG offers its low-budget signatories is the *deferment* option, which allows you to withhold pay to the actor for a predefined period of time. Lots of folks seem to be under the impression that "deferred pay" means "no pay." The fact of the matter is that deferment is nothing more than a budgeting tool, and it must be used strategically.

For starters, you will need to pay *something* upfront and commit to paying the rest before the film is exhibited, you're not avoiding the cost, you're just delaying it. In fact, SAG won't let you release the film commercially unless all of the salaries have been paid, along with the 18% Pension & Health (P&H) payments, Social Security, taxes, disability insurance, unemployment, overtime, reimbursements, per diem and liquidated damages, among others. The point I am making here is this: don't think of deferment as a money-saving option because it's not. SAG can be expensive, and you need to be aware of the cost before you commit to working with them.

Location Scouting

Assuming that you don't have the budget to hire a location scout, how do you go about finding locations? Whether they're free locations or locations you have to pay for—the scouting process is generally the same, and the answer is, however you can.

For *Pickings*, we knew that we were going to shoot a big chunk of the film inside a bar, it was practically a *character* in our movie. It couldn't be a New York City bar because the place had to be somewhat isolated and our budget was pretty tight, to say the least. So my first task was to write down a *Must List*, an itemized checklist that included the following:

Country bar, 7 days of filming, $500 a day.

1) Isolated.
2) Must be able to shoot for 12 hours a day, at the least.
3) Must accommodate a $500 a day budget.
4) Must be easily accessible, ideally within a 30-mile radius.
5) Must have a back alley.
6) Must have a back office.
7) Must have a stage for on-screen performers.
8) Must have a backdoor or a back entrance.
9) Must have a cellar.

Our film's budget and logistics called for items 1-4 while the screenplay (the story) called for items 5-9. I started searching for neighborhood bars in Staten Island, Yonkers, Jersey, and Connecticut. I created an Excel spreadsheet and made a lot of phone calls, sent a lot of emails, and reached out to *every* place I could find within a 30-mile radius. To say that you need to be fastidious in this line of work would be an understatement. The fact of the matter is that location scouting can be painstaking work. However, one of the many benefits of working in the movie business is that most people get *excited* about the prospect of being included in your project, specifically when it comes to bars, restaurants and other small businesses. The right movie can generate a good deal of exposure, it's effectively a perpetual ad campaign that *pays* the business, instead of the other way around. So when I called and presented myself as a film producer on the lookout for a new location, I was generally met with enthusiasm. I went into every bar I could find, looking around, taking pictures, asking questions, and doing my homework as scrupulously as I could, and I quickly realized that I'd have no choice but to compromise on my *Must List*. I had found some great bars that met *some* of my criteria, but lacked a few important features such as the cellar, the alley, or the back office. So the thought of "cheating for camera" came into play, and some of my *Musts* turned into *Shoulds*. The big question I had to ask myself whenever I visited a new location was: *How do we film around it? How do we make this space look like something it's not?* This is one of those classic cases when creativity and self-efficacy can come together to solve problems and "save your movie" in pre-production.

Ultimately, our search led us to a beautiful Irish bar in Yonkers, New York. We learned that during the week, this particular bar closed its doors at around midnight, which meant that we could potentially use the space overnight. The delightful couple who owned the bar were more than willing to accommodate our shoot (despite our less than ideal budget) and we asked if they could close the place a little early so that our crew could start setting things up—giving us about 12 hours of work per-night, and to my amazement, they said yes!

Now, compromise was inevitable, and we ended up having to rent a separate location for the cellar. But since the bar had its fair share of doors, we could "cheat" the space and make it look like our characters were walking *from* the cellar *to* the bar upstairs with a simple cut. We also had to "set-design" one of the bar's VIP rooms to make it look like a back office. We added furniture, stacked beer boxes and loaded up the space with as many knick-knacks and novelty item as we could find to make it feel authentic. It worked out quite nicely.

On cellar location in Staten Island, $100 per day

I followed the same (*Must List*) approach when scouting for our other locations. Some were free (exteriors), some were *really* cheap (we found a creepy-lookin' cellar in a creepy-lookin' house for $100 a day—what a bargain!), and others were open to negotiation. Our character's home was found on Airbnb for less than $300 a day. We secured our mobster's restaurant in Staten Island by calling places we found on Yelp and asking if they were "smoker friendly." We secured another bar by complete happenstance as we were driving past it on our way back home from another location.

Basically, what I'm trying to say here is this: location scouting doesn't have to be expensive or complicated, it's a lot of work, but it's *manageable* work. You shouldn't strive to check every single item on your location's *Must List*; instead try putting your creativity to work and figure out how to "cheat" by using doors, stairs, and creative set design to make your space work for your story. A door in one location can lead to a door in another, *the only limitation is your imagination.*

Our Yonkers bar, rented for $500 per day

We turned this VIP room into an office. It's amazing what creative set design can do.

"When I'm dissatisfied with a location scout, I go on Google Earth. It's an amazing tool."
~ Niels Arden Oplev

Budgeting

Creating a movie budget is a pretty straightforward process, although it might seem a bit daunting if you've never actually seen one before. Today, every person who has access to the internet can find a multitude of sources designed to help indie filmmakers in the creation of industry-standard movie budgets, as well as guide them through the detail and terminology typically found within these budgets.

However, not many sources dive into the *strategy* behind the financial planning of a low-budget indie film; and I believe that the true value of a budget is not in its composition, but rather in its efficacy. Anyone can download a budgeting template and write a bunch of numbers in it, but doing so without proper research and without a sensible strategy can lead to a guaranteed disaster. A poorly researched budget will kill your movie and blow a hole through your pocket before you ever turn your camera on.

The purpose of this chapter is to give you a basic rundown of what a typical movie budget looks like, but more importantly, it'll give you an in-depth look into your *budgeting strategy*. Specifically, in this chapter, I'll show you what I would do if tasked with the creation of a $10,000 feature film budget. The approach presented in this chapter can easily be applied to any movie, regardless of its budget.

It's Easier to Make a $10,000 Film Than a $300,000 Film

A lack of resources often gives birth to innovative ideas, and oftentimes, low-budget filmmakers are forced to come up with creative solutions to problems that otherwise would have cost a small fortune to resolve. This is why movie studios love to hire them, they know how to save a dollar. The general idea is that the less money you have to work with, the more effective you must become. In our case, that means fewer locations, fewer actors, and a smaller footprint.

The 80/20 Rule

Whether you are working on a $5,000 budget or a $50,000 budget, if you plan to *fund* and *distribute* your upcoming film yourself, or retain distribution rights until a sale is made, then you *must* adhere to the following rule:

The 80/20 Budget Rule says that you must allocate at least 20% of your film's budget towards marketing, distribution, and unforeseen emergencies.

The chances that a first-time filmmaker who operates without the assistance of an experienced Line Producer (or Production Accountant) will exceed their proposed budget is quite high. Plenty of first-time filmmakers go over budget, and when they do – bad things happen. Filmmakers could max out credit cards and go into debt (not recommended), and once they're out of resources, they're screwed! Without any money to put back into the project, they are forced to shut it down. This is why *strategic budgeting* is so important. You never want to put yourself in a situation where you're going broke because of a movie you're trying to make. Your art shouldn't destroy your finances and ruin your credit, and if it does – you're doing it wrong! The best piece of advice I can give you is this: if you have a $10,000 budget, make a movie for $8,000. If you have a $50,000 budget, make it for $40,000. Always put 20% of your budget to the side.

First, it will teach you how to be more *disciplined*, which is crucial if you ever want to succeed in this business. Second, it will give you *leverage* once your movie is done. You'll be in a better place to negotiate terms with distributors and will have the option to self-distribute if no good deals come your way. It'll give you the freedom to invest in the release of the film, which is just as important as the making of it. Putting 20% of your film's budget towards marketing and distribution will give you a *huge* advantage, putting you and your movie way ahead of the competition. We'll cover the specific use of those 20% later in this chapter.

Above the Line: The Cast

Under the SAG Low Budget Agreement, you are required to pay your actors a minimum of $125 per day. So if you're trying to make a one-location film for under $10,000, you need to keep in mind that on a five-day shoot, five actors will run you around $3,125 (assuming no one is operating under "deferred payment"). Add $701 in taxes, Social Security, payroll, and Workers Comp; plus, another 18% for Pension & Health contributions ($562). You are now looking at $4,388, and that doesn't include overtime, per diems, travel and gas compensation. In total, you'll need to put aside around 50% of your film's budget to pay for five SAG actors.

Alternatively, you can opt to hire some non-union actors for less and not have to deal with the union, or you can choose to write a more "contained" script that centers around one or two characters (in which case, SAG becomes affordable). Watch some highly contained movies like *Before Midnight, Following, Phone Booth, Buried, Locke, Panic Room,* and *Zulo* for inspiration. These "contained" stories generally revolve around one or two characters and take place in a single location. They are easier, faster, and cheaper to make, and in my opinion, they're the perfect first film for a newbie filmmaker.

Above the Line: Your Assistant Director

As I mentioned before, a good AD can save your life, and so it's crucial that you do your homework before you hire anyone and don't be afraid to ask for references. In the low-budget indie world, a good AD will run you around $100 per planning day and $250 per shooting day, but with ADs, you can often work out a deal where they get paid a single lump sum for the duration of the project. The AD will be with you from pre-production and stay by your side until the day you wrap. Some ADs stay on for post as well but that's not as common in the low-budget indie world.

The Director Does the Budget, Too

If you're an indie filmmaker, chances are you are creating and managing your own budget when you shoot; however, if you are a hired director, you may feel inclined to "not care" about the budget since it's not your money, not your problem. But, if you want to be hired again, and if you want your financiers to love you (and you do), you need to be heavily involved in the budgeting process. Ask to sit in on financial meetings and get to know the film's budget, intimately. As a creative person, you have the power to envision alternatives to budgetary issues that producers and money people may not be able to. Combining shots, alternating between props, and fixing problems in pre-production are going to ultimately save the production a lot of money, and a smart director will get involved with the specifics as soon as possible so that (a) he/she has a say as far as how the money is being spent, and (b) so that his/her artistic decisions won't be compromised due to financial restrictions and poor financial planning. The role of a DIY filmmaker is to handle *everything*, and the minute you show your face in the morning, you'll get bombarded with questions and problems that you have to solve. The smaller the set, the fewer problems you ideally have, but problems arise either way. *Problem-solving is a reality that you have to learn to accept and try and master.* Watching the bottom line is a daily concern, and it's something that you have to keep an eye on, every day, from the minute you start pre-production until the minute you release your film to theaters. Whether you have to report to financiers or yourself, keeping your film under budget requires careful planning, and it's something that you need to be good at, even if it's not your job.

Designate a Production Accountant,
Even if You Have No Money

This may seem like an oxymoron, and I know that a Production Accountant probably sounds like a luxury your little movie cannot afford – but trust me, you don't have to afford it, you just have to *designate* it. The main role of a Production Accountant is to control the cash flow (many times, your Line Producer will take on that role), basically, it's their job to make sure that you don't bounce checks. On a low-budget indie film, they'll be the ones writing the checks and keeping balances. On a big feature film, their job is a lot more complicated. But just because you can't afford a Production Accountant doesn't mean you shouldn't have one. Ask your Line Producer to take on that role, if you have one, or invent a character named Mary Sue (she's British), who sits in an office in Los Angeles somewhere and let her be the film's Production Accountant, while you secretly do the task at the end of the day. Hire your mom, your sister, your uncle, or that childhood friend of yours to be your film's Production Accountant. The reason why you *should not* be in charge of cutting checks and dealing with money while on set is clear to anyone who has ever worked on a low-budget shoot and understands how human beings behave; but if you haven't had the pleasure, let me guide you through it. You are the writer, director, producer of the film – it's day 15, and you're about to shoot a very intense and very important scene. You're about to walk up to the actress and guide her through her mental state for that scene and explain the camera move to her when suddenly you are stopped and approached by a cast/crew/team member who tells you that they need an advance on their pay, or that he/she is working too hard for too little and is demanding that you pay them more, right now! What do you do? Do you argue? Do you take the time to diffuse the situation? If the situation becomes dicey, and the person is combative, you are now in *an argument* in front of your cast and crew, seconds before you are supposed to shoot a scene. Your head will not be in the right place, and that could mess up your day, fast!

Someone told me it was going to happen, and I brushed it off with, "Nah, it'll never happen to me." And then it did, and I had to get into an argument with a crew member minutes before I was supposed to shoot a scene. The crew member was fired the next day, but that messed up everyone's day and definitely got in the way of me being able to direct a scene properly. So take it from me, if you are a one man/woman show, people will approach you about money at the *worst* possible time! And if you are kind enough to accommodate a request, I can pretty much guarantee that another member of your team will approach you with a similar demand. This is where the option of saying, "Email Janet, I don't handle the money" is a blessing.

Designating someone who isn't *physically present* on set as your Production Accountant will free you from that responsibility. In most low-budget films, that role will be given to the Line Producer, and that Line Producer is tough as nails. That person will send an email to everyone a day or two before the shoot begins with instructions on how to handle complaints, questions, and other problems that may arise on set (including questions about money). So try to avoid being the money person on set; it'll solve a lot of problems.

Below the Line: The Production Designer / Art Director

Your Production Designer is as much your "creative partner" as the cinematographer – it's his/her job to hire and manage your art department (people and budgets) and to make sure that your film stays consistent with its visual theme, from locations and sets to props and costumes. They are in that "first hire" cluster, meaning they get involved shortly after you've started pre-production. Most low-budget indie filmmakers will merge the Production Designer's responsibilities with those of the Set Designer and Art Director – and just hire them as "Art Directors." On the very low end of the spectrum, an amateur Production Designer will run you around $100 per day (including prep days), but much like the Sound Mixer and Cinematographers, you can opt for someone more experienced and strike a deal "per project" if the film is shot for more than a week and if the script is amazing. $200-400 per day is what you can expect from a Production Designer who knows what he/she is doing. Also, keep in mind – that person is going to need an Art Budget.

Below the Line: The Camera Package

When a low-budget indie filmmaker hires a Director of Photography, they'll hire someone who has his/her own camera package. That camera package will most likely include the basics: The camera, storage (SD Cards, C-Fast, Red-Mags, etc.), lenses (at the very least you'll get two lenses: a long lens and a short lens), and some basic camera operating gear like a rig, tripod, shoulder mount, and slider. The more money you have, the bigger the package and the more accessories you get with it. The smaller the budget, the more creative you have to be with what you have. Now, there's an ongoing debate in the filmmaking community about which camera you ought to be using for your low-budget feature film – to me that debate is flat-out ridiculous because it's not nearly as important as many gearheads think it is.

Stop Obsessing Over Gear

Plenty of indie filmmakers are *obsessed* with the camera they're using, but you – as the film's screenwriter, director, and producer – shouldn't be nearly as obsessed with the camera because you are already obsessed with the *story*, and that's infinitely more important than how many details you have in your shadows. Your obsession should be with your screenplay, your cast, your visual style, your story—not the machine with which you use to capture it.

There's a common saying that you can give an IMAX camera package to an amateur filmmaker and an iPhone 4 to Steven Spielberg and see who makes the better movie. The point is to just go out there and tell a *great* story, get attention, and use that attention to get money for your next story (which will ideally have the budget you need to work with the camera of your dreams). That's the game plan, so stop obsessing over the camera and instead focus your attention on the story.

If you live in a big city (like NYC or LA), you can find a great DP with a 4K camera package for $250-500 a day, and when working on a seven-day shoot, that comes up to a total of $1,750-3,500. The decision whether or not to hire a DP is ultimately up to you, and while it's very important to have a DP on set, it's not as if you can't shoot a movie without one. Plenty of filmmakers DP their own films, and if you are confident enough in your own abilities to light a scene and op the camera, then by all means, be your own DP. Otherwise, you might want to hire someone, and hire someone with a decent kit who knows what they're doing. Let them obsess over their camera, and you keep your eyes on the story.

Below the Line: What Camera to Use

Steven Soderbergh's movie *Unsane* was shot on an iPhone 7, and it was a pretty bad-ass film. Sean Baker made *Tangerine* on the iPhone 5s and went on to win the NEXT award at the 2015 Sundance Film Festival. Now, would I personally ever shoot a movie on an iPhone? Most likely not, and not because I don't think I can do it, but rather because there are better options out there that will cost me next to nothing in the camera department.

Assuming you decided not to hire a DP but to shoot your own film instead, then you can rent a decent 4K package for very little money, and the results will be infinitely better than an iPhone. Keep in mind that most big city rental facilities work on a five-day week basis. That means you can take equipment out on a Friday and return it Monday morning and only pay for a single day of rental, that's one *powerful* loophole that you can take advantage of. If you choose to only shoot on weekends, you can save a lot of money on camera rentals. There are plenty of filmmakers who opt to shoot their films on weekends. They'll pick up their gear every Friday morning, shoot over the weekend, and return it first thing Monday morning and be charged for a single rental day. On a fifteen-day shoot, you only paid out of pocket for five days of rental. That's not a bad deal.

Free Gear

This trick is also pretty cool, and it's a strategy often used by low-budget or no-budget indie filmmakers, and although it is a little sneaky, it's far from illegal. You can buy a decent camera from a store that has a return policy, shoot with it, and then return it before the 30-day period ends, and you only have to pay a fraction of its cost on shipping and returns. The only caveat here is that you must bring it back in the same condition you bought it, and it must be done within the return period, and, of course, the cost of the camera is paid upfront and then returned to you when you send the merchandise back – but even so, the fact that you end up spending next to nothing on your gear is pretty amazing.

Should You Buy Gear?

The question of whether you need to buy your own equipment is one that a lot of people are asking, and the answer to me is very simple: *if it costs less to own it, buy it.* But if you're only going to use the camera for a week and then send it back to the rental place and never have to touch it again, then it makes no sense to spend all that money on a brand-new camera. I run a little side business where I sell cinematic stock footage online, so it made sense for me to buy. Whenever I don't use the camera, I rent it out to other people on camera rental websites like KitSplit. The investment in gear only makes sense if you shoot a lot of content or if you rent it out for extra income.

Camera Rentals

So, if you decide to DP your own film, then you are now facing the dreaded question that has been pestering YouTubers and gear-heads since the birth of DSLRs: "Which camera should I get?" to which the only reasonable answer could be: "Whichever camera you can afford, obviously." However, nowadays, depending on your budget, there might be plenty of options for you to choose from, and so I'm going to give you my two cents on cinema camera package rentals. Note the word "cinema," i.e., narrative, story, fiction, anything that's shot listed and lit for cinematic effect. The reason I make this distinction is that not every camera which can shoot video should be used to make a cinematic film, and today you can probably afford to rent a wide variety of cinematic cameras, even if you have very little money to spend.

> Note – it's important to understand that not every camera will be suited for every situation, as every shoot requires a different set of parameters. Some cameras work well in low light, others have better colors and nicer skin tone, some cameras have full frame sensors, and others have crop sensors. Some cameras are smaller, others are heavier, some are more suited for run and gun situations, and others need more time to set up. So whatever I write in here is based on the assumption that you are shooting a narrative feature film with 50% exteriors, 50% interiors, 25% night exteriors, 25% night interiors. It's split evenly down the middle. That's a heck of an assumption, but it's one I need to make in order for this to make sense. This is also based on my own personal opinion, so please take it with a grain of salt.

Anything under $500

If your camera rental budget stands on $500 or less, you can rent out an A7s II kit with a basic lens, a tripod, two SD cards, and two lenses on KitSplit for $50 per day, which should be enough for a twelve-day shoot (ten days of filming + two weekend days). Alternatively, if you *only* choose to shoot on weekends, you could increase your daily budget to $125 and get a better kit. Also, the Blackmagic Pocket Cinema Camera should cost you around the same price. For $65 a day on KitSplit, we found the Blackmagic Pocket Cinema Camera 4K, packaged with a Rokinon lens, a Gini Rig w/follow focus, a Magnus VT4000 Tripod, a Rode Video shotgun mic + mini boom pole, SD Cards, four batteries, and accessories. This pricing will vary to an extent, depending on what part of the country you're in.

If you want to add some stabilization, you might have to pick up a gimbal. Both the A7S II and the Pocket will work fine with a Ronin S, which runs about $50 per day. If I were to shoot a simple film tomorrow with a $500 camera budget, either one of those would most likely be my choice for a kit. However, if I had a light kit budget, or if I was shooting outdoors during the day, I would most likely choose to shoot with the Pocket 4K since the colors are going to be a lot nicer and the image overall is far more cinematic. The A7s II is great, but it's not a cinema camera. It has a horrible rolling shutter problem and color grading is going to be a challenge. Again, for a $500 budget it doesn't really matter that much, just get the story in the can, and you'll be fine.

Anything under $1,000

Most low-budget indie films are shot in around ten to fifteen days or so, so a $1,000 camera package budget lands right on the sweet spot. For a ten-day shoot (eight + weekend) you can afford up to $125 per day if you choose to shoot it consecutively, in which case I'll be picking up the same kit as the $500 or less but will probably get an extra lens, a slider, or a gimbal. However, if again, you opt to only shoot your film on weekends, then you have a little more wiggle room, in which case, ten days of shooting filmed over the course of four weekends (it'll actually get rounded up to twelve, so you have twelve days of shooting) will give you a camera budget of $250 per day. For $250 per day, we found a C300 kit on KitSplit that includes the camera, lenses, batteries, cards, a tripod, external recorder, and lights. For $200 a day, we found a Blackmagic Cinema Camera package that included the 4.6K camera, batteries, chargers, cards, and a set of Rokinon Lenses. Now keep in mind, if you have no light budget or sound budget, it might be wiser to combine these and get a package that includes the lights and sound within the camera package.

Anything under $3,000

If you're shooting on a $3,000 camera budget, you are now in a place where you can afford to rent way better gear with high-quality lenses. For an eight to ten-day shoot, $3,000 will grant you a $375 daily budget when shot consecutively, and if you choose to only shoot on weekends, that'll be twelve days of shooting filmed over the course of four weekends, which will give you access to some real gear at $750 per day. In most likelihood, for $750 per day, you'll end up getting a Red Epic kit with some cinema lenses, a tripod, slider or a Dana Dolly, and some accessories to boot. Or you could simply choose to hire a professional cinematographer and save yourself the hassle.

"In the finished Annabelle 2 there's one Blackmagic Pocket camera shot and one Ursa Mini 4.6K shot. Let's see if people can spot them." ~ David Sandberg

Below the Line: Gaffer / Light Package

So, once you have your camera package secured, your next step would be to hire a gaffer. It's the gaffer's job to execute the DP's "lighting vision;" they're the head electrician, the ones checking the fuse box when you go into a new location. Gaffers are also responsible for overseeing the grips and in big cities, gaffers will bring interns with them, sometimes for $0 cost to you. An experienced gaffer will come with a light truck, and in a big city like NYC or LA, you can get a decent gaffer for as little as $200-300 per day (I'm talking about an experienced gaffer who knows what he/she is doing. You can clearly hire an amateur for $100 a day). A more experienced gaffer will bring more equipment, work faster but will charge more (you're looking at $400-$600 per day).

However, if you are working as your own DP, you might as well look into either renting or buying a lighting package, and if you're working on a low-budget DIY indie film, you're most likely going to buy a very basic LED/Tungsten kit and rely more heavily on practical lights and natural daylight for the rest. Unlike the super exciting world of cameras, there aren't nearly as many gearheads out there talking about the "best light", simply because there are so many options and variations when it comes to light, and good lighting can come from anywhere. Cinematographer Shane Hulbert has an online seminar where he lights a scene with a high-end lighting kit and then takes it apart and relights the same scene with a $100 Home Depot light kit – the results are amazingly close, and that's the beautiful thing about light: you don't *need* a super expensive light kit to make a good movie. In fact, I can name many films that are not "beautifully lit" but are otherwise amazing films.

Now, keep in mind that the gaffer brings more than just a light to the set, and you're going to need to have access to the rest of the stuff: C-stands, light stands, flags, gaff tapes, gobos, ND gels, black cloth, zip-ties, apple boxes, etc. Most of these can be purchased or rented quite cheaply and be resold at the end of the shoot.

Get a Grip

If you choose to gaff the film on your own, I highly recommend that you hire a grip. They'll save you a lot of time and energy on set, which is something you really *need*. Shooting a film is exhausting enough as it is, but having to move the light, walk back and check the camera, then move the light again all on your own is going to kill you after about three hours. Hire a grip! In big cities, you can find inexperienced grips for free, but considering how hard they work, you might want to give them something at the end of the day. Also, keep in mind that if you have a few people behind the camera, it gives your film a sense of legitimacy, and it makes people put more trust in you. On small shoots, I'll hire a Swing (someone who does grip as well as fill other duties) and a PA/assistant for the cost of a stipend.

Pack a Goodie Bag

Whether I'm filming with a big crew or just on my own, whether I'm the DP or the director, you'll never find me on set without my goodie bag. It has saved my life on numerous occasions, and since it's such a random little bag, it often contains within it items that other people never thought about bringing with them to the set that day. If something goes wrong or a gaffer misplaces an item, I'll have a spare in my bag and save them the fifteen minutes it'll take to find where they've put it. My goodie bag includes a gaff tape, tape measure, a multi-bit screwdriver set, a small LED light, batteries, clapperboard, clamps, lens cleaner, macro tube, zip ties, gels, black cloth, a small foldable green screen, diffusers, HDMI cables, and a small monitor, among other items.

> "It's far better to shoot a good picture than a good-looking picture." ~ Robert Richardson

Below the Line: Sound

At the end of the day, you can have the best picture quality in the world, but bad sound will make any movie unwatchable. Sound is something that you should give as much attention to as anything else in your film, and the person responsible for that sound can be a very dangerous hire. Sound isn't something that can be easily observed on set. It's not constantly being checked by a group of technicians. There's a certain degree of trust that must exist between the sound mixer and the filmmaker, which makes the process of hiring a sound mixer all the scarier. Oftentimes, you won't have any idea what the scene actually sounds like until you drop the files into your editing software, and by that point, it's way too late to do anything about it. Therefore, it is crucial that you hire a sound mixer that you can trust – someone with high standards, someone who, believe it or not, *loves* sound! A sound mixer who has high standards might be an annoying presence to some people on set, muttering "hold for sound" every time they hear an abnormality. I personally don't find it annoying at all because I know that a sound mixer's job is *internal*.

Unlike a makeup artist, a DP, or a costume designer, a sound mixer works in relative isolation. They have their headphones on from the minute you yell "roll sound" to the minute you yell "cut," and when it's all said and done, nobody else is exposed to the quality of their work. They run their own quality control.

Almost every sound mixer/boom operator will have their own kit, generally a boom, a mixer, and a few lavalier mics. The particulars of their kit will change based on the parameters of the scenes in your film, because some scenes are harder to mic than others. A scene with five talking heads on the beach is going to be way harder to mic than a living room dialogue scene between two people. The more talking heads, the more lavalier mics they need and the trickier their job becomes. And that is why I'm not a fan of doing your own sound work on set. For starters, it only works in medium/close-up shots and in fairly quiet environments (I'll rig the mic to the top of the camera and hook it up to a Zoom recorder), but that means that you can forget about wide shot dialogue scenes, or shots where the character is talking and walking away from the camera. So do yourself a favor and hire a great sound mixer, they can make or break your film. A good sound mixer is going to cost you anywhere from $200-500 a day. You can probably find someone on Craigslist for $100 a day, but keep in mind that if you make the wrong choice, the entire picture could be ruined. You don't want to have to "save your sound" and be dependent on ADR.

What if You Have No Money for Sound?

In my opinion, sound should be one of those things that comes above all else in the Below the Line budget, simply because it's so darn important. But what happens if you have $500 or less to spend on sound for your shoot? On a ten-day shoot, that's not going to be enough for a sound person, and if you can't hire someone under deferment (basically agree to pay them later), then your only other option would be to rent/buy sound equipment and utilize whatever tools you have to capture the best sound you can.

A used Zoom H4N Pro recorder will run you about $150. Add to that a Rhode Shotgun mic, and a few lavalier mics from Amazon, and you can spend less than $400 on a decent sound kit. And when it comes to setting up the mic in your scene, you'll need to get creative. Know the blocking ahead of time and plan your mic setup accordingly. You can have the PA run the boom and listen to the sound on their headphones; you can also have a shotgun mic mounted to your camera, thus capturing two sound sources. The lavalier mics can be hidden on your actors, and the wires hidden under their clothes and plugged to their phones. Apps like Voice Record Pro will actually yield some amazing results with these lavalier mics. However, this process comes with its own set of difficulties and creative challenges that you'll need to figure out how to solve before you start shooting.

Under the Line: Makeup

One of the first people to show up on set every morning and one of the last people to leave at the end of the day is the makeup artist. I have a lot of respect for makeup artists, and I really enjoy the ones who have a *passion* for it. So, unless you're making a fantasy, sci-fi, or horror, your makeup department isn't going to be a full-time nuthouse. The basic setup for most low-budget indie films will include one to two makeup and hair artists. The more characters, blood and special effects you have, the more people you'll need in makeup. But if you're keeping it simple, if you're making a $10,000, one-location romance film, then you're probably looking at hiring one head makeup artist who also does hair. That makeup artist will most likely bring an assistant which you'll get at a discounted rate. So, a beginner may charge you $100 per day, assuming that there's no need for blood or crazy SFX makeup, but a *good* makeup artist will cost you anywhere from $250 to $400 a day (again, long shoots will qualify you for a discount). So, if you keep your makeup to a minimum, you're looking at anywhere from $1,000 to $4,000 for a ten-day shoot.

Your $10,000, One-Location Feature Film

So, what would I do if I needed to shoot a one-location, low-budget indie feature film for $10,000? Well, for starters, I have some experience in the cinematography department, and if I didn't, I would probably take the time to *learn* as much as I could; but the bottom line is that for $10K, I am *not* hiring a cinematographer. Also, I am only giving myself $8K-8.5K to work with, following the 80/20 rule I had established earlier. That extra $2k will be spent on festivals, marketing, and if I can't sell it – distribution. Also, for that budget, I might be able to get away with a seven-day shoot (five days + weekend, Wednesday morning to Sunday night) and would have to opt for a one-location film with a few scenes shot in my area of residence and a few scenes shot outdoors. I'd run a skeleton crew and a skeleton cast and keep things as minimal as I can.

On a $10K shoot I might have to go with non-union actors, since going SAG could double my hiring cost. If I budget $2,000 for cast, then that's my cast budget. But if I decide to make it a SAG film, I'll have to add an extra $1,500 to my cost just to cover their fees and taxes. If you have more than two actors on a $10,000 film, you might want to think twice about SAG, especially if you've never worked with them before. Now, if you can get a SAG cast and get them to agree to a partial deferment, then you could potentially shoot this film as a SAG picture. But again – I'd recommend getting experienced with SAG before you make the commitment.

Let's say I choose to write, direct, and produce a *Before Midnight* type of story (with a twist) – a lady checking into an Airbnb has a passionate, drunken, one-night-stand with her Airbnb host. Things get complicated when we learn that the host is engaged to be married and the lady is a distant relative of the bride to be. Cool story, right? I'd probably want to spend half my time shooting inside my own apartment, half the time will be spent shooting outside on the streets of NYC, and maybe one scene will be shot at a local bar (if I can get it for no charge). I'm not going to shoot a wedding scene and will be keeping wardrobe and makeup to a minimum. Also, absolutely no transportation; we'll be filming the whole thing in and around my home. So, let's take a look at my budget:

"To be honest, I've always made films and I never really stopped, starting with little stop-motion experiments using my dad's Super 8 camera. In my mind, it's all one big continuum of filmmaking and I've never changed." ~ Christopher Nolan

Above the Line

Development Costs	Rate	Total
Setting Up the LLC (Legal)	$225.00	$225.00
Script Copies	$25.00	$25.00
Copyright & WGA Registration	$50.00	$50.00
Subtotal:		**$300.00**

Production Team	Amount	Unit	X	Rate	Total
Producer	X	X	X	$0.00	$0.00
Line Producer	X	X	X	$0.00	$0.00
Subtotal:					**$0.00**

Cast	Amnt	Unit	X	Rate	Total
The Leading Lady (6 out of the 7 days)	6 Days	Days	X	$125.00	$750.00
The Leading Man (5 out of the 7 days)	5 Days	Days	X	$125.00	$625.00
The Wife	2 Days	Days	X	$125.00	$250.00
The Girl's Best Friend	1 Days	Days	X	$125.00	$125.00
The Guy's Best Friend	1 Days	Days	X	$125.00	$125.00
Extra Characters * Non-Union			X	$0.00	$0.00
Cost of Casting / Auditions			X	$50.00	$50.00
Subtotal:					**$1,925.00**

So, if I tell this story from the girl's perspective, that means I probably have more scenes with her than I do with anyone else. I divide my time between the leading man and his best friend, the leading lady and her best friend, the conflict with the wife, maybe bring in the parents, add a few unpaid day players and some extras to make it interesting. Thus far, I'm above the line at $2,225, and I have $5,775 to go.

Below the Line

Set Hires & Operations	Unit	X	Rate	Total
Camera Package: Blackmagic Pocket Cinema Kit with 2 Lenses, Tripod, Cage & ND Filters	7 Days	X	$80.00	$400.00
Light Kit (I'll purchase a basic Kit)		X	$250.00	$250.00
Sound Mixer	7 Days	X	$150.00	$1,050.00
Makeup Artist (won't use her every day)	6 Days	X	$100.00	$600.00
Swing / Grip	7 Days	X	$100.00	$700.00
Production manager (Doubling as Assistant Director)	7 Days	X	$1,000.00	$1,000.00
Food Budget	7 Days	X	$120.00	$850.00
Props Budget (Purchase/ Rental)	X	X	$200.00	$200.00
Misc. incidentals, etc.	X	X	$500.00	$500.00
Subtotal:				**$5,550.00**

Above the Line	$2,225.00
Below the Line	$5,550.00
Subtotal:	**$7,775.00**

So, if I had $10,000 to work with, I would aim to shoot my film for 80% of the budget (came close at $7,775). I would utilize free locations, rent a very basic camera package, hire only essential personnel on the days that I need them, but pay them, feed them well, and do what I could to make this film look as professional as possible. If you own your gear, then you might be able to spend the extra money on SAG, and write in a role for a TV actor, at $500-800 a day and shoot his/her scene on the last day of the shoot. This will help you get your film noticed and get you into festivals. I have created this budget under the assumption that you have access to a home or an apartment, that you have access to a laptop and a printer, some hard drives for storage and an editing software. I'm also assuming that you know your way around post-production, and that you don't have to hire people to finish your film. This is a true DIY indie film; all the balls are in your court.

If my math is correct – there's $2,575 left in the budget. What are we going with that? First of all, that money should *not* be touched during the production of your film unless something horrible happens and your entire shoot is threatened. In which case, it's better to break the piggy bank and pay up rather than lose the entire film. If you've managed to get through your shoot without going over budget, and you find yourself in post-production with that 20% intact, here's what I would do with it:

Post & Release	Amnt	Unit	X	Rate	Total
Music Budget (5 Tracks @ Audiojungle)	5	Tracks	X	$25	$125
Festival Submissions (Early)	20	Festivals	X	$25	$500
Subtotal:					$625.00

Distribution *If I didn't sell the film* *at a festival*	Amnt	Unit	X	Rate	Total
Wix Website (6 months)	6	Months	X	$14	$84
Quiver Digital (Sell Directly on iTunes & Google Play)	X	X	X	$1,200	$1,200
Sell on Amazon – Free	X	X	X	$0	$0
Advertising on AMS Amazon	30	Days	X	$10	$300
Subtotal:					**$1,584.00**

I have also taken into consideration that you don't have any friends in the music business, in which case you have no choice but to pay for music. When I made *Pickings*, I received several offers to contribute music for $0 in return for a shared promotion or an on-screen credit and a mention on our social media pages.

Okay, so I guess the purpose of this budget is to show you that with $10K, you can make an ultra-low non-union film and have the money left over to distribute it yourself (if needed). And if you can make a $10,000 film for $8,000, then you can make a $500K film for $450K, and a $3m film for $2.5m – and *that* is a skill that studios and financiers will cherish. It's a skill that will keep you employed forever and keep you and your moviemaking business profitable.

"I feel that your ambitions should always exceed the budget." ~ Guillermo del Toro

Side Note – Why I Love Shooting in New York City

There are many reasons to love New York City. For one thing, it's the biggest and most recognizable movie set in the world. It's also a very *cinematic* city and transportation is super-cheap, but all that is just a bonus. There are a few reasons why New York City is film-making heaven (to me, at least), and here are just some of them:

> *1. Free to Shoot.* In New York City, as previously mentioned, if you're not blocking the sidewalk or using any of the city parks at night, you're most likely going to apply for an "optional permit," which is another way of saying that it's free. Skeleton crews and small productions don't require a permit to film in the city, but if you want to cover your ass and get one, it's 100% free. Now, whenever permits are not optional in New York City (meaning you *need* a permit), the cost is fairly cheap as well ($300 one-time fee per production) when compared to other cities (where you pay per day).

> *2. Free Police Presence.* If you're filming a scene in New York City that requires a special permit, like when an actor has a gun on set, you'll find that the city provides you with police presence for no extra charge. When we filmed *Pickings* in Yonkers, NY, we had to pay for a police officer to come to set whenever a blank firearm was discharged, and we paid by the hour. You pay anywhere between $400-$800 a day to have police present on set in other places, in addition to the permit fees, and it's even worse in other states that aren't as film friendly. So, the fact that your $300 permit comes with a friendly NYPD officer is a blessing.

3. Plenty of Options to Choose From. Have you ever tried holding a casting session in a small town? I have. In 2010, I was in pre-production for a horror film that never came to fruition, and I held auditions in Fort Wayne, Indiana. Around twelve actors applied, and many of them came from many miles away. In New York City, however, you put one ad out there, and you get inundated with submissions: actors, crew, post; everyone has a home in New York City.

4. Free Locations. I already mentioned that NYC is one of the best movie sets in the world, meaning you can step outside with a camera and shoot in Chinatown, Little Italy, The Village, Wall Street, Upper West Side, Harlem, etc., but the city also offers a wide array of free locations. If you visit www1.nyc.gov/site/mome/resources/location-library.page, you can find a list of free NYC locations to film in.

5. Made in NY. Movies made in New York are eligible for participation in the Made in NY program, which gives filmmakers access to discounts from vendors, free publicity, and advertising on the subway system, as well as hiring opportunities for PAs and hardworking folks from low-income areas who want to get into the movie business and be a part of your set.

6. Tax Credits. NYC filmmakers are eligible to receive a fully refundable credit of up to 30% of their production and post-production costs. You should check out their website for more info on that; it's designed for bigger budget films, but it's still pretty amazing.

Planning Our $10K Shoot

The Shot List

Before I do a lick of planning, I'll sit down and visualize the film. I'll break the script down and make note of each and every shot I need to tell the story the way I want to tell it. I don't adhere to the wide, medium, close-up rule and I'm not too rigid about my shot list either. I know that things change, and as I see new locations and get exposed to the actor's blocking, my vision of a scene or a line of dialogue may change with it. So, step one – shot list!

Planning Your Own Shooting Schedule

Since I put some money aside for an AD/UPM, my life is going to be made somewhat easier on this shoot. I design the schedule based on my shot list. I usually give myself thirty to forty-five minutes per shot (depending on the size of the crew and the complexity of the shot; some shots need more time, some need less). This is also why one-location films are so darn effective; you have no travel dates. Setting up new scenes is a breeze because all of the gear is already on-location, and you don't need to haul everything in every day. Everything is done in less time. Sure, you may switch locations when you go from the bedroom to the living room but, ultimately, you're inside the same house.

> *"I have a notebook, and I know what decisions will be made in pre-production. Everything is pre-determined in the pre-production period. I visually design the whole thing, and I know when things will happen." ~ Alejandro Gonzalez Inarritu*

The Call Sheet Template

Getting your call sheet-making skills under control will be the thing that'll make the difference between a successful shoot or a production nightmare. Being organized isn't optional, and I don't care if you're calling sixty people, or two people, the quality of your call sheet and the way that they are organized will be the biggest factor in how well your movie is progressing. Your chances to stay on schedule are usually measured by the quality of your call sheets. Here's an example of a call sheet from my first feature film, *Pickings*.

Simple Script Breakdown
"PICKINGS"

Day: #1	Date: 03/02/2016	Location(s): INT. CELLAR - NIGHT	Scenes: S01

Description: Jo Lee-Haywood pontificates on the virtues of pain vs. pleasure before executing Jimmy.

Cast	Props	Production + Crew	Set	SFX	Hair / Makeup
JO	Chairs (X2)	Director	Workshop tools	Gun fires blanks	Jimmy FX Makeup
BOONE	Cigarettes, Rolled	AD + PM	Red chairs	Earplugs	Momo FX Makeup
JIMMY	Revolver – Blank Firing	DP + Gaffer		Dusk masks	Blood, lots of it!
MOMO	Revolver Bullets	PAs (X2)		Blood squibs	
	Rope (Extra Bloody)	HMU (X4)		Blood on Boots	
Minors?	Tooth (Bloody)	Grip + Assist (X2)		Smoke machine	
None	Boone's Lighter	Crafty (X1)		Dust, lots of dust!	
	Jo's Lighter	Weapon Handler (X1)			
		Police Officer (X1)			

Wardrobe

JO, OUTFIT #1	BOONE, OUTFIT #3	JIMMY, OUTFIT #2	MOMO, OUTFIT #2
Red, long skirt	Plaid shirt	White Dress Shirt	Blue, Dress Shirt
Red, see-through jacket	Jeans	(Very bloody)	(very bloody)
Red, lipstick	Brown, leather jacket	Black, Dress Pants	Blue, suit jacket
White Boots + Spurs	Stetson cowboy hat	Black, Dress shoes	Black, dress pants
(Blood on boots)	Cowboy boots		Black, dress shoes
			Black, skinny tie

Camera Department	Grip / Electric / Cranes	Vehicles	Others
Camera Kit + Accessories	Light kit	15 Pass Van (1)	NYPD Permits Needed
Lens Kit		Light Truck (1)	
"Falling tripod stunt"		DOP Car (1)	

Be a Disciplined Shot Lister

Every amateur film director knows the feeling – you have a shot list, you get to the set, things happen, the day gets longer, and you start your first shot a little later than expected. CUT TO four hours later, and you're behind schedule. You were supposed to be on shot 15, but instead, you are on shot 10. You are now forced to abandon the shots you missed because you ran out of time, and you have to move on to another scene and leave the location. Planning and sticking to a shot list is an act that requires *discipline*, and if you can develop that discipline, you will ultimately become a better filmmaker. Your end product is going to look more like what you originally envisioned, and you will have become a master of your craft. Shot listing is an artform unto itself, one that puts your creative juices in a state of constant conflict against time and resources. It's not unusual for first-time filmmakers to plan out thirty to forty shots per day, only to go on set and come back with ten to twenty, or alternatively, get forty shots but be under such heavy time constraints that the shots turn out sloppy, and the actors don't really get a chance to act. The desire to have all these different shots from different angles ultimately stems from a *lack of confidence*. The filmmaker is either trying to be "cool" by planning various ECUs and crazy camera movements, or they are afraid of "not getting what they need," so they over-compensate by shooting the scene from a million different angles.

This lack of confidence can only set the stage for disappointment, and I'm talking from experience. In my first few projects, I was going after the wrong kind of coverage – the "cool" or "safe" kind – but since then, I think I've developed the discipline and the ability to shoot wisely and plan out my shot list from the point of view of a storyteller, not someone who's out to look cool. *What is the purpose of the shot?* What is it supposed to make you feel? Is the character scary? Or scared? Are they feeling small? Or big? Isolated? Or loved? Every shot is a painting, designed to convey information, to move the story along, and give us a glimpse into the character's experience.

The "Rules" of Shot Listing

Every four-year film school in the country spends a good deal of time teaching its students a somewhat outdated approach to preparing a shot list, and I'm sure that you are aware of it. It goes a little something like this: "Get the master, then go for the medium or over the shoulder, and if you have time, go for the close-up." This approach to shot listing was and to this day is still used by filmmakers around the world because it is simple and safe. The master is your backup; it allows you to run the entire scene from beginning to end on a wide angle lens. The medium/OTS is what you cut to; each character gets a medium shot, and then you get the close-up – reactions, key lines, etc. It's been the drill on movie sets since the dawn of time and for a good reason: *it's effective.* However, filmmakers should treat cinema as an artform, not a technical experiment in capturing the same types of shots over and over again from different angles. Filmmakers ought to experiment with the way they shoot, the way they edit, the way they frame, and the way they direct their movies, and this is where a *confident* filmmaker stands out from the crowd.

Directing is an extension of screenwriting; and so you should be mindful of the writer's *purpose* in a scene and apply it to the various elements that construct the whole (the individual shots). The purpose of a shot is to *convey information*; camera movements should have a purpose, and your framing will have all sorts of symbols attached to it when done correctly. It's ultimately up to you to decide how to use the camera, the blocking and the stillness or movement of the camera to convey an emotion, and what meaning you want to give each shot in your film. So, shooting a wide, when a wide is not needed, is a waste of time, and shooting a close-up in a scene where the actor is running might also be a waste of time. Don't follow the wide, medium, close-up rule blindly – use it at your discretion.

Every film is going to be handled differently, and every filmmaker is going to tell a story in their own way. No one rule applies to all moviemaking, and if you follow the rule blindly and shoot wide, medium, and close-up on a scene that really *only* needs a close-up, you might find yourself out of time by the time you get to the close-up, and you go home without the shot you *really* needed.

So, forget the rules, focus on *meaning* instead. For example, you can give this scene to fifteen different filmmakers: "A character slowly walks from her bedroom to the kitchen after hearing a strange sound in the middle of the night." Every one of those fifteen filmmakers will come back with a different result, and a few of them will be way better than the rest. Why is that? The answer lies within the shot list (obviously sound and visuals play a role, too). One filmmaker will choose to track the woman from the minute she gets out of bed to the minute she gets to the kitchen, walking behind her with a Steadicam in a single shot, following her gaze into different rooms as she walks around the house, slowly. Another filmmaker will take the wide, medium, close-up route – and the scene will be cutty – and that's fine, if it's done for a *purpose*. But the reason should never be that the filmmaker was too scared to go for what he or she really wanted first, so they ran out of time.

Don't Lose Shots, Combine Them

Running out of time *sucks!* Whether the sky changes, your location time runs out, or you can't afford the SAG overtime, and the pressure is mounting – it sucks! Even the best and brightest will have off days and will run out of time on occasion. What lots of folks do is opt to scratch the shot (which is why it's so important to get the shots you want *first* and keep the safe shots for later). But you don't really have to scratch the shots; you can opt to do some *oners* – basically a single shot that includes all of the shots you needed in a single take. You put the camera on a Steadicam or handheld it and let the scene run, going from wide to medium to close-up (not necessarily in that order). You do the second take from a different angle so that you have something to cut to. On days where I'm running late, I'll sometimes call action and, without cutting, have the actors run through the scene a couple of times, capturing three or four shots in a single take; again – there are no rules. If you have thirty minutes left, and you're missing five shots, run the scene, don't stop, capture it from various angles, and let it run until you're out of card space or time runs out.

ECUs Inserts and Cutaways

If you watch any of my films, you'll see inserts, close-ups, and ECUs peppered throughout; they all serve an *important purpose* – to save your butt in the editing room. I will often wrap a scene with five to ten minutes to spare for inserts, close-ups, and ECUs because I know how valuable they are. Having something to cut to when the edit isn't working is a life-saving habit that I'm glad to say I've mastered to a degree. The name of the game is *coverage*, and I never leave a location without getting as much of it as I can. For me, it's been a lifesaver, and it makes the esthetic of my film a little more interesting. Try adding a few minutes for ECUs, inserts, and cutaways at the end of every location or scene before you move on to the next. Each shot shouldn't be longer than a few seconds, but that extra coverage can save your life in the edit room. You most likely won't it use unless you want to call attention to something, but when you *really* need it – it's there.

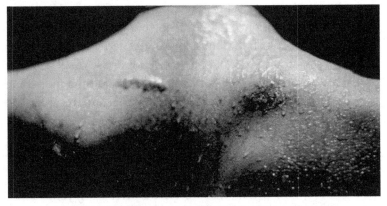

A close-up shot from the movie "Pickings". Close-up shots can serve you well in the editing room, never leave the set without them.

The Ultimate Filmmaking Masterclass

What follows is a great shot list/framing masterclass for people who want to learn to direct film masterfully. *This* is what I think they should be teaching students in film school: Go online and find a screenplay to a movie that you haven't seen but want to watch. It can be something old, something new, or in between. Read the script and pick your favorite scene, then put your friends in a room, take a camera if you have one or use the camera on your phone, and shoot the scene, beginning to end, with slates, from different angles, just like you would on an actual movie set. Make a shot list, take notes on how you want your actors to perform, figure out the purpose of the scene, the blocking, etc., and *film it.* Then go into Adobe Premiere or any other editing software and edit the scene; put it together – watch it. Then go rent the film and watch what that filmmaker did differently. That is the *ultimate* filmmaking masterclass, and the experience you get by doing it will far surpass any other course or class you can take. Do that exercise ten to fifteen times, with different films in different periods, different styles, looks, and locations if you can, and as you go deeper and deeper into these projects, you become a little better with each one, and by the last short exercise, you've filmed a Hitchcock scene and sound designed it, lit it all on your own, and maybe added a special effect – and it looks amazing! After each exercise you do, you'll start to improve, and by the tenth one – you'll be ready to make a feature. It's a free exercise that takes nothing more than time and dedication to the craft of filmmaking, and, regardless of how much experience you think you have, this is an exercise worth doing.

"To question your own process is a necessity. If you don't question yourself, it's impossible to improve."
~ *Alejandro Gonzalez Inarritu*

Framing / Storyboarding

One of my favorite parts of film directing by far is framing. The quality of your framing ultimately comes back to *meaning*. The best directors are the ones who can convey a lot of information in a single shot without the character saying a word or the actor doing a lick of acting. Study the works of Sergio Leone, Alfred Hitchcock, Stanly Kubrick, Quentin Tarantino, Buster Keaton, Steven Spielberg, and Martin Scorsese to see how they choose to compose their shots and move the camera to tell a story. The one thing I would say about storyboarding and shot listing is that you should never be married to it. Sometimes, you go on location, and a shot that you thought you could get won't work, or you see a potential for an amazing shot that you didn't think of before – don't do what some other filmmakers do and become a slave to your own shot list. When you see a location and new ideas come to mind, revise accordingly.

When it comes to storyboards, I generally storyboard my scenes using 3DS-Max or Autodesk Maya, but you can storyboard using a pen and paper. Sometimes, the old-fashioned way works best (*there are no rules*). The purpose of a storyboard is to help you visualize your shot list and communicate your ideas to your team, so whatever course you take to achieve that is irrelevant. Some great apps for storyboarding include Shotpro, Frameforge, Storyboarder (free), Canva, and Boords.

Storyboard for Dual Action. Created with 3DS-Max

Research Artwork

These days, all you have to do is visit Google, and get access to a million-and-one artworks crafted by artists from around the world since the beginning of time. When I dig into the visual planning of a movie, I'll typically search for inspiration in artwork, paintings, murals and artistic photographs. I'll create a "visual inspiration board" on a Word doc, print it out and put it up on my wall. Each artwork represents a feeling, a theme, a color pallet, or an idea that I want to capture. Getting exposed to art will help spark your imagination and serve as a major source of inspiration. Color pallets, themes, and other creative ideas get boosted by the observation of related artwork. And while most people get those inspirations from other films (myself included), the exposure to other forms of art can often serve you more. It's something that I picked up from cinematographer Shane Hulbert and I've been applying to my films for quite a while. Wes Anderson does the same thing, and his artwork speaks for itself. I personally favor the work of artists such as Dorothea Lange, André Kertész, Annie Leibovitz, and Brassaï. I recommend you Google their names and see if you find their work as entrancing as I do. You never know where inspiration could come from.

Ahead of Schedule, Under Budget

I think that there should be a special awards category for filmmakers who finish their film under budget or ahead of schedule, and that's because there are so many films made every year that go *over* budget and get pushed back due to production delays. In most cases, the ability to stay under budget comes down to *discipline* and *planning*. Accidents will always happen, and there is no telling how a production is going to go when you first get into it, but those who plan ahead, those who stay organized and understand their product, and those who are *disciplined* will be on schedule and on budget. Likewise, those who plan to go under budget will, and those who plan to be ahead of schedule have a greater chance to.

Planning, Planning, Planning

Alfred Hitchcock used to say that it's better to lose $100,000 in pre-production than a million shooting something that isn't ready to be shot. If you are unhappy with your script, unsatisfied with your plan, your actors, your team, or don't have a total grasp of your schedule – stop! Take a breath, and figure out if it's worth pushing or postponing your schedule. It's not a good idea going into principal photography for a project that has unresolved issues in pre-production; the whole "we'll figure it out when we get to it" is a recipe for disaster. The minute you set foot inside that set is the minute the clock starts ticking. You have a certain number of hours to get the shots you need and move on to the next piece, and the more you plan ahead, the greater your chances of walking out with the raw material you need to make your movie happen. Going into principal photography without doing diligent planning is a death wish and is something that I'll never indulge in again (I've had some painful experiences that resulted from a lack of planning). If you're lighting your own film, you must have a light schematic plan in place; you should know how you're going to light the space ahead of time. The last thing in the world you want to do is get to set without a plan; that could steal hours from your day and set you off to a rocky start. Doing your homework and planning your shoot properly will help ensure that your time on set is utilized properly and that no time is wasted. So, visit your location before you shoot, figure out which lights you're going to use and where are you going to put them, figure out the blocking in advance, run a camera test at the location before you shoot – do it! If you can bring your actors and rehearse the scene, do that. Planning and organization shouldn't be on your "nice to have" list; the success of your shoot is literally dependent on your ability to plan and stay organized. And lighting can be a big time thief if not carefully planned ahead of time. So, plan out your shots and plan out your lighting by creating a light schematic (check out the *Shot Designer* and *Shot Pro* apps on the iPhone / Android).

Bring Two of Everything You Can't Live Without

Every movie you make serves as a masterclass in filmmaking, and these masterclasses often teach you what you can or cannot do, what you're good at, what you're bad at, where you need improving, and what you should or should never attempt to do on a movie set. As I was writing this book, I went through a "troubling" experience on set, and something happened that I could never have anticipated (which is why books like these are important: they teach you how to expect the unexpected). We were filming a beautiful short film called *Windblown* in a gorgeous Rhode Island town called Charlestown (it's about three hours away from New York City). We were sleeping in the cottage where most of the filming took place and ended up staying on location for five days. And being the experienced crew that we are, we made sure we had every piece of gear we needed. We planned it thoroughly, got permits, notified the police, had a good-looking shot list, booked all of our vendors and suppliers in advance, and had hired some wonderful SAG actors. We arrived on location, and everything was going smoothly, aside from the lack of sleep – we were moving along, and every day was wrapped ahead of schedule – something that is quite rare on indie sets like ours. Then, at the end of Day 3, something unexpected happened. Our C-fast Card Reader died. For those of you who don't know, C-Fast 2.0 cards are small, expensive, and really fast recording media cards for cinema cameras like the Ursa Mini and the Alexa cinema cameras. Luckily for us, the card reader died at the end of the day after we had wrapped principal photography for the day. However, unfortunately for us, Rhode Island doesn't really have a whole lot of places where one could buy a C-fast card reader. We spent the entire night and a portion of the following morning making phone calls to every camera store we could find, and we couldn't find anything within a 50-mile radius. In other words, it looked like we were in *real* trouble. If this was New York City, a quick run to B&H would have solved the problem, and I would have had the solution within a matter of minutes, but because we were filming on location, that wasn't possible. We ended up sending our location manager (a man who was kind enough to let us use his location for free) on a hunt all the way to Boston – a two-hour drive each way. We were very close to running out of card space when the time came to break for lunch, and our savior returned with the card reader from Boston. The lesson here is this: if you're filming in any other city or town, make sure that you either (a) have the contact information of a local camera rental facility that has the equipment you need in case anything breaks down; or (b) bring two of everything that you can't live without.

Your Pre-Production Checklist

Before we finally pull the trigger, it's time to run through a checklist of everything we need to wrap our pre-production process and move into the production phase of our film.

1. Get Your Feet Wet – Make a $0 Short Film.
Create a $0 short film for the sole purpose of educating yourself on the process of making films from start to finish; nothing beats real-world experience. Try the "Film Directing Masterclass" I mentioned earlier.

2. Get Some Post-Production Experience.
Get some practice and experience with Photoshop, Premiere, After Effects, or similar software, and get yourself familiar with the post-production process. You can learn everything you need to learn in 2 weeks or less.

3. A Polished Screenplay, Obviously.
At least three to five drafts, and keep editing until you're *happy* with the results. Check for exposition, character development, etc. Read it aloud, make sure it gets the job done. Anything short of great isn't good enough.

4. Logline.
A strong logline should describe the central conflict and hook the reader. You'll put it up on your IMDB page, your website, social media, etc.

5. Synopsis.
A brief description of the main characters and the film's conflict; end it with a cliffhanger.

6. Budget.
Create your first film budget on Celtx, Excel, or other budgeting app.

7. Script Breakdown.
Break down your script and make a line-item description of your film.

8. Create a Shot List and Schedule.
Go over your shots and plan your day meticulously. Keep SAG rules in mind if you're working under SAG contracts.

9. Visualize.
It's time to visualize your film, create a storyboard, and shoot rehearsal videos for complicated action sequences.

10. Table Read.
Bring your friends, family, actors, producers, etc. and run through a table read.

11. Post-Table Read Rewrite.
Take notes during your table read and make the appropriate changes, if needed.

12. Business Plan / Marketing Plan.
Define your strategy for funding, making, and marketing your film.

13. Set Up an LLC and Prep Contracts.

Protect yourself and make your film legit. Sign up with the state as an LLC, start preparing contacts for actors, crew people, producers, locations, vendors, and others.

14. Set Up a Bank Account.

Create a bank account for your LLC and get a checkbook/debit card. This will help you keep track of your budget and will make financial reporting and handling a lot easier.

15. Copyright Your Script.

Send your script to the copyright office and submit it to the WGA.

16. Build a Website.

Use Wix or some other web-building app to create a good-looking website. If you have no money to spare you can create a website using Wordpress for free.

17. Create a Social Media Presence.

Create a Facebook, Instagram, and Twitter account; create a logo in Photoshop and share it with the world.

18. Create an IMDB Page.

Visit the Contributor Zone and create a page for your film.

19. Create a Concept Poster.

Use your newly found Photoshop skills to create an awesome concept poster or visit freelancer websites like Fiverr to create one for you.

20. Hire Your Above the Line People.

Hire your Producer, Line Producer, AD, and designate an off-set Production Accountant.

21. Hire Your Cast.

Hold casting sessions and assemble your cast. If you are casting SAG, you need to become a signatory and submit their paperwork at least three weeks before principal photography begins.

22. Set Up Payroll and Insurance.

Work with an Entertainment Payroll provider (when doing SAG), or pay everyone via MISC 1099. Whatever you do – just make sure you do it *on the books*. Secure your insurance if you can afford it.

23. Post-Casting Table Read.

If you can't afford a rehearsal session, invite your actors to a table read. Take notes.

24. Hire Your Crew.

Hire your Department Heads: DP, Makeup, Sound, etc.

25. Hold Your First Production Meeting.

Bring your department heads together in a room. Print copies of the script for everyone and do a reading of the script from top to bottom. This is their opportunity to plan, ask questions, and get an idea from you about your vision for the film, wardrobe, makeup, hair, light, etc. (Make sure you have plenty of coffee and some snacks; it could go on for a while.)

26. Hire Your PAs.

Hire your head PA, and task him/her with finding free interns, behind-the-scenes shooters, and people who want to help make movies happen.

27. Location Scouting.

If you're not filming a movie in a location to which you already have access, you'll need to scout and secure locations; hire a location scout/manager or do it yourself.

28. DP One-on-One Meeting.

Meet with your cinematographer and go over the shot list and storyboards (don't do this during the production meeting; it'll waste everyone else's time. This meeting is all about the director and his DP coming together and deciding on the film's look, color pallet, light themes, challenges, etc.). If you happen to be your own DP, it's time to hire your crew, specifically, your key grip, gaffer, and AC. It's also time to secure your camera and light package.

29. Secure Permits.

Make sure each location is signed under contract, has a certificate of insurance, and that you have a permit to shoot there. This varies depending on your budget, but you should take every measure possible to ensure that you're operating legitimately and responsibly. Never shoot gun scenes or stunt scenes without a permit, and don't do anything stupid like block the sidewalk or shoot on a railway track without permission.

30. Secure Food & Crafty.

Make sure you have enough food, snacks, coffee, and tea to feed your hungry cast and crew for the duration of the day.

31. Greenlight.

The moment of truth: time to lock the shooting schedule, make a commitment, and send out call sheets to everyone. This is also the time to pay all the bills that need paying, upfront payments to vendors, props, wardrobe, locations, 15-pass rentals, security deposits, gear, and equipment, etc. On *Pickings* we did this about two weeks before principal photography began; however, that will vary from shoot to shoot.

32. Early Publicity.

I'll dive into the specifics of publicity in later chapters, but keep this in mind. While you're shooting, you need to get as many BTS photos and videos as possible, and if you have the budget to hire a publicist, hire them before you start shooting. You can use your own social media to post photos and create hype during the shoot to get those followers interested.

33. A Toast!

Invite everyone, and I mean *everyone*, to a celebratory drink at a local bar a few days before the shoot. It's time to say "good luck!" and thank everyone for taking part in your project. If you can't do it before the shoot, get a bottle of champagne or wine and give a toast on set at the end (or start) of day one – a tiny glass of wine wouldn't do any damage, but the gesture will go a long way.

"In order to write scripts, you must first study the great novels and dramas of the world. You must consider why they are great. Where does the emotion come from that you feel as you read them? What degree of passion did the author have to have, what level of meticulousness did he have to command, in order to portray the characters and events as he did? You must read thoroughly, to the point where you can grasp all these things. You must also see the great films. You must read the great screenplays and study the film theories of the great directors. If your goal is to become a film director, you must master screenwriting." ~ Akira Kurosawa

The Ultimate Gear Checklist

So, you're three days away from on-location principal photography, and you need to make a list of everything you need to bring with you to the set; here's your chance. I'm going to assume that you're DP'ing and directing your own film. Now keep in mind – if you don't have all of these things, that doesn't really matter. Bring what you do have, and try to have some fun!

Camera & Audio Gear	*Lights & Grip*
Camera & sound Kit	Basic lighting kit
Lenses	Clamps, C47's
HDD storage + card readers	Eyelight / catchlight
Batteries & chargers	Gels & filters
Slider / tripod / stabilizer	Diffs, silk & bounce
HDMI cables	C Stands / light stands
Laptop with USB 3 or faster	Rain covers (if needed)
Portable generator	Green screen (if needed)
Clapperboard, markers	Goodie bags
Splitters & extension cords	Apple boxes
Pelican cases or bags	Sandbags
On camera mic / recorder	Gaff tape, marker tape
XLR cables	Tape measurer
Headphones	Black cloth / duvetine
Lens cleaners	

When Shooting Far Away From Home

Foldable chairs	Garbage bags
Small foldable tale	First aid kit
Paper towels	EZ Pass
Zip ties	Coffee maker, thermos
Portable cooler	Driving music!!

PART FIVE
Production

Rehearse, Please!

Most low-budget indie filmmakers never put the money aside for rehearsal because they are under the impression that they cannot afford it. But the truth is – they need it! And it's often more affordable than you think. Rehearsal helps you make a better movie, and that's just a fact. For starters, when you rehearse, you get to know your actors better; you get to develop a relationship with them, and you build a stronger rapport with them, which will be a lifesaver once you start shooting. Rehearsal helps you refine the scenes, the dialogue, and the characters. It is the actor's opportunity to ask you questions about the scenes and better understand their purpose and intention for each moment. Each line is looked at carefully, and the collaboration is being utilized to its max potential. Rehearsal also allows you to *brainstorm* with the actor, to come up with ideas, solutions, thoughts, and basically just work together to perfect the actor's connection with the character he/she is playing. For my money, I will always opt to rehearse when shooting a dialogue-heavy short or a feature film.

Rehearsal Tips and Tricks

1) When you read through the scene for the second time with your actors (whether on set, on the day, or during rehearsal), let them walk around the room while they act. This will help you better visualize your blocking and maybe give you some last-minute ideas you could use to improve the flow of the scene.

2) Have your script handy with a pen, take notes on the first run, then go back and address them one by one. Don't interrupt the first read; let your actors do their thing.

3) Keep in mind that some actors respond better to intention (this is what your character is feeling), while others respond better to direct emotive, like "sadder," "more intense," etc. The majority of actors will respond better to the former.

4) If camera movement is necessary, and if you are working with a camera operator, shoot the scene in rehearsal with an iPhone, so that your operator knows how they're supposed to move the camera.

Trapped Inside Rehearsal (Top) vs. On Set (Bottom)

Carefully Plan Your Rehearsal Schedule

If you choose to rehearse a dialogue-heavy scene, make sure you do it a day or two before you shoot. I made the mistake of rehearsing a dialogue-heavy scene with an actor for two straight days. He read it and rehearsed it so many times that by the time we started shooting, he knew the dialogue inside and out; the only problem: he was scheduled to shoot at *the end* of our thirty-five-day shoot, and since production got delayed, it took about three months before the actor found himself on set – totally unprepared. He couldn't remember any of his lines, and the ones he could were rushed through nervously. Now, sure, everyone else on set blamed the actor – I mean, how can you come to set and not know your lines? However, I was the only one blaming myself, and for a good reason. Had I taken two to three days to rehearse the scenes with him again before we shot his scene, I would have seen that he was unprepared and would have taken drastic measures to either replace him or make sure he knew his lines. At the end of the day, I had to completely scrap his character in post which totally messed up my storyline (since he was an important character), and this seemingly small error in judgment was a big source of frustration. It ended up costing me a lot of time and money that we didn't have to spare and completely annihilated my original vision for the film.

Always Have Food!

Whenever you're filming anything, you should always have food! If you're on a professional set and you keep a craft services table, they should make sure that coffee, snacks, or some "thing" is always available and that you're never looking at an empty table. Craft services should be the first person on set. Coffee has to be ready before makeup and grip ever step foot inside your set, and it has to be hot, fresh, and available until the last person has left the set. If you're working on a small, low-budget shoot, the same rule applies, and if you don't have a craft services person, get a PA to do it or do it yourself. Nobody does any work before they've had a sip of coffee, and people working on sets that feed them well tend to be more productive. SAG rules dictate that lunch must be served every six hours, but my rule says that there should always be something to snack on-set, and there's a nice treat in between "lunch" and "wrap." If you arrive to set at 9:00 a.m., eat lunch at 2:00 p.m., then you should send a PA to get something delicious for the team at 11:00 a.m. and again at 5:00 p.m. (not pizza or anything that'll put people to sleep; beware too much salt or too much sugar). The bottom line is this: feed your people well, and they'll be happy.

Try Shot Lister

One app that has proven to be very useful on set for me is an app called Shot Lister. Shot Lister allows you to schedule your shoot and follow up on your shot list in real time. During the shoot, you can mark good/bad takes and get a picture of how well you're doing with regard to schedule. This is particularly effective if you don't have a big crew, and you have to rely on yourself to look at the schedule at the end of each and every shot. It takes a while to input everything into the app during pre-production, but it's well worth the time.

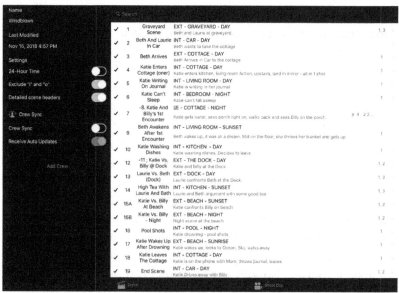

Shoot Smart

Plenty of inexperienced filmmakers will make the mistake of either planning too many shots per day or too little, and I've made that mistake myself in the beginning. And when people ask me how many shots per day I recommend shooting, I never know what to tell them because – and this is important – every scene is different, every shot is different, every day is different, and every crew is different. It's easier to get forty shots a day if you're shooting all of them in the same room, but it's not as easy to get forty shots per day if you have to change rooms, change wardrobe, if you have any stunts, FX, lots of dialogue, emotional scenes, makeup touch-ups, etc. This is where filming your movie in pre-production on an iPhone as an animatic/rehearsal helps, as it gives you a sense of timing.

Solving Problems

There's no escaping it – it doesn't matter how well-prepared you are, and how much homework you've done, how professional your crew and how experienced you are as a filmmaker. Problems always arise on set, and your job as the Director/Producer is to resolve them. Now, the more experienced your team, the better equipped they are with handling problems, but also – the bigger your team, the bigger your production, which means you get more problems. It's actually easier to film with a tiny footprint since there are way less moving parts and, therefore, you encounter fewer problems. So, get ready to have problems and get ready to solve them. It's a part of the job.

Control Your Emotions

A movie set can sometimes turn into a war-zone, and you can find yourself on the verge of breaking. Whether it's another person that's getting on your nerves, a technical malfunction, or a time-stealing problem that knocks you off your course, these "challenges" can test your patience and trigger all sorts of unhappy thoughts and feelings inside you. There are many instances of film directors blowing their tops, screaming at the top of their lungs, getting into loud arguments, and reacting poorly to these situations. The one important thing to keep in mind is this: your movie set is *your* movie set, you are the boss, you are the person in charge, and your energy will dictate everyone else's energy on set. If you're mad, depressed, or upset, the people you work with will sense it and act accordingly, turning your movie set into a tense, joyless, unhappy place to work. And if you're happy, upbeat, excited, and energetic – they sense that, too! *Your excitement infects everyone around you,* and people walking onto your set will feel that sense of excitement and can't help but feel the same way, too. Whatever you're feeling when you work on set is being amplified and reverberated around the room. It's magnetic, and you need to be painfully aware of it.

I once had a rotten, horrible day on set when nothing was working the way I wanted it to, and I noticed that when I was feeling bad, everyone around me was looking like their puppy died. It wasn't something I did consciously, but a cast member brought it to my attention – and ever since then I have made a conscious effort to keep a positive attitude on set, at all costs, while repressing the negative and keeping it hidden from sight on set. While it's inevitable to have a bad day every once in a while, you should keep in mind that you'll have all the time in the world to get angry, depressed, or feel sorry for yourself – but when you're on set, *that cannot happen.* You have to, for the sake of your cast and crew, control your emotions and never, ever lose your cool. Getting into a screaming match with a cast member or yelling and insulting people is how you lose everyone's respect and get people to resent you and work against you. When you scream at someone, you're screaming at everyone, and negative energies begin to spread, people lose their faith in you, and they could eventually revolt against you.

Embrace Collaborations

Filmmaking, at its core, is a collaborative effort. You're collaborating with your cast, your crew, your DP, your producers – everyone is working together to turn *your* vision into reality. You need to be aware of that fact, first – because you want to keep in mind that people have a *need for acknowledgment* and want to feel like they're contributing to your project, and second – because if you treat your team with respect and listen to their ideas, they'll be more inclined to share those ideas with you, and you will gain access to their genius. You should have a strong vision and stick to your guns in general, but keep your mind open to collaborations, listen to the people you hire, listen to their advice, and make up your own mind.

Present the Take

This tip lands in the "love it" or "hate it" branch of moviemaking tips, but it's one that became a favorite thing to do on set, mainly because it has so many benefits. At the end of a take (usually in a scene where the actor is supposed to evoke an emotion), after yelling "Cut!," I'll often invite the actor over to look at the shot in the camera's monitor. Five times out of ten, the actor would look at me and ask if they can do it again, sometimes exclaiming, "I can do it better." Showing your actor what they look like on camera and, more importantly, what their action and facial expressions are doing on the screen, will motivate them to give you 150% on the next take. If they're happy with the result, then it is up to you to decide if you want to move on to the next shot, or if another take is needed. Sharing the magic of the moment with an actor after a take can yield powerful results, but keep in mind that not all actors follow the same rules. Some of them will regard this practice as distracting; others will cherish the opportunity to see themselves and make an effort to give you more on the next take.

Make a Playlist

Another habit of mine, one that I developed during the making of my first feature film, was to produce a playlist for the movie (many times I'll do this while writing and revisit the playlist a few days before principal photography is scheduled to commence). I'll often pick and choose songs to put people (and myself) in the "mood." And when we're on set, I'll play music during setups. It helps keep the crew in a good mood, and it gives everyone a sense of rhythm on set. In addition, it can help the actors get in the right mindset for the upcoming scene. This is especially useful when working on genre sets, horror, noir, comedies, etc. However, you should always be respectful of your location and consider the atmosphere. I'll never play music before a very emotional scene since that can distract the actor, and I'll always think twice before playing music on a quiet, serene location. Sometimes, it's better to feel the silence and enjoy the atmosphere, and music can ruin that – use at your discretion.

Follow Up On Requests

This is an important lesson I learned on the set of *Pickings*. If you have a scene where an actor is acting with a cat, dog, horse, donkey, whatever, and you want it to appear as if they have an established relationship (which you should, if it's the character's pet), then you must allow and allocate an hour for the actor to bond with the animal prior to shooting their scene together. When we were making *Pickings*, one of our child actors was supposed to have a scene with a kitten. The kitten in the film was the character's pet, so it would make sense for her character to know how to handle the cat, how to hold it, pet it, engage with it, etc. Upon arrival on set that day, I asked my animal wrangler to introduce the cat to the actress before makeup. It was crucial to me that the kid feel comfortable with the animal; a certain person on set (doesn't matter who) was supposed to be on top of it. When the time came to shoot the scene, I learned that both the wrangler and the person I tasked with this mission had neglected to do as I instructed, and the actress didn't have as much as a minute with the kitten before the scene was shot. Unsurprisingly, the scene didn't work, the tiny kitten didn't feel comfortable with the actor, and the actor didn't feel comfortable with the cat, which resulted in us having to shoot around the animal, and I didn't get the shot I wanted. I was furious, but I realized that the blame for this situation was ultimately my own – telling someone to do something is great, but when something is very important to *my* scene, then it is my responsibility to follow up and make sure that it gets done, especially when it's not something obvious like that. If you ask for something once and never follow up, there's a chance it won't get done, particularly when working on a low-budget film with an inexperienced crew.

End the Day On a Positive Note

If you're shooting a film over the course of several days, it is important to wrap the day on a *good note*. Whether you break out a bottle of wine and commiserate with your cast and crew, play Mafia (it's ever so addictive), or show your favorite highlights from the day (or all of the above, whenever possible), doing something fun after you wrap for the day will keep everyone in good spirits, and would definitely encourage folks who might otherwise flake to return to your set the following day. Overall, it adds to the moviemaking experience and gives people the opportunity to relax. I had to learn this lesson the hard way, trust me. It's a habit worth forming. If you're spending the night on set, and people want to stick around for a while after wrap (and the schedule allows for it), let them. In fact, be the leader of the tribe and open a bottle of wine if you can. Filmmaking is a *people business*, and as the person in charge of these people, you need to understand that people need to de-stress, and if you can help them de-stress, they'll appreciate you more and be easier to work with the following day.

Don't be Afraid to Fire People

I *hate* firing people on movie sets, but sometimes it's an absolute necessity. I was surprised to learn, however, that there are a lot of people out there who refuse to fire a person who isn't working out simply because they don't want to "cause trouble." Let's get this straight – firing people sucks! For starters, it hurts morale, but more importantly – you *need* that person there. If he or she gets fired at the end of the day, you need to have an alternative or someone else who's ready to do his/her job the next day or after the weekend. For example, firing a focus puller is easy; firing an actor is a different story altogether. But if there's one thing I learned, if you don't fire a person that isn't working out, the damage that person is capable of causing may put your *entire* production at risk. Think about this: if you hire an actor who shows up on his first day on set – and surprise! – he starts treating people disrespectfully, or he/she doesn't know their lines, then that actor must be removed from your set as soon as possible. *You must kill negativity the second it hits your set; otherwise, you and your movie are going to suffer.* The longer you delay, the worse it's going to get. If you're scared of firing people because you don't think that you could find a replacement – that's rarely the case because anyone and everyone can be replaced. Of course, you should always try to diffuse the situation before you fire anyone, but if it comes down to it, you can't be afraid of letting someone go.

If you do end up sending someone home, make sure you do it at the end of the day, whenever possible. It's better to tell someone that they're not needed tomorrow than to send them home after they've made the trip. Especially if you're shooting on location, and the person has to ride with you in the van at the end of the day. In that case, just call him/her when you get back, or if you know the person isn't going to be confrontational, do it in person at the end of the day. Avoid firing someone in front of other people – unless the situation is dire.

Firing for Moral

On very rare occasions, firing someone in front of the cast and crew can be a good thing. I won't say his name, but a well-known NYC director recently fired a grip in front of everyone after he behaved like an absolute jerk to one of the actresses and actually went as far as making her cry. The director "lost it," screamed at the guy, fired him, and had him kicked off the set, and everyone started clapping; the rest of the day had a different type of energy. I had to fire a trainer who showed up late to set and started screaming at my Production Manager (the sweetest, most non-confrontational person you can imagine) for leaving the pickup spot without him. I had to fire him in front of our production staff – and while it wasn't pleasant for anyone, it did improve morale among the team for the next few days. Apparently, the guy was very abrasive and was treating our female producers with a certain level of contempt and disrespect, which I won't stand for. However, 99% of the time, when it's time for a member of your team to be let go, do so in secrecy.

Firing an Actor

Oh boy, this is a tough one. While I hope you never have to be put in a position where you are forced to fire an actor, sometimes these situations do pop up, and you feel as if there's no other choice but to get rid of the person and replace them with someone else. If you haven't started shooting yet, then firing an actor is fairly easy; you just say "goodbye!," find someone else, and move on. If that ends up pushing your start date, so be it – *it's better to start late with the right people than to start now with the wrong ones.* But, if you've already shot scenes with that actor, things can get a little more complicated. It is now your job to figure out the pros and cons of keeping the actor around versus letting them go. The calculation is fairly simple: (1) How important is the character to your story? (2) How long will it take to cast and re-shoot? (3) How much will it cost? (4) Can you recast the actor and re-shoot his scenes at the end of the shoot? (5) If other actors' schedules won't work, can you shoot his/her scenes without the need to have everyone else in the room? (Meaning, use camera magic to film that person's scenes in a creative way) For example, you can choose to film their scenes in singles (when shooting singles, each character has their own frame, and so you can shoot one character on Day #1, and the character sitting across from them on Day #12, and no one will know). Replacing an actor in a movie isn't as hard as it used to be. At any rate – this is where your problem-solving skills are being tested. If you have no other choice but to get rid of the actor, find a creative way of re-shooting their scenes without adding to the budget or delaying the schedule.

Always Have a Plan B

The bigger the production, the higher the chances that something might go wrong in the course of filming, so a lesson I've learned in the making of *Pickings* is to *always* have a Plan B before you start shooting. Keep an Excel file with names of boom operators and sound mixers, key grips, swings, interns, costume designers, makeup artists, etc. You should even go a step further and keep a list of ADs, Production Managers, Cinematographers, Camera Operators, Actors, Extras, and Producers. Keep the names you get during your hiring process and put the ones with promise in your Plan B. Generally, when a person quits, flakes, or has to be fired during the course of production, it is the department head's responsibility to find a replacement. When a key grip quits, the DP should have someone there the next day to take his/her place; when a makeup artist isn't doing her job, the Head Makeup should have a replacement ready before the end of the day. In the low-budget indie world, it might be you who has to find the replacement, so a list of Plan Bs is a must. The same applies when a key department head quits or leaves; a responsible department head will give you the courtesy of a replacement. Since their departure from the project could cause delays and be a great source of loss for the film, they are supposed to find (and train) a competent replacement upon departing. However, if that key department head isn't willing to do that, you would be very glad to have had a Plan B. Someone who can pick up their slack and jump into the previous person's shoes is now a phone call away. This is why you need a really good Line Producer – a delay caused by a replacement of a key department head will go unnoticed in the hands of a good Line Producer, who can rearrange the schedule without skipping a beat.

Don't Forget the Eye Light

One of the most important pieces of the storytelling puzzle is the actor's ability to convey information and evoke an emotion on screen, and that emotion takes place, first and foremost, in the actor's face, particularly their eyes. You could write the best script ever written and hire the most prolific actors, but if you can't see their eyes when they act, it'll feel flat and be a big waste of a good opportunity. If you're the DP, you should always, always, always, always make sure you check for that eye light before you yell action! Eye light (also known as catch light) can be produced by anything that shines light really because eyes are so reflective, so it's not a difficult task – but it is an important one. The YouTube channel "DedoWeigertFilm" has a beautiful, in-depth video that deals with the specifics of catchlights called "The Light in Your Eye." It's definitely worth watching.

Set Up a DIT Corner

One of the worst things that could possibly happen to any filmmaker is when a DIT messes something up, and footage is lost. Losing footage is by far the biggest crime you can commit on a movie set - the shot was captured, the money was spent, and the footage is lost. One way to make sure that it *never* happens is to set up a DIT corner, and double, triple, quadruple check it every time you dump footage. You set up a corner on every set with a laptop, connected to two hard drives, and when one card is full – you dump the footage and make a copy. *Always make a copy* – your footage doesn't exist unless it's sitting on two hard drives. So, get the shots, dump the footage, and check it twice before you take the card out. Most professional sets have a DIT person who dumps the footage and checks it while everyone else is filming, so if you can afford someone you trust – hire them. Otherwise, do it yourself, and do it carefully.

Dropbox

One way to make sure that you never have to worry about deleting the wrong folder, or losing footage is to connect your computer to a Business Dropbox account. It's a little more expensive than a regular Dropbox account (costs $40 per month for unlimited storage) – but it is a lifesaver. My entire computer is sitting on the cloud as well as on physical hard drives, and when I edit, when I shoot, dump footage, or work on VFX, sound, 3D, etc. – everything gets automatically saved to my Dropbox folder, and if anything gets deleted – recovery is a click away.

Mark Your Media

If you're doing your own DIT and have to dump the footage yourself, you're most likely going to have more than one card when you go to dump footage. Realistically, you can't go to the DIT spot every time the card gets full; that's a big waste of time. So, whenever a card is full, take it out of the camera and *mark it* with a green piece of gaff tape. If it's a small SD card, then you can mark it with a little sticker. This will ensure that you won't have a situation where you dump six cards at once and just happen to "miss one" by accident – you may think it won't happen, but I'm telling you that it *could*. When you're on set, and there are a million things happening at once, you might make a mistake – so why risk it? Mark your cards until the footage is dumped, then remove the sticker and put it aside.

Don't Leave the Set without Your Footage

Every day, no matter how late you wrap it, should end with you or your DIT – dumping all of the footage you captured that day into two separate hard drives (a main one, and a backup). This includes camera footage as well as audio. I don't care how much you trust your sound guy or how tired they are, never, ever leave the set without taking their card and dumping the files. This is one rule that you are not allowed to break.

Hiring a Behind the Scenes Person

The moviemaking process is tasking; there are a lot of moving parts, there is a lot going on inside your head, and sometimes you just can't take the time to worry about capturing behind the scenes (BTS) footage or taking stills, not to mention that the best BTS footage takes place *while* you're in action, and your attention is needed on the shot. So, hire a BTS person to cover your shoot. Now I'm sure that the "what is it going to cost me?" bell is loudly ringing in your ear right about now, but you'll be surprised at how cheap a good BTS person can be, and you'll also be surprised to learn that many film sets have *free* BTS people. Yeah – they're not trained professionals, but they are curious, quiet, and polite and will do the job for a credit. It's really easy to find a free BTS person who has his/her own camera (it's usually a T4i or something like that, but hey – beggars can't be choosers). Just make sure to feed that person, treat them well, make them feel valued, and you'll be fine. Keep in mind that press photos, BTS clips, and on-set interviews will be used *extensively* during your film's marketing campaign. It's not optional – do it!

> *"For me, filmmaking combines everything. That's the reason I've made cinema my life's work. In films, painting and literature, theatre and music come together."* ~ Akira Kurosawa

Phones on Set

I had to fire a focus puller on a film because he was looking at his screen while we were shooting a scene. It took everything in me not to scream aggressively at that person right there and then (keep your cool, remember?). The topic of "phones on set" is a highly contested one, and it's something that every filmmaker has a different opinion on, so I won't bore you with the "right" or "wrong" approach to cell phones on set because there is none. Some filmmakers vow by the no-phone policy; for others, it's a stupid rule that doesn't make any sense. For me, it all depends on the project I'm working on. I'll sometimes ask people not to take photos of a set or a scene because I don't want to reveal information about the film that ought to be kept secret. In other cases, I won't really care if people have their phones on them. But I do have a *no cell phone while filming* rule, and it's a rule I adhere to quite rigidly. From the moment I yell "action" to the second I yell "cut!" I don't want to see a glare, hear a ding, or see someone looking at something that they're not supposed to be looking at unless the phone is a part of the scene.

Communication is Key

You are the filmmaker, which means that you are tasked with executing your own vision. It also means that you probably have a picture in your head of what the scene is supposed to look like, what the actors are supposed to do, how the camera is supposed to move, and what the scene is supposed to "feel" like. So, when you first put on your "filmmaker hat," you can get so excited or distracted by the ambiance that you might forget to cover the basics, and end up yelling "action!" prematurely. Chances are this will lead to a moment where something doesn't sync; the camera, the actor, the prop, something isn't going to work, and you'll have to reset and start over. The risk of rushing into action to save time could backfire and cost you more time in the long run. At first, I thought that habit belonged exclusively in the realm of amateur filmmaking, but I was surprised to see professional filmmakers under the stress of time rush into action only to cut a few minutes later, revisit a camera move, and give it another go. If they had taken a moment to rehearse the camera move beforehand, they wouldn't have to waste a take. And if you think that wasting digital takes isn't the end of the world, try shooting on location with a limited number of available media cards and a broken card reader. The funny thing about it is that I sometimes catch myself doing the exact same thing as well. The point here is this: before you yell action, take the time to run through the scene, listen to your actors, follow the beat of the scene, make sure nobody has any questions, and then – yell "action!"

Answer Questions "Creatively"

While we're on the topic of communications, you will sometimes be confronted with a question that challenges a creative decision you've made, and you are then forced to justify it to the actor, the editor, the cinematographer, or whoever it is who approaches you with it in order for the day to proceed and for the creatives you work with to have faith and an understanding of your vision. For example, as I was walking an actor through a certain shot, I was confronted with the "why" question, the dreaded "what's my character's motivation?" question. The actor appeared a tad frustrated that I would take a shot of her feet, slowly walking towards the source of an ominous sound. "You already have a shot of my face reacting to the sound and walking towards it, so why do you need a shot of my feet as well?" Lots of filmmakers could get frustrated by these types of questions, and I understand why. In fact, it was the "thing" that people told me I'd hate most about working with actors; it was the element that made Hitchcock famously refer to his actors as "sheep." The motivation question will always pop up, regardless of how celebrated you are or how much some actors may adore you. You will always have an experience with an actor who wants to better understand your reason for doing the things that you want them to do. Instead of giving them a sour face and resorting to the "because I said so" comment, instead of bulldozing my way through the actor, I played the game. I proceeded to explain to the actor, off the cuff, the significance of the shot, and why it was important. I told her the reason why the camera needs to capture that moment in time, how I am going to intercut this with the other shot, the sound effects I'll use, the movement of the camera, and how the shallow depth of field is going to raise the stakes and make the audience fear what they can't see – in other words, I gave her a creative response to a creative challenge. The question of why you do the things that you do should have an answer in your head when you do them, and if you don't – make something up. As long as it makes sense, and it sounds like you know what you're doing, people will accept it, and their confidence in you will grow.

Protect Your Actors

The most important person on set, aside from yourself, is your actor as, without an actor to breathe life into your character, you have no movie. I am amazed at filmmakers who look down on actors, and as someone who regards himself an "actor's film director" – I have an immense amount of respect for actors. I honestly love and appreciate their craft; I enjoy watching them work, and I credit much of the film's success to the actors who inhabit its characters. This is why I never tolerate any disrespect or any form of harassment towards my actors. I make a conscious effort to make sure that they have the tools they need to do their jobs in the best way possible. If an actor likes to carry around his gun to inhabit the character, but the prop guy is giving me a sour face, I'll get to work on convincing the prop guy to agree instead of asking the actor to forget about it. If an actor needs five minutes of silence before an important shot, and my AD is yelling in my ear about the lack of time, I'll take responsibility for the five minutes of silence and give the actor what they need to do their job. The same rule applies to their communication and state of mind on set. I always make an effort to put on a serious face whenever a serious scene is taking place; no music, no goofy slates. I'll take precautions to give the actor the space they need to do their job. Some actors can tune out the goofiness that takes place on a movie set before a serious scene, and other actors need their atmosphere to align with their state of mind. If you take the steps required to protect your actor, they will reward you and your film with a great performance.

Eat Together, Share Stills, Get Excited!

During the early days of making *Pickings*, I made the mistake of keeping myself somewhat isolated in my DIT corner during lunch hour, but I have since learned the value of sharing my experiences on set with my cast and crew during our thirty-minute meal time. Now, whenever possible, we dine together. I share some still photos from the day's shoot, and if possible, play a clip. Maintaining a certain comradery among your cast and crew is vital if you plan to keep morale up and get everyone excited about the project you are working on. This habit now goes hand in hand with my belief that everyone who works on my set is a part of my world and a contributor to my film. Sharing a meal with a person allows me to get to know them better, get to know their strengths, weaknesses, what they like, what they hate, and what kind of ideas they have. It makes people feel special. It may not be the same for you, but if you give it a shot, you'll be surprised by how well people react to your presence on crafty.

Capture PG Trailer Lines

As I was crafting the first trailer for *Pickings*, I had a line of dialogue that I really, really wanted to use, but couldn't, since it contained the f-word. I had a feeling – on the day of shooting that scene – that I'd end up using it in the trailer because it was so iconic and so perfectly embodied the idea behind the film. It was only after realizing that I couldn't use it that I saw a film trailer where the actor said the word "damn," which was replaced with the f-word in the actual movie. So – next time, if I know a line is going to make its way to the trailer, I'll shoot it twice, once as intended and once with a PG filter. It's the little things you never think about that end up serving as the biggest lessons in the world of moviemaking.

Wrap Parties and Why They're Important

Moviemaking is a collaborative effort, but the results are almost always attributed and credited to the person in charge; that's *you* – the writer/director/producer. You're the one who's going to own this movie once it's all said and done; you're the one who's going to reap the reward, collect the awards, gain the publicity, and have notoriety as a result of this project. In other words – most of the credit goes to you. So, once principal photography is concluded, it is more than expected for the filmmaker to show their appreciation for their cast and crew via a wrap party. Unlike an actual job (that when you leave it, you feel comfortable telling people what you really think of them), in the movie business it's always advisable to end things on a good note, mostly because (a) you're most likely going to end up working with these people again in the future; (b) NYC and LA may feel like big cities, but in a way – everybody knows everybody, and reputations go a long way; if you end things on a good note with someone you clashed with on set (someone who wasn't fired, obviously), their opinion of you and your project is going to change, and when your film comes out, they'll show up to support it; (c) the people who worked with you on your shoot are going to remain a part of your project long after you wrap it. Whether you need them to show up for ADRs, or just show up at a festival to help promote the film – being *kind* and ending things on a good note is vital to maintaining good relationships with the people you work with. Another thing that wrap parties do is create a buzz around the film. When we held our *Pickings* wrap party, we had balloons and cake with the *Pickings* logo on it. We took over the bar and showed the trailer to people in the monitors – the atmosphere was amazing!

Give Yourself 48 Hours to Relax Before
Scheduling Anything Post Picture-Wrap

I was smart enough to book our *Pickings* wrap party the night after our last day of filming – BIG MISTAKE. Our last day was an overnight shoot, which meant that I had to go home, sleep for a few hours, and then be ready that night for the wrap party, but I didn't count on so many things going wrong. Living in NYC and traveling back from location to my home, I was stuck in traffic for three hours, then I had to return the van, go to Queens and return our gun props, and pick up the slack left by a crew member who misplaced an important piece of gear on set, so that stole a big chunk of my day. Before I knew it, it was 5 p.m., and the cake I had ordered came in late, the driver got into an accident, and everything that could have gone wrong, went wrong. I ended up with zero hours of sleep, having to go to a party in NYC and celebrate all night long. However – the overall experience was fun! My cast and crew all bonded over a crazy night in New York City, and I ended up going to bed after being awake for forty-three hours straight, so yeah... fun!

"Filmmaking is a miracle of collaboration."
~ James McAvoy

PART SIX
Post-Production

Figure Out Your Workflow

Before you start editing, before you start playing around with your footage – you need to figure out and plan your Post-Production Workflow. What software are you going to be working on for each step of the process? How do you plan to handle your picture edit, sound design, visual effects, color, and titles? If you've followed my advice and taken the steps required to master software like Adobe Premiere, After Effects, etc., then you have no need to worry. Please keep in mind that this is not a "How to Edit a Movie" book, so I won't teach you how to edit your film, but rather show you how generally I go about my own workflow and hope that you can derive some value from my experience.

Step 01. Dump Footage
I start by dumping all the footage and all the sound files in my hard drive to a working edit drive (any fast, external hard drive connected via USB 3.0 or faster).

Step 02. Proxies
I don't care how fast my computer is, if I've shot a feature film on RED, Alexa, Ursa, or any other cinema camera, I'll always make proxies, put those inside a folder, and arrange them by DAY.

Step 03. Organize Neatly
Organization is extremely important. If you're working on a big feature film with lots of moving pieces, it's going to get really messy really soon – a lack of organization will result in hours lost in post and will make your whole experience a whole lot less fun! There's nothing worse than having to spend hours looking for stuff that you otherwise would have had easy access to. One of the first things I do is arrange my footage per day (DAY 1, DAY 2, etc.) and within each day, I'll have a folder called *Footage*, and a folder called *Audio*.

Step 04. Import Footage

Once I import everything into Premiere, I'm going to start renaming the files within the software (that way it's non-destructive), and follow the same organizational structure – but instead of creating folders per days, I'm going to create them *per scene*, watching the clip, renaming the file, and sending it to the correct folder (For example, Scene 12 take 3 will be called S12T03); each folder will also contain VFX files and various timelines for cuts.

Step 05. The Edit

Once all the files and folders are organized neatly, I'm going to throw everything into a timeline that I call "DUMP," and every folder will have a DUMP timeline, and within it, I will begin to sync the audio and video together, watching the footage and taking notes while I do it, color favorite clips in Green, interesting takes in Purple, and unusable takes in Black. Everything that isn't Black gets moved to a new timeline called SELECTS – and it is from that timeline that I begin to assemble my edit. There is no right or wrong here, by the way – it's just a matter of preference.

Step 06. Test Screening

I am a big believer in conducting test screenings and doing so fairly early in the process gives people the impression that they are contributing to the making of your movie, which is 100% true. My first screening will typically be with friends or family. I'll gather around twenty people at my place, half of them are in the movie business (actors, directors, producers), and the other half are my *target audience* (if I'm making a horror film, it'll be horror fans, etc.). I'll create a test audience form, print out copies, and hand them out. You'll usually find a few bottles of wine on the table, some snacks and popcorn, juice, etc. Before the test screening starts, I'll show an early cut of the trailer and get their thoughts and opinions on its efficiency in selling the movie (this will be *crucial* during your marketing and advertising campaign). There will be a short Q&A about the trailer before we start the screening (basically I'm trying to give them the same information they would have found out if they had seen the trailer on Facebook and gone to the website to learn more; I'm not revealing anything about the movie yet). Once I'm done with the trailer, I'll screen the film; watching people watch a work-in-progress cut of my movie is always nerve-wracking. I want people to have a good time, and I want them to enjoy the product, but I also picked people who I know will be *brutally* honest – so I'm on edge throughout the screening, looking at people's faces and watching them write notes throughout. Once the screening is over, I give them time to fill out the forms, and we then follow up with a quick discussion and a "thank you" toast.

A Note on Test Screenings

Test screenings are nerve-wracking, but they serve a very important purpose. Not only do they give you an idea of what your target audience thinks about your movie, where you can improve, what parts they like, dislike, what they thought of the pacing, the editing, the acting, and the visuals – but they also give you information that you can and should use during your film's marketing campaign. Knowing who your target market is, is crucial to the success of your film, and if you know what your target audience loves most about your movie and what's most important to them in a film, you can design your marketing campaign to fit their desires and, by doing so, sell a whole lot more movies. Of course, you *must* pick people who you know will give you their unbiased, honest opinion. You need people who aren't afraid to tell you if your product sucks, and if they tell you that it was amazing, you'll know they're not sugar-coating it.

Once you have your first test screening, you go back to the edit, work it, and about a month later, you'd probably come back and run another test screening, but this one will be to a select audience, people you don't know and who don't know you. There are services out to help filmmakers conduct test screenings, but I find it more effective to just rent out a space and do it yourself.

Step 07. Final Delivery

After a few months in post-production, my film will be ready for festivals; it's at this point that I'll upload it to a password-protected Vimeo link or a Dropbox, go to a website like FilmFreeway and start submitting it to select festivals (not without a festival strategy, of course – more on that in the following chapters).

Watch Movies

Every movie is different and calls for a different post-process. When I'm cutting a movie all by myself, I'll work differently than when I do so with another editor, but one thing I always find myself doing is watching movies in between editing sessions (generally films that are in the same vein as what I'm working on, or films that were nominated for "Best Editing" in the previous year). I take notes, write down thoughts, and keep my eyes open to interesting musical choices. Something happens to your brain when you spend twelve hours in post every day, and if you ask most people if they want to watch a movie after staring at the screen for all that time, they'll tell you to go to hell. However, when you watch movies during that time, your brain keeps all that information in your head; it's like watching a movie after taking a cinematography class – you can't help but look at the lighting in every shot you see. The same goes with editing; your brain is looking for cuts, inspirations, ideas, thoughts, and you'll be surprised at how many times you find yourself pausing the film and writing notes for tomorrow's session. I watched a movie about editing movies before I started editing my film *Prego* back in 2015, and then, subconsciously, two years later before I started editing *Pickings*. Since then I've made it a ritual, and every once in a while, I'll watch a documentary film called *The Cutting Edge* for inspiration. It's narrated by Kathie Bates and stars plenty of famous film directors and movie editors – to me, that movie is equivalent to watching a motivational video; it really puts you in the right mindset and kind of makes you want to go out there and edit a movie.

Three Cuts in Three Weeks

Generally speaking, I try my best to deliver the rough cut on the first week, so it takes me seven days to compile a rough cut of my film. Once the rough cut is done, I'll start making edits, changes, and improvements to bring it down to a manageable length. (PS – my rough cuts are always very long. For *Pickings*, it was nearly three hours long). Once the third cut is complete, I take a few days off, clear my head, and come back for a fourth cut. You need that time apart to gain some perspective and watch it again fresh.

Guest Editors

When I have the budget to work with an editor, I do, and when I don't, I bring them in as guest editors. This only happens if I have a problem that I don't know how to solve. Instead of brainstorming on my own, I'll bring a friend who's a filmmaker or someone who's a *professional editor* as a consultant. I'll show them the cut, discuss the scene, and ask for feedback. I've done this numerous times, and I have to say that sitting and talking about your movie with an actor, an editor, or an experienced film director gives you a fresh perspective on your film and can help you improve the overall quality of your work. Also, it's nice in general to speak with a cinephile about a movie that you happen to be making.

Go for Walks

Sitting in front of the computer for so many hours isn't just bad for your health, it's also bad for your brain and can hurt the quality of your work. Post-production demands that you keep an open mind and have the liberty to *think*, contemplate choices, and brainstorm new ideas. And there's no better way to do that than to stop working every two hours, put on your headphones and go out for a ten-minute walk. Listen to some music, get away from the computer, and let your mind go where it may. If you listen to your own movie's soundtrack, you'll start noticing pictures coming into your head as you're walking – there's a lot of power in that, and one of my favorite sequences in *Pickings* was created after I went out for a walk, listened to the soundtrack we were using to cut the scene, and saw a new sequence in my head.

PPDS – The Post-Production Depression Syndrome

Well before making my own film, I'd heard tales of famous film-makers who said they wanted to "kill themselves" during the post-production process, and as I went into my own post process, I began to empathize with them; this shit was rough! Watching the first cut of my film for the first time left me in a state of shock. The movie was so far away from what I had envisioned, and it was so *not* what I intended to make that I honestly gave true thought to either getting funding and re-shooting parts of it or taking my name off the film entirely. I consider myself a very upbeat and positive person, but for the first time in my life, I felt as if I was sinking into a state of depression (over a fucking movie). I know it sounds ridiculous, but I felt as if I was forced to mourn the death of my vision for a long period of time, and had to do a lot of "mental adjustments" in my head. I spent a great deal of time in post before I could create a cut of the movie that I didn't hate. Tracing back the source of the problem is easy now. I can name each and every single one of the problems that led to that result (and already have, in this book). From having to cut a key character out of the

194

film because the actor portraying him couldn't do his job to losing an important piece of our production midway through filming, every problem I encountered had a creative cause and effect that influenced the way in which the film was shot, and the quality of the shots we ended up with. It was towards the end of the editing process when I heard Ron Howard speak about his own post-production process and how he approaches these types of situations where you don't have what you want in post because something went wrong during the making of the movie. His approach is a simple, yet hard to swallow solution – "You have what you have, find a way to make it work, write down the reasons why it didn't work out and be better prepared when you step foot onto your next movie project." Such is the value of education, I guess.

Sound, Grading, and VFX

Because I work in Adobe, this process is made a little easier. I don't have to export my files from one software to another. I just click a button, and it's there – automatically. The only time I export anything is when I work on VFX and when I do my color grading. I usually color with Adobe Premiere or Davinci Resolve, VFX is done with a combination of software like Maya, 3Ds Max, After Effects, Photoshop, and Houdini, but it all comes back to Premiere via After Effects at the end of the day.

Music Clearance

If you were making a low-budget, indie film twenty years ago, you wouldn't have even considered the possibility of having real licensed music in your film, but things have changed for the music industry in the past few years. The internet has created a vast market for indie filmmakers with small budgets who want to use music in their film. So nowadays, you can license music from websites like *Greenlight Rights* ($2,000 plus per song), *The Music Bed* (around $1,500 per song, roughly), *BeatPick* and *Marmoset Music* ($100-$400 per song), *Audiosocket* ($50-$500 per track), *Neo-*

Sounds ($30-$300), and *AudioJungle* ($10-300), etc. When dealing with smaller websites like *AudioJungle* and *NeoSounds,* the process is fast and easy. You can download low-res samples of the songs you want to use – they're less likely to have real bands and more likely to feature instrumental music, with some exceptions.

Websites like *The Music Bed, Marmoset Music,* and *BeatPick* will feature some amazing indie bands and some actual musicians like Johnny Cash and Charlie Feathers, while websites like *Greenlight Rights* will grant you access to any song you can possibly think of (Eminem, Katie Perry, etc.) but at a higher cost. Another option at your fingertips is to go hunting for a local band willing to contribute their music to your film for the publicity. Or to write your own music into the film and hire actors who can sing, which is what we did for *Pickings.* In that case, my actress / co-producer Katie Vincent wrote and performed all of the music for the film, and a bunch of people contributed free tracks as well (because they wanted the exposure). We even published and sold an original soundtrack called *Pickings – Music From the Motion Picture.*

Hiring a Composer – Beware the Temp Music

Many filmmakers who hire film composers will edit their film to a temp track (something they don't own from another movie or an album they like) with the intention of replacing the track with whatever the composer they hire will provide them with later. The one thing I learned about this process is that when you send a scene with a pre-existing track to a composer, that music is now in his/her head, and the results will be exceptionally similar, 95% of the time.

So, it's a rule of law in music departments that you should avoid sending a scene with pre-existing temp music to a composer. Their artform involves watching the scene *without music* and creating something original based on the cut; don't kill their creativity by adding temp music to your edit. You can still cut your film to temp music, but make sure you mute that channel before you send it out.

Keep Everything M&E Friendly

Generally speaking, when you sign with a foreign sales agent, when you sell to a distributor, or when you make a foreign sale on your own, you will be asked to deliver an M&E track – M&E is a series of audio tracks consisting of all the sounds, music, and effects in your film *minus* any on-screen dialogue, so basically the M&E track is how foreign distributors are able to dub a different language over the dialogue without having to mute the original track. When you edit your film, make sure you keep your audio stems separate and organized. That way, when the time comes to deliver an M&E track, all you need to do is hit the "mute" button and hit "export," and you're good to go.

"First cuts are a bitch for a director, because it's been so many months and you put your trust in your editor and you're going to see your film assembled for the first time. You look at it and go, This is terrible. I hate it." ~ Richard Donner

PART SEVEN
Festivals

So, you finally finished your film. You have all of your ducks in a row, you're getting ready to send it out into the world, win awards, and hopefully sell it at a movie festival to a serious distributor, and if you can't, you still have 20% of your budget left to distribute the film on your own. However, like everything else in this process, festival submissions need to be done *strategically*. You are now at the point where you go from "filmmaker" to "film-marketer."

Remember that marketing plan you created at the beginning of this book? Well, it's time to dust that old thing off and put it to use because now is the time to start digging into film sales, distribution, marketing, and delivery – the not-so-glamorous yet extremely educational process that will set you on the course to theatrical distribution.

The Biggest Marketing Mistake I Made on Pickings

At the end of the day, a festival is a festival, and all film festivals exist primarily to give filmmakers a platform to showcase their art and talent to the world. That exposure is generally exploited in two ways: *publicity* and *acquisition*. Film festivals are essentially a marketplace for film distributors who are out to acquire the rights to award-winning films. The marketability of these films is affected by the reputation of the festival itself, so a film winning "Best Picture" at a small movie festival in the middle of nowhere isn't nearly as newsworthy as if that same film had won "Best Picture" at Sundance, which is why distributors flock to these big festivals with the intention of buying film. I don't think I fully realized that fact when I completed my first feature film, *Pickings* – because before the film was even sent to festivals, I made the mistake of announcing the fact that we had a distributor attached to the film and announced the film's release date –*big mistake*. Most legitimate film festivals stay clear of films that have already sold the rights to a distributor. The result was eighty-one festival rejections (with only twenty-six watching the film on Vimeo). In the beginning, I believed this pattern of rejection was due to the quality of my film, but after speaking with a person who had an "in" with a festival that rejected our film, I learned that they never even watched it – they rejected it purely because it already had distribution and a theatrical release date; a few months later, my sales agent confirmed my suspicion. What I should have done and will do next time is keep my mouth shut, take the film on the festival tour, and then announce the release date (or sell it, if I get a good offer). Announcing a release date before the festival tour begins is definitely a big *no*!

Festival Submission Schedule

So, before you submit your film to any film festival, you need to figure out your submission schedule. And this process is basically broken down into a few simple steps: First – you need to register with a submission website (Filmfreeway). Once you have an account, you need to do some research – make a list of every film festival that caters to your target audience. What do I mean by that? If you shot a horror film, make a list of film festivals that accept horror films, if you made a family-friendly film, make a list of family-friendly film festivals. The purpose of this list is to include every film festival that your movie has a chance of getting into. The list can be as short as 20 or as long as 400 – as long as the festival shows *your kind* of movies – it goes on the list. Now – if you have some extra money, add your dream festivals to the list. These are the movie festivals that everyone and their mother is trying to get into: Sundance, Cannes, Toronto, Telluride, Austin, Tribeca, and Venice, to name a few.

Festival	Deadline	Notification	Running	Status	Spent	Success!	Lost!
Telluride Film Festival	4/1/2017	8/1/2017	9/1/2017	Accepted!	$95	$95	
Toronto Film Festival	4/1/2017	8/22/2017	9/7/2017	Denied :(	$85		$85
Raindance Film Festival	4/1/2017	8/31/2017	9/20/2017	Pending	$55		
Fantastic Fest	4/1/2017	8/21/2017	9/21/2017	Pending	$50		
Montreal	5/1/2017	9/15/2017	10/4/2017	Pending	$40		
New Orleans Film Festival	5/1/2017	8/2/2017	10/11/2017	Pending	$60		
Cambridge Film Festival	5/1/2017	9/11/2017	10/19/2017	Pending	$45		
St. Louis International Film Festival	5/1/2017	9/30/2017	11/2/2017	Submitted	$110		
The Yonkers Film Festival	5/1/2017	9/8/2017	11/3/2017	Submitted	$45		
Leeds International Film Festival	6/1/2017	9/14/2017	11/1/2017	Submitted	$85		
Hamptons International Film Festival	6/1/2017	9/18/2017	10/5/2017	Submitted	$55		
Another Hole in the Head	6/1/2017	10/7/2017	10/25/2017	Submitted	$45		
New Hampshire Film Festival	6/1/2017	9/30/2017	10/12/2017	Submitted	$40		
Austin Film Festival	6/1/2017	9/26/2017	10/26/2017	Submitted	$60		
Big Apple Film Festival	6/1/2017	9/15/2017	12/31/2017	Submitted	$60		
St. Cloud Film Festival	6/1/2017	9/30/2017	11/4/2017	Submitted	$20		
Manhattan Film Festival	7/1/2017	10/8/2017	10/19/2017	Submitted	$65		
Hollywood Film Festival	7/1/2017	10/5/2017	10/19/2017	Submitted	$85		
AFI Fest	7/1/2017	10/13/2017	11/9/2017	Submitted	$65		

Now, duplicate that list, and start arranging your movie festivals from BIG to SMALL – the biggest festivals go on top, and the smallest festivals are underneath. The order of the small ones isn't all that important – it's the ones that demand "world premiere" or "city/state premiere" that you have to pay attention to. In order for the Sundance Film Festival to accept your movie, you have to be willing to give them your *world premiere*, meaning, the movie cannot be premiered anywhere else prior to the release date. So, since Sundance is playing at the end of January, you cannot have another festival screening around that date, which means that Sundance comes first. You cannot submit to a film festival that has a December date; you can only submit to film festivals that, if accepted, will show your film after the Sundance date. So, if your movie is ready to be sent out in August, and you really want to get into a film festival that's playing in December, you have to choose between that festival and Sundance.

Do Your Research

Once you have a list of desired film festivals, it is your job to start researching these festivals individually, nit-picking and narrowing down that list to a manageable size. When you pick and choose only the right type of festivals, do your research and get picky with the festivals you want to submit to – you will have a higher success rate. If I make an R-rated horror film and submit it to thirty-five film festivals without doing my research, I have no way of knowing what these festivals' criteria is. Are they family friendly? Are they only looking for films that adhere to certain morals? Are they interested in stories about the human condition? Immigration? Love? Or are they primarily festivals that screen horror films? If you send a horror film to thirty-five pre-screened horror film festivals, you'll have a higher success rate than if you sent it randomly to some film festivals you know nothing about.

Stick to Your Budget

There's an emotional element to film festivals that doesn't really rear its ugly head until you're actually *in* the submission process. When you spend $1,000 submitting your film to thirty festivals, and you start getting rejection letters it takes everything in your system to fight the urge to go back to the website and submit your film to another thirty festivals. My advice to you is to *wait it out.* Don't assume a 100% rejection rate before you actually get to a 100% rejection rate. Going over budget during your festival submission process is very easy, so I implore you to use caution and stick to your budget.

Be Realistic

Now that you have "the list," it's time to get realistic, and, much like when you had to cut scenes from your script when you couldn't afford to shoot them, you are going to have to cut festivals that you don't think you can get into or festivals that are not within your budget. The cost of submitting to Sundance is $65, Toronto is $85, and Telluride is $95. On their own, it's not that bad, but when you combine them with thirty to forty other film festivals, it quickly becomes overwhelmingly expensive. So, this is the point where you have to pick and choose. Do you go for big film festivals and put your film on hold until you either get a solid "yes" from one of them or "no" from all of them? Or do you pick your top indie 40-100 film festivals that don't require a world premiere and are easier to get into? There are no right or wrong answers; you do whatever you think works best for your film and your budget.

"A director must be a policeman, a midwife, a psychoanalyst, a sycophant and a bastard."
~ Billy Wilder

Be Early

Most film festivals will offer four submission deadlines: the Early Bird, Regular Deadline, Late Deadline, and The Extended Deadline. Because your end game is to be cost-effective and have a higher acceptance rate, you should only be on the lookout for film festivals that land within the early bird-regular deadline, since these are (a) the cheapest options, and (b) give you a greater chance of having your film seen by a programmer. Filmmakers who submit early have a higher chance of getting in because they are making "first impressions" and are getting viewed before all the thousands of other submissions kick in.

Create a Festival Spreadsheet

So, let's say you have a super-scary, one-location, R-rated thriller and a $1,000 festival budget. How do you know which festivals to submit your film to? Where would you get the most bang for your buck and have the highest chances of success? Well, this is where research and proper planning comes into play. Your first step would be to create an Excel spreadsheet (like the one below); the spreadsheet will have the following seven columns:

> 1) <u>Festival:</u> Your first step would be to populate this column with film festivals by (a) visiting one of the many submission websites (like Filmfreeway). They keep organized lists of festivals, and you can search for festivals based on certain parameters like genre, cost, submission deadline, etc. (b) Just Google "best film festivals" or "best horror film festivals," or whatever your genre is, and you'll find plenty of lists online. (c) *Moviemaker Magazine* publishes an article in April every year titled "50 Film Festivals Worth the Entry Fee." When you type a festival name into a festival submission site, the site will display everything you need to know about the festivals, their rules, regulations, what type of films they're looking for, timelines, deadlines, and festival dates.

2) <u>Date:</u> Next to each festival, write down its date – when is the festival actually running? Most festivals run for several days, but all you need to worry about right now is its launch date, i.e. – Day #1.

3) <u>Notification:</u> Every film festival will publish two important dates: the running date and the notification date. The notification date is the deadline for notifying filmmakers who got accepted or denied. This is crucial information because it will help you create a realistic timeline for your film's release.

4) <u>Cost:</u> This is where you list the cost of submission.

5) <u>Status:</u> This is where you update your submission status (pending, accepted, denied).

The Selection Strategy

This is where you start to narrow your list down. Visit the festival's FilmFreeway page and keep an eye out for (a) what kind of films they're looking for; (b) the deadline and the cost; (c) their rules and regulations (no nudity, no R rated. Do they only accept female filmmakers, foreign filmmakers? Are they focused on family-friendly content? Or are they focused on horror?). This form of research will help eliminate a great deal of festivals that are just not suited to your film. Next, you want to research the competition – what similar films to yours were released last year? And what was their festival circuit like? You can visit any film on IMDB and see a list of every festival they were in and every award they won. This type of research will help you focus your attention on film festivals that are searching for *your* kind of content. Next, you want to arrange the remaining film festivals by size. The festivals that are well-established (the ones that have been running for ten years or more) are generally harder to get into, but they are a big deal if you do. Any first-year film festival will most likely accept your film, and if you submit and get accepted, your movie will play along with other amateur filmmakers and will likely get no press as a result of a win; therefore, I recommend you focus your attention on the established festivals first.

Diversifying Festivals

So, the final step would be to diversify your list to ensure a higher acceptance rate. A diversified festival run will look like this:

<u>20% Big Festivals and Oscar Qualifiers</u>
These are your Toronto Film Festival, Sundance, Austin, etc. Your chances of getting in are smaller, but if you don't submit, you'll never get in anyway, so you might as well try.

<u>30% Niche Festivals</u>
Niche festivals are great because they are being run by people who are actively seeking your movie. A niche festival is the perfect home for a niche film; these are your Shriekfests, the Chicago Comedy Film Festivals, California Women's Film Festival, Annecy International Animated Film Festival, etc.

<u>30% "Popular Festivals"</u>
These are popular film festivals that are not "Oscar qualifying." They generally accept every genre on the list, and you'll find them on those "best film festival" lists every year. These include film festivals like the Atlanta Film Festival, Brooklyn Film Festival, Cleveland International, Chicago Underground, etc.

<u>20% Small / Local Film Festivals</u>
These are the "small but promising" film festivals, and every city has them. What you are looking for in particular is a film festival that's been around for at least three

years, one that has a solid-looking website and more than fifty fans on Facebook. Do your research, see what films and filmmakers they've hosted in the past (websites like FilmFreeway offer reviews, so that's powerful). The second thing to consider is whether or not that small film festival is local – local film festivals are great because they give you a chance to network, meet people, and get exposed to folks who are trying to do what you do in this business. Small/local film festivals are more likely to accept your film and you probably won't get any publicity, but you can capitalize on the social network to create a buzz if you win some of these festivals. It's worth looking into.

Publicity – Press Kits

The first stage of any film publicity campaign is the creation of the film's press kit. Your press kit is used to "sell" your film to film festivals, journalists, bloggers, film reviewers, and acquisition executives. A good press kit consists of a synopsis, a list of cast and crew and their bios, a Director's Statement or an FAQ, publicity stills, behind the scenes content, film reviews, trailers, 30-second ads, clips, interviews, third-party endorsements, and links to the websites, IMDB, Rotten Tomatoes, etc. Many websites offering festival submissions will allow you to build your EPK online, but you still need the materials, so I suggest starting by creating an actual press kit using software like Photoshop or InDesign. Here is a sample of a press kit for my feature film, *Pickings*:

FILM TITLE
Pickings

LOGLINE
Still Waters Run Deep

CONTACT INFO
Dark Passage Films
Attn: Usher Morgan
(Address)
www.PICKINGSFILM.com
www.DARKPASSAGEFILMS.com

USHER MORGAN
WRITER, DIRECTOR, PRODUCER
(Phone Number)
(Email)

TECHNICAL INFORMATION
Original Cut
TRT: 103 Minutes
Exhibition Format: DVD, Blu-Ray, DCP, MOV
Aspect Ratio: 1.85
Shooting Format: RED
Color, English

FROM SCRIPT TO SCREEN

After completing his award-winning short film *Prego*; writer, director, and producer Usher Morgan teamed up with cinematographer Louis Obioha and actors Elyse Price, Katie Vincent, and Joel Bernard to bring to life an exciting new feature film, entitled "*Pickings.*"

An intoxicating, yet toilsome, year-long practice in indie filmmaking took this project from concept to reality, and finally, after two industrious years, *Pickings* was ready to be unleashed. This neo-noir meets spaghetti western crime drama pushes the boundaries of style and takes the viewers on a thrilling ride into the story of Jo Lee Haywood — a single mother and neighborhood bar owner who spent years trying to escape her violent past. But when a local mobster and his gang of thugs come knocking on her door, Jo is forced to embrace her inner demons and confront her deadly history in order to protect her family and property. Still waters run deep in this stylistic, neo-noir crime saga.

As pre-production commenced in January of 2016, Morgan and cinematographer Louis Obioha decided to film *Pickings* on the Red Epic camera, with additional night shots filmed on the Sony A7S II, using old vintage lenses. Principal photography began in March of 2016 under a shooting budget of $350,000. The film was shot in Yonkers, New York City, Southampton Village, and Staten Island for a total of 35 days, and post production was concluded in November of 2017.

The film's ensemble cast includes Elyse Price, Joel Bernard, Katie Vincent (who also served as the film's associate producer and music supervisor), Joe Trombino, Emil Ferzola, Yaron Urbas, Michael Gentile, Christopher Liam Gentry, and Samantha Zaino, among others. Morgan turned to his frequent collaborator, Katie Vincent, to write, compose, and perform many of the film's original songs. Dark Passage Films will handle the release and distribution of the film's original soundtrack.

For additional information concerning the film's theatrical release schedule, and a list of theaters, cities, and general release information, please visit our website, www.PickingsFilm.com, or follow the film on Facebook @ www.Facebook.com/PickingsFilm. You may also follow the filmmakers on Instagram @ushermorgan, @kitkat2290, @iamcleverchimp

AWARDS

HBO Urban Action Showcase And Expo
Best Feature Film
Best Actor (Elyse Price)
Best Action Sequence

Tampa Bay Underground Film Festival
Best Leading Actress (Elyse Price)
Best Cinematography (Louis Obioha)
Best Feature Film Director (Usher Morgan)

Greenpoint Film Festival
Best Feature Narrative Film

New Filmmakers NYC
Best Narrative Feature Film

Midwest Weirdfest
Best Feature Film

Long Island International Film Expo
Best Feature Film (Nominated)

Riverside International Film Festival
Best Screenplay
Best Editing
Best Cinematography

ACCOLADES

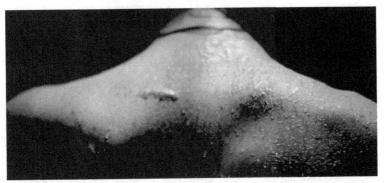

"The visually arresting, wickedly entertaining crime drama "Pickings" marks an impressive narrative feature directing debut by Usher Morgan, who also wrote, edited and produced. He's a talent to watch."
~ THE LOS ANGELES TIMES

"It immediately hearkens back to classic film noir or, more recently, the films of the Coen Brothers. The dialogue, meanwhile, with its tongue-in-cheek references, is somewhere closer to a Tarantino film. Even the main character herself, who we soon come to learn is named Jo, is somewhat reminiscent of Uma Thurman's Bride from the Kill Bill series."
~ FILM INQUIRY

"I'd be lying if I said that I didn't think this film was an absolute blast to watch, from start to finish. It's slick, unique, incredibly confident in its presentation and just so entertaining to watch."
~ HIDDEN REMOTE

213

THEATRICAL RELEASE

Following a red carpet world premiere on Feb. 23rd at the prestigious AMC Loews Lincoln Square in New York City's Lincoln Square – *Pickings* will open to 10 theaters in 6 major cities on March 2nd, 2018.

FILMMAKER'S BIO

USHER MORGAN
WRITER, DIRECTOR, PRODUCER

Usher Morgan is an award-winning screenwriter, film director, producer, and studio executive residing in New York City. Morgan started his career in book publishing and later became involved with film production and distribution. He produced his first documentary film *The Thought Exchange* starring David Friedman and Lucie Arnaz in 2012, followed by his directorial debut, the award-winning short film *Prego*.

Morgan's first feature film, *Pickings* will be released to AMC theaters on March 2nd, 2018 and will be making its way to VOD in August of 2018. His directing style is influenced primarily by film-noir and spaghetti westerns. *The Los Angeles Times* calls Usher Morgan "a talent to watch."

ELYSE PRICE
JO LEE-HAYWOOD

Classically trained, Elyse Price has played roles from Shakespeare to Tennessee Williams, performing in major American repertory theaters, the Moscow Art Theatre, and Theatre Calgary. Most recently Elyse performed in Shaw's *Major Barbara* (A.C.T.) and *Pygmalion* (California Shakespeare Theater), the original cast of *Steve Yocky's Very Still and Hard to See*, and the American premiere of *Phantom Pains* by Vasily Sigarev. Elyse received her MFA from the American Conservatory Theater and her BA from Queens College in 2010.

KATIE VINCENT
SCARLET / PRODUCER / MUSIC SUPERVISOR

Katie Vincent is an NYC-based actor, writer, producer, musician, and all around maker of stuff. Past film credits include: *Prego* (Usher Morgan), *Death (and Disco Fries)* (Dennis Cahlo), *Before The Snow* (Manmade Productions), *Hotel* (Manmade), *BadPuss: A Popumentary* (Emily Weist), among other titles. She received her BFA in Drama from Tisch NYU.

JOEL BERNARD
BOONE

Joel is an American actor, voice artist, and co-artistic director of Benefit of the Doubt Theatre Company. Film and TV credits include *Law and Order: SVU*, *Silent Hill: Downpour*, *Fine Dining*, and the upcoming feature film *Mouse*. Joel trained at LaGuardia High School for the Performing Arts, The Moscow Art Theater, received a BA from Queens College, and an MFA from the American Conservatory Theater.

YARON URBAS
SAM "HOLLYWOOD" BARONE

A versatile and talented actor, Yaron Urbas has played everything from working class hero, soldier, mobster to cultured entrepreneur in various roles for feature films and television. He is known best for his appearance in *Orange is the New Black*, *Gotham*, *The Blacklist* and the *Jim Gaffigan Show*, among others.

CONTACTS

USHER MORGAN
Writer, Director, Producer
(email / Phone Number)
Instagram: @ushermorgan
WWW.USHERMORGAN.COM

KATIE VINCENT
Producer
(email / Phone Number)
Instagram: @KatieVincentNYC
WWW.KATIEVINCENT.COM

DARK PASSAGE FILMS
Distribution Company
(email / Phone Number)
WWW.DARKPASSAGEFILMS.COM

STILLS

Festival Submissions

So, you have your press kit, and now you are ready to start submitting your film to the festivals you've selected. As long as you stay true to the plan and stick to the budget and the pre-proposed list of film festivals, you should be fine. The desire to go on a shopping frenzy will arise, especially once you start getting rejection letters, but that's one desire that can blow a big hole through your piggy bank, so make a conscious effort to resist it. Don't blow all your money on film festival submissions; small film festivals are not as likely to make the difference between getting picked up by a film distributor or not, but I do recognize the fact that winning awards can increase your chances of selling the movie down the line, so I understand the temptation; it's well justified – believe me. You are now entering into somewhat of a "downtime," but that doesn't mean that it's time to relax. On the contrary – while you wait for your festival's tour to materialize, you need to start preparing your publicity assets and set an imaginary, private release date for your film (one that goes unannounced to the world) and start planning for the release of your film.

"Rejection is a common occurrence. Learning that
early and often will help you build up the tolerance
and resistance to keep going and keep trying."
~ Kevin Feige

PART EIGHT
Distribution

So your film got accepted into festivals, and you've sold the rights to a big distributor... awesome! The information herein will help you utilize the situation and maximize you and your distributor's efforts as you take the film into VOD, DVD, and Blu-Ray. However, let's assume for a moment that your film got accepted into film festivals (or not), and you didn't make a sale. Now what? First of all, don't view this situation as a failure, but rather as an opportunity – this is actually what happens to *most* indie filmmakers, especially first-time filmmakers. There are filmmakers who end up at Sundance and Tribeca who never get picked up as well, so you're not alone. The difference now is going to be between you (who is now set for self-distribution) and the other guys, who plan to give away their film to a vanity distributor and receive nothing in return. Now it's *your* job, your goal, your mission to make sure that the movie you created is being watched, reviewed, and talked about by as many people as possible. That's the *end game*. Reach as many people as possible. Which leads us to this final chapter – Distribution.

Now, they say that a movie is made when it's written, when it's shot, and when it's edited – and to that, I would add, a movie is made when it's released. Your film doesn't really exist unless people watch it and experience it, and this is where *publicity* comes into play. There are many ways to "publicize" a film; there's the "free" way, which you are already aware of – that's Facebook, Instagram, Twitter, talking about your film, and sharing interesting content online, something that you already do by default. Then there's the "expensive way," which involves hiring a publicist, spending money on ads, and doing paid marketing work to call attention to your film. The latter is obviously effective, and if you have the budget for it – do it! But this book is dedicated to the low-budget, indie filmmaker. I want to teach you how to get the publicity and distribute your film without going broke in the process.

Your Online Publicity Schedule

A publicity schedule is a "calendar" designed to break down your publicity goals into daily/weekly/monthly actions, from content creation to pitching deadlines. The ultimate purpose of a publicity schedule is to "plan out" your publicity actions over the course of the film's release schedule. If you have a dedicated publicist, he/she will create one for you, and if you don't – you'll need to create one on your own. An average indie film will need at least three to four months of active publicity prior to its release date. That means that if your film is scheduled to be released on April 15th, you're pitching it to the press in January. This is where it gets tough, and that's where you need to get creative; the plan you create isn't as much a "plan" as it is an "answer," an answer to the question: "How do I get my film noticed?" What are the individual steps I have to take to make sure that people know about my film and that people will go out to watch it? Here's an example of a Publicity Plan for our feature film, *Pickings*:

January

2018

Sunday	Monday	Tuesday	Wednesday	Thursday	Friday	Saturday
				1	2 Announce Trailer	3
4	5 Official Trailer Release	6	7	8	9	10
11	12	13	14 Picture from the Trailer, Plus Quote	15	16	17
18 Trailer Boomerang with Quote From Movie	19	20	21	22	23	24
25 Thanks for 10,000 Fans Post!	26	27	28 News Story, Pickings is coming.			

February 2018

Sunday	Monday	Tuesday	Wednesday	Thursday	Friday	Saturday
				1 Coming to Theaters Announcement; Review Spot	2	3
4	5 Featurette #1 - About the Movie | Comic Book Strip Graphic	6 Character Box – Introduce Jo. | Katie Vincent Blooper Video	7 BTS Photos | Review Post / News Article	8 Merchandise Promotion | BTS Throwback Thursday	9 BTS Stills | Announce List of Cities	10 Box Poster - Publish List of Theaters
11	12 **30 Second Spot #1** | Facebook Live Premiere Announce	13 Tickets Lottery | Gift Bags Giveaway	14 Reviews, Print promo cards; giveaway	15 Character Posters | 30 Second Clip From the Film	16 One Week to Premiere! Announce	17 Something Red, Cocktail Recipe
18 Character Intro (Uncle Boone) - Video	19 10 Second Mini Trailer	20 Official Posters, Promote	21 Box Poster – Movie Quote | Official Movie Website Promotion	22 **Soundtrack Pre-Orders Go Live!**	23 Facebook Live Event. Red Carpet	24 10 Second Mini-Trailer; Share Stills from Red Carpet
25	26 Box Poster - Don's Miss this "Date Night Movie"	27 Viral Marketing Campaign (newspaper)	28 30 Second Review Ad!			

March 2018

Sunday	Monday	Tuesday	Wednesday	Thursday	Friday (Release)	Saturday
				1 Boomerangs; 15 Second Spots; Film Opens Tomorrow!	2 **Opening Night.** Tag a Friend (Picture of Stub) + Promo	3 30 Second Spot - Now Playing	Boomerang Video - Now Playing
4 Buy the Soundtrack; Box Poster	Featurette #3 – BTS	5 Movie Stub Pic Contest	Box Poster - Quote from the movie	6 Box Poster – Festivals	Update Theatrical List – Expanding?	7 Boomerang Gif, Quote From Movie	BIG SCREEN Promo	8 Boomerang (Now Playing)	Interview with Cast	9 Movie Review Quote Box Poster	Week 2?	10 Pre-Order on DVD/Blu-Ray/On Demand
11 Best Indie Movies of 2018 List - News Story	12 Blooper Reel	Behind the Scenes	13 Still playing in BK, promote!	Soundtrack News	14 Poster giveaway	T-shirts	Taking pics at AMC Theaters	15 Times Square ad	Promotion on Instagram	16 Theaters in Brooklyn, Promote!	17 Neo-noir news
18	19 Behind the cinematography video	20 New 30 second ad, promote pre-orders DVD / Blu-Ray	21 Film review box; summary of reviews. Must see!	22 Big poster giveaway; after-party pictures with winners!	23 Katie Vincent Rockwood Show Announce!	24
25	26 Magazine Publicity Publish	27 Awards and accolades! Critics are talking, graphics	28 10 second spot! Pre-orders	Still playing, tickets in BK giveaway			

225

Preparing Publicity Assets

Whether or not your film sells to a film distributor, or if you end up distributing the film on your own, you will need to start building your press assets. These are crucial marketing tools that you'll spread around social media, YouTube, Facebook, Instagram, Twitter, and post on your website. Press assets help create interest and will ultimately be used as an advertising tool that will raise awareness for your film and create buzz.

Publicity assets consist of videos:

- Teaser trailers and 2-minute trailers
- 30-Second Teasers
- Video commercials, interviews, press junkets, and BTS
- Announcement videos (coming soon, festival wins, nominations, etc.)
- Movie clips and promo clips.

And photos, lots and lots of photos:

- Still photos and posters
- BTS photos and on-set photos
- Memes, humorous pictures and viral-worthy content.
- Announcement graphics and GIFs (coming soon, festival wins, nominations, etc.)
- Review graphics (graphics with review quotes)
- Own it graphics
- Competition graphics

Here are some publicity materials we used on *Pickings*. As of right now, your job would be to start creating these types of materials, and it is the purpose of your **Publicity Calendar** to tell you when and how to publish them.

Festival Promos

Review Graphics

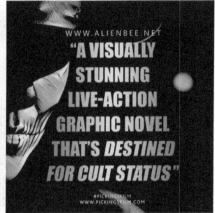

Theatrical Announcements

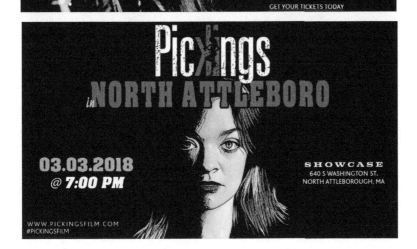

Building a Media List

Once you have a calendar, a step-by-step schedule, and lots of publicity assets, the time has come to build a media list. A media list is basically a big list consisting of names, emails, and contact information of members of the press to whom you plan to solicit your film for reviews, interviews, features, or press release distribution. So how do you get these lists? Well, you can go the expensive route, and sign up to a company like Cision or Meltwater, which will give you access to thousands of reporters' emails, phone numbers, and mailing addresses, but it will cost you around $6,000 to $15,000; or alternatively, you can go the DIY route, which involves you doing your own research and creating a personalized media press kit in an Excel sheet. Which is what we did for *Pickings*. For us, it was about going to a newspaper we wanted to be featured in, let's say, *The Hollywood Reporter*, then tracking down the editor's email address (usually found in the "Contact us" portion of the website), and sending them a well-crafted email with a one-sheet attachment and a link to all of our press coverage. It looks a little something like this:

(SEE NEXT PAGE)

Film Review Email Template

Dear Mr. X,
For your consideration, we would like to submit a review copy of our upcoming feature film, *Pickings*. Our film will be released to theaters on March 2nd, 2018 (limited).

Film Title: Pickings
Genre: Crime Drama
Running Time: 102 Minutes
Budget: $350,000
Cast: Elyse Price, Joel Bernard, Katie Vincent, Emil Ferzola
Written, Directed, Edited and Produced by: Usher Morgan
Original Music by: Katie Vincent
Release Date: March 2nd, 2018

Screener Link: _____
Screener Pass: _____
(If you'd like to receive a DVD or Blu-Ray copy instead, please let me know and we'll ship it to you.)

Trailer: https://www.youtube.com/watch?v=y1f_PS3zA8Y
Press Kit: www.PickingsFilm.com/Press
IMDB: www.imdb.com/title/tt4789822/
Website: www.PickingsFilm.com
Facebook: www.Facebook.com/PickingsFilm
Instagram: www.Instagram.com/PickingsFilm

To download high-res stills, posters, trailers, one-sheets, and for additional press information, visit
www.pickingsfilm.com/press

About *Pickings*: Pickings is a neo-noir crime film that tells the story of Jo Lee Haywood – a single mother and neighborhood bar owner who spent years trying to escape her violent past. But when a local mobster and his gang of thugs come knocking on her door, Jo is forced to embrace her inner demons and confront her deadly history in order to protect her family and property. Still waters run deep in this stylistic, neo-noir crime saga.

Please let me know if you have any questions.

Thank you,

This is how we got reviewed in the *LA Times*, *Hidden Remote*, *The 405*, *Huffington Post*, etc., by just sending out a ton of emails and doing lots of follow-ups. In the first few months building up to the release of the film, we didn't have the budget to hire a real publicist (since those cost $10K a month in New York City), so instead of "hiring" a publicist, we consulted one. I put up an ad on Craigslist looking to hire a publicist as a consultant, meaning we'd bring her in once a week for one hour to check on our progress, give us advice, and help us plan out our press strategy and pay $200 for the privilege. She was kind enough to give us names of reporters that we couldn't find contact information for and pointed us in the direction of a very helpful little website called **PressRush**, which does pretty much what the big guys do, but instead of costing $6,000 a month, it costs $45 a month. PressRush isn't a well-known service, and I hope that changes soon; they have a wealth of media contacts there. It's where we got most of our phone numbers, emails, and press contacts, people that we didn't even think of reaching out to. I recommend you sign up for it and add the names to your Excel sheet.

Creating a Rotten Tomatoes Page

When I did the festival tour for *Pickings*, I met a lot of indie filmmakers who were obsessed with the idea of having a Rotten Tomatoes page for their film. Many people asked me how in the world did I pull that off? Well, first of all, just so you know, you don't need a Rotten Tomatoes page for the *LA Times* or the *New York Times* to write a review about your film. When a magazine or blogger with a Rotten Tomatoes Certified account decides to write a review about your film, they will automatically create a page for you. But in my case, the RT page was there long before anyone contributed to it, and because I know that a lot of filmmakers are obsessed with it, I'll reveal the secret as to how I pulled it off. The secret, regretfully, is not a secret at all; it's just hidden in plain sight, and it's called – metadata. Every time a company (small, big, or independent) makes a movie, produces a song, or publishes a book, they will utilize the services of "metadata companies" whose sole purpose is to distribute the product's data across various platforms and websites, essentially setting the stage for the release of the product, informing websites via feed that a new product is about to be launched. IMDB is one of them, by the way. So, to send your information to a metadata company it will either cost you nothing ($0) or a lot more than nothing (thousands a month, roughly). Companies like Rovi and Neilson, for example, charge movie studios thousands of dollars in return for extensive metadata distribution. They will take a movie trailer and populate it over the web in places to which access seems exclusive (Yahoo Movies, JoBlo, Coming Soon.net, etc.), but there are some metadata companies that will do so for free. They're not that extensive, but they're also free, so who cares? Companies like IMDB and TMDB are "movie databases," and a lot of websites take their movie metadata directly from them, but there are also companies like Internet Video Archives and Baseline Studio Systems (Gracenote) that will help you distribute your metadata for no charge. Internet Video Archives is the easier to use of the group, and they pride themselves in helping filmmakers to promote and distribute their metadata content for free (trailers, clips, 30-second spots, etc.). So, if you visit www.internetvideo-archive.com/promote/ and select "movies," you'll be given access to a submission form where you can upload all of your movie's technical information, as well as upload your film's trailer. Hit the submit button – and voila! One week later, your trailer appears on Rotten Tomatoes, and your film has its very own RT page. You'll have to reach out to Rotten Tomatoes via email later to ask them to add pictures and correct any information that isn't relevant, but that's easy.

> *"What I'm looking for is a self-promoting film; a*
> *movie which immediately gets people's imagination*
> *going - a project which writes its own publicity."*
> *~ Jeremy Thomas*

Festival Publicity

So, you've submitted your film to fifty festivals, and the rejections keep coming in, but out of every few rejections, you get an admission – someone says "yes!" to your movie. They send you that congratulations email. How exciting! Every "yes" and every "no" will go into the Excel sheet you've created, and before long you will have a clear picture of your upcoming festival tour. You now know what festivals you are going to attend, where your film is going to screen, and how your festival tour is going to go, and this is the point where you go out and hire a publicist, or alternatively, if you're doing your own publicity – this is the point where you create a publicity schedule and start prepping your release (even if you land a distributor, they would highly appreciate the preliminary marketing work you've done, and if you don't – you'd have your basics covered). Announcing your nominations and sharing your award wins with the world is important, and that is generally the point where you start to accumulate buzz, when you start building a followership on social media. This is also the point where knowledge and understanding of Photoshop is going to save your life.

Your Release Strategy

As your festival tour is beginning to wind down, you'll need to start working on your release plan. How are you going to release the film? Where are you going to sell it? And how are you going to convince people to actually buy it, watch it, and create demand for it? Unless you've made a movie with a well-known actor, chances are you're going to have to get very creative and overcome some challenges that films with bigger names don't really have to worry about.

Should You Go to Theaters?

Before you decide to schedule a theatrical release for your film, you need to ask yourself whether or not your film should actually be released to theaters. I know it sounds like a defeating question to ask, but the truth of the matter is, "straight to video" exists for a reason. Not every movie can or should perform in theaters, and most low-budget indie films will end up losing money during their theatrical release. However, there are exceptions to that rule, and there are many benefits to actually releasing your film to theaters. The greatest pro to getting your film to play in a real movie theater is the fact that it makes it eligible for reviews in bigger and more noteworthy periodicals: *NY Times, LA Times, Chicago Tribune*, lots of big-name newspapers will review movies that land in their local theaters, even if that film is really small. It's not a guarantee – but your chances of getting reviewed while in theaters are far greater than if you go straight to DVD. Most of the film reviews we received for *Pickings* happened during our theatrical release. The other pro is that, if done correctly, a theatrical release can actually make money, but keep in mind that a theatrical release calls for a great deal of constraint and strategy on your part. You could find yourself at a place where an opportunity presents itself to expand your release to more theaters than it should probably be released to, and the need to appear big can easily cloud your financial wit and end up costing you big time, which brings me to:

Your Theatrical Release Strategy

If you decide to release your film to theaters, you must be able to justify it. For *Pickings*, my reasoning was based entirely on (a) reviews and (b) ego. On the review front, we did great! And because of the ego, I lost money where otherwise I could have profited. My theatrical release strategy was simple – release the movie in New York City because I know I can sell it there. I have a lot of friends who live in New York City, and our cast and crew network alone (friends, family, friends of family, etc.) is huge. I knew that releasing the film to NYC theaters would make money, and I was right – a big chunk of our revenue came from New York City. I also knew that I needed to release the film in Boston because a few of my actors reside there, and I knew that their personal network would generate a great deal of revenue, and I was right – we couldn't get any Boston theaters to play the film, so we ended up doing a "Four-Wall deal" with a local theater; rented the movie theater for a week and let it pay for it myself. That paid off – big time. My actors and their friends/family came through, and I covered the cost of the four-wall. Next, I knew that LA was a great market and that I could get some good reviews in LA – so I released the film in LA as well. We didn't do so well financially there, but the reviews from the *LA Times* and other periodicals more than made up for the cost. That's three locations that strategically we should have released the film in. In reality, my ego got in the way, and when we got picked up by AMC independent, they gave us a choice of *any city* we wanted, and my ego was screaming! Eventually, we ended up releasing the film to fourteen theaters in eight cities: New York, Burbank, Norwalk, Los Angeles, Boston, Chicago, Dallas, and Houston, and for good measure – some indie movie theaters in and around NYC (Brooklyn and Queens). Guess what? Whatever money we made in New York, LA and Boston was lost in Burbank, Norwalk, Chicago, Dallas, and Houston – and for good reason – those cities weren't on my strategy because I didn't have leverage there. I don't know a whole lot of people in Houston, Chicago, or Dallas; we don't have a whole lot of actors living there, and I didn't play in any festivals there. This was my ego, plain and simple, and it got in my way and taught me some important lessons. Going to theaters costs money. Even if the theater is willing to do a shared-revenue deal with you, you still need to pay for marketing, local advertising, DCP printing and shipping, posters, materials, etc. So, if my ego didn't get in the way, *Pickings* would have been more profitable in theaters.

Picking Cities

The process by which you pick the cities where you want your movie to play is quite simple; all you have to do is follow the instructions above. You need to only pick cities where you have *leverage*, meaning places where you know you can bring a large audience of people to watch your film. If you have a vast network in your hometown – that's your leverage. Big movies have a lot of leverage; they have big names, big budgets, and plenty of P&A money to go around. Smaller movies have less leverage, so they count on names and reviews to draw audiences to the theater. Ultra-low-budget indie films with no names attached must rely on reviews and personal networks to attract audiences since their marketing budgets are pretty small. So, only pick the cities where you know you can draw an audience. Then use whatever budget you have to secure theaters, do your marketing and advertising in advance, and start getting people excited about your release in that city using social media and press.

AMC Independent

The process of booking theaters demands patience, dedication, willpower, and the ability to handle rejection because theater programmers have pretty busy schedules, and lots of films to consider on a weekly basis. The truth of the matter is that if you have no names in your film, it means that it's probably not on the top of their list. So, how do you pick the right theater? Do you approach a movie chain? Or reach out to independent theaters? Well, I took the same approach to booking theaters as I did to film festivals, meaning the "big guys" get dibs, so I reach out to them first, and if they say no, then it's open season, and I can approach the smaller theaters. So, my first step was to reach out to the biggest movie chain in NYC, and that's AMC. For those of you who are unaware, AMC has a program called "AMC Independent" where they give indie films a chance to play in their theaters. Every year, AMC Independent releases a handful of films to their local theaters, some under "revenue share," others under "four-walling" contracts. You can submit your film to AMC by visiting their website here: www.amctheatres.com/programs/independent/submit-your-film

Your Marketing Plan

Now, finding AMC and submitting your content is easy, but getting in is a different story. Remember in the early chapter on "planning" when you had to create a marketing plan for the film? Well, this is where you're going to need to send it out to people. AMC Independent, Regal, and Showcase Cinemas all ask that you send them a copy of your marketing plan, detailing how you plan to get people to leave their house and pay money to watch your film in their movie theater. A good marketing plan should be updated and revisited once in a while during pre-production, production, and in post – so by the time you get to a release, it's up-to-date and ready to be sent. So, what are they looking to see in your plan? What information should you give them? Well – here is a sample of our marketing plan for *Pickings*. Some information was removed for privacy, but it'll give you a good picture of what's expected:

"No person who is enthusiastic about his work has anything to fear from life. All the opportunities in the world are waiting to be grasped by people who are in love with what they're doing."
~ Samuel Goldwyn

Pickings

Marketing Plan
COMING MARCH 2ND, 2018

Written, Directed and Produced by
USHER MORGAN

Starring
ELYSE PRICE
JOEL BERNARD
KATIE VINCENT
YARON URBAS
JOE TROMBINO
MICHAEL GENTILE
EMIL FERZOLA

THE FILM

Cast:
* Elyse Price
* Joel Bernard
* Katie Vincent
* Yaron Urbas
* Joe Trombino
* Michael Gentile
* Taso Mikroulis
* Christopher Liam Gentry
* Samantha Zaino
* Michelle Holland
* Lynne Jordan
* Emil Ferzola
* Meghan Corry

PLOT

Jo Lee-Haywood (Elyse Price), a single mother and neighborhood bar owner, has spent years trying to escape her violent past. But when a local mobster and his gang of thugs come knocking on her door, Jo is forced to embrace her inner demons and confront her deadly history in order to protect her family and her property. Still waters run deep in this stylistic, neo-noir crime saga.

Rating: R Rated
Genre: Neo-Noir Crime Film
Cities for Release: New York (Primary), Los Angeles, Austin, Dallas, Boston, Chicago.
Release Date, Theatrical: March 2, 2018
Release Date, VOD/DVD/BLU-RAY: August 3, 2018

Marketing Objectives:

* Theatrical Distribution
* Pre-Distribution & Pre-Sales of DVD, Blu-Ray
* 10,000 organic fans on Facebook Upon Launch
* 100k Trailer Views Upon Launch

Taglines:

* They Just Messed with the Wrong Family
* Still Waters Run Deep

Websites, Social Media, Links:

Official Website: www.pickingsfilm.com
Facebook: www.facebook.com/pickingsfilm
Instagram: www.instagram.com/pickingsfilm
Twitter: www.Twitter.com/pickingsfilm
IMDB: www.imdb.com/title/tt4789822
Wikipedia: https://en.wikipedia.org/wiki/Pickings_(film)
Official Trailer: www.youtube.com/watch?v=y1f_PS3zA8Y
Rotten Tomatoes: www.rottentomatoes.com/m/pickings/

Early Reviews, Press and Media Links:

(List Your Reviews Here)

MARKETING

Budget:

Principal and Post Budget: _____
Marketing Budget: $_____
Breakdown:

January	$XXXXX
Facebook, $X per day, 5,000 Likes	$XXX
YouTube Trailer Ads, $X a day	$XXX

February	$XXXXX
Facebook, $X per day	$XXX
YouTube Ads, $X a day	$XXX
Others	$XXX
March (Release Date)	$XXXXX
Facebook, Twitter & Instagram $X per day	$XXX
YouTube Ads, $X a day	$XXX
Filmmaker Magazine	$XXX
Newspaper Ads	$XXX
NYC Street Campaign (Newspapers, Fliers)	$XXX
Additional Ads & Marketing Budget	$XXX

April / May (Downtime)	$XXXXX
Facebook, $XX per day	$XXX
Additional Advertising	$XXX

Blu-Ray, VOD, DVD Release, P&A Budget: $XXXXXXX

June	$XXXXX
Facebook, $XXX per day	$XXX
In House Publicist	$XXX
Newspaper Ads	$XXX
Graphic Novel Release & Promotion	$XXX

Summary	
Release P&A	$XXX
Downtime P&A	$XXX
VOD P&A	$XXX
Fringes	$XXX
Total P&A Budget	$XXXXXX

Specific Channels:

* Pickings Official Facebook Page
* Official Website
* YouTube Channel
* Library Tales Publishing (Tie in Book Release)
* Cast Facebook Pages
* Partners Facebook Pages
* Original Soundtrack on Amazon/iTunes/etc.

Blogs:

* The Guardian (mix ads and content submission to editorial)
* Featurette submission via Internet Video Archives, Rovi
* Interview requests submissions, press junket clip distribution
* Invites to Red Carpet Premiere

YouTube Promotion:

* Trailer, featurettes and behind the scenes videos – distribution and advertising
* YouTube channel set up, uploading videos under the Pickings Film branded YouTube Page
* Music video distribution (original songs)
* Trailer submissions to popular channels
* Promotion tie-in with Library Tales Publishing for "The Pickings Novel" via YouTube and social media.

Festivals (Submitted):
(List Your Festivals Here)

STRATEGY

- Plane ticket and premiere attendance, meet the cast
- Free copies of the soundtrack (Signed vinyl)
- Pickings Shirts & Hats
- Jo's Spur Shoes
- Free Book Screenplay
- Pickings Guitars
- Live Red Carpet event
- Use Twitter & Instagram to Promote Facebook Marketing
- Advertise Teaser Trailer / Feature Trailer
- Street Art / Floor Chalk Paints
- Book tie-in, social media marketing via LTP (the publisher)

Online Marketing

- Releasing & Distributing Content
(Articles, Videos, News Mentions, Press, Posters)
- Releasing Trailer
- Competition/Giveaway
- Exclusive "Behind the Scenes Content"

Video Marketing

- Post Trailer to YouTube, Vimeo, Facebook, Twitter, Instagram, Archives, Rovi, Baseline, Websites, etc.
- Post Interviews with Cast and the Director
- Use Viral marketing Services

Viral Marketing

- Create a fake newspaper (Port City Times) with interesting headlines, give away at the NYC subway.
- Publish Pickings Novel, 2020.
- Print Posters and Marketing Materials
- Roadshow Promotion, BK theater
- Hire Publicist to Promote VOD release

Advertising

- IMDB Ads
- Facebook and social media
- Print Posters and Hang Around NYC
- TV ads / Radio ads

Cast & Crew Marketing

- Create Poster for Each Character, Post Online
- Ask Cast & Crew to Post with Hashtag #PickingsFilm
- Cast Interviews
(Press, Articles, Q&A's, Press Releases, Video, Radio)
- Produce "Behind the Lens" with Cinematographer

Behind the Scenes Materials

- Release Behind the Scenes B-Roll
- Release Interviews & BTS Footage
- Release Post Production BTS

Revenue Generating

- Release to Theaters
- DVD, Blu-Ray, VOD (Pre-Sales)
- Streaming VOD Services
- Produce and Sell Soundtrack
- Publish Novel (2020)
- Sell to Cable
- Foreign Sales
- Sell to Drive-Ins
- BK Road Show
- Sponsorships

Music, Soundtrack and DVD:

- Release Soundtrack
- Music Video

THE MARKET

Target Audience

- Men and women, 18-45.
- Females (25-45) at 72% Facebook engagements.
- Greater reach in big cities (NYC, LA, Dallas)
- Crime Thriller Fans / Sin City Fans / Kill Bill / Tarantino
- Female Character Driven Film Fans
- Female Heroes Fans

Movie Comparisons

- Sin City
- Kill Bill
- Blue Ruin
- The Drop
- John Wick
- Out of the Furnace

Why Should Audiences Watch the Film?

- Positive Reviews (LA Times)
- Publicity
- Personal Network of Actors, Friends and Family
- 19,000 Facebook fans
- This Isn't Your Average Indie
- Music Videos
(The Movie has an AMAZING Soundtrack)
- Parody Ads and Clever Marketing (Newspaper)

# # #

Your marketing plan is your *guidebook*, and it should be written with the particulars of your film in mind.

Adding Indie Theaters to Your Theatrical Run

There are many benefits to working with small, independent movie theaters. For one, your cut of the profits is going to be higher, and your release schedule could be a lot longer. AMC and other chains will either give you a "no commitment deal" (meaning they can't promise the film will be in theaters for more than a couple of days), or a "one week minimum" deal. But even if you score a "one week minimum" deal, your film could still get pulled at the end of the week, effectively ending your theatrical release without notice. This is why it's important to program your film with smaller, indie theaters. Indie theaters will give you more wiggle room, workarounds are faster, and more often than not, they'd be willing to share your trailer (as well as your other marketing materials) on their social media platforms. Big chains will give you in-theater marketing but won't really push your film on social media unless it features a recognizable name. With indie theaters, especially small, local theaters, you have a partner who is as invested in your theatrical run as you are. They may be small, but they count for a lot. So, how do you pitch to indie theaters? The same way you pitch to everyone else — send emails, make phone calls, follow up, follow up, follow up.

MPAA Ratings – Do You Need It?

I was always under the assumption that I couldn't release my film to theaters unless it had an official MPAA rating. In my mind, that green/red rating card presented in trailer lead-ins was a mandatory piece of the puzzle. If I was going to bring my movie into theaters, I had to get it approved by the Motion Picture Association of America. However, it wasn't until I started handling the distribution of my film that I learned that movie theaters don't really care about your MPAA rating (or the lack thereof). Especially when you're in the business of making low budget indie films. From what I gather, MPAA doesn't really apply to low-budget films because their market is pretty limited. However, it's hard for me to say what the MPAA rating gave me because I had it, so I didn't get approached by anyone saying, "Sorry, we can't do X because you don't have a rating."

My rule of thumb concerning MPAA has changed to: "If you're making a movie for the masses, get an MPAA rating. But if you're making a low-budget, neo-noir indie film with no names and no plans to gross $20m in the box office, don't bother. Save the $3,000 and spend it elsewhere."

Pickings – Our Viral Marketing Campaign

How do you push people who are walking down the street into the theater where your movie is playing? What do you do to convince people who don't know anything about your film to pay $10 for a movie ticket? Well, I can't tell you *how* to think creatively, but I can tell you what we did on our end when the time came to promote our film.

> 1) Fake newspaper. One of the things we did was to manufacture a fake newspaper and give it away at the entrance to the NYC subway. The fake paper served as an ad in disguise for the movie. It was filled with humorous articles about certain events that transpired in our movie world as well as ads for fictional products like Cowboy Jo and the fictional *Pickings* bar. Interns would scream, "Mafia boss gone missing!" and hand out newspapers with the same title on the cover and a picture of the actor playing the lead mobster in the film. The stories all tie-in with the film's plot without giving anything away, and as you read the newspaper, you'd soon realize what was going on. On the very last page, there was a list of theaters playing the movie in the city, and on the other side of the spread, a huge movie ad for Subway commuters to see. Lots of people came into our Times Square location holding copies of that newspaper. It was as guerilla marketing as guerilla marketing gets.

2) Setting up a table at AMC Times Square. We had a big table set up on the first floor of AMC Times Square. People who walked through the door got a chance to enter a competition, win free tickets, and some really cool merchandise. AMC Times Square was one of the theaters where our movie was most popular because it's one of the biggest movie theaters in the country, and it is at the heart of New York City, so all of our friends, family members, and acquaintances came to see the movie there.

3) Flyer giveaway. Since our film was also playing in Brooklyn, we had to walk around and give people flyers with information about the film, giving away free T-shirts, posters, guitar picks, and koozies.

4) Live from the Red Carpet. The good folks at AMC were kind enough to allow us to hold a red carpet premiere at the prestigious AMC Loews Lincoln Square 13 in the heart of New York City. It did come at a cost, but it didn't cost nearly as much as I thought it would. Giving us access to AMC Lincoln Square resulted in an "unexpected" viral marketing campaign. The amount of people walking in and out of that theater on a daily basis is gargantuan, and AMC gave us the opportunity to hold our red carpet premiere there. And not only that, they decorated the space with posters, signs, and marketing materials a few days before the event and kept them up for an *entire week*. If we wanted to run an ad on a bus stop in Lincoln Center, that would have cost more than twice the cost of our red carpet premiere. So, by giving us access to that theater and allowing us to hold a proper film release, *Pickings* became "legit." All of a sudden, press contacts who wouldn't return our calls earlier were now agreeing to come by and watch the film, our social media presence exploded, and Knocktournal Mag-

azine agreed to sponsor the red carpet event. Combined with our AMC release, the red carpet event gave us a much-needed publicity boost and added the film to a lot of people's watch list, especially New Yorkers who were walking by the theater during that seven-day period. People who were at the theater on the day of the event caught glimpses of our posters and engaged with our marketing materials. We saw people taking pictures of us on the red carpet from the escalators and checking out our posters – all because it looked like a big event. It looked like something was happening, and people thought it was cool.

Last Thoughts on AMC Independent

In the 80s and 90s Kodak was giving away free film to film students who were attending classes in various universities across the country. Four years later, when the time came for those former students to buy film, they bought... Kodak! That was a huge corporation buying the loyalty of its future clients while they were still in training. I am of the personal belief that AMC is heading in a similar direction. I was surprised at how accommodating a big corporation like AMC was when the time came to release our film, and this is the only justification in my mind – *they're treating us well so that we come back for more.* Ever since the popularization of "straight to streaming" films, movie theaters have been working to keep filmmakers loyal to the movie theater experience, and I think that AMC Independent had found the right way to go about it. When loyal filmmakers release their films, they'll hold their red carpet premieres at AMC theaters, they'll do Q&A's, they'll pop in to surprise fans and view the theater as an equal partner. I have become an *advocate* for AMC and AMC Independent. I became convinced that the movie theater experience should be expanded to include more low-budget indie films. Filmmakers have a responsibility to keep the art alive by making their films available to movie-goers in theaters.

DCP Prints

When a movie goes to print these days, it goes to print on a DCP, which stands for Digital Cinema Package. DCPs are printed on specialized hard drives called CRU Data Ports, and all a projectionist has to do is take the drive, insert it into their system, and it's ready to be ingested and tested for the screen. If you're not too worried about color replication (making sure that the movie looks exactly the same on screen as it does on your computer), then you can probably go the cheaper route and use Adobe Premiere to export your film to a DCP format, then send it to a company that can manufacture it and ship it out to theaters. If you are familiar with the process of creating professional DCPs, then, by all means, go for it. I wasn't and didn't really have the time to learn or experiment, so I ended up hiring a company to create my DCPs and send them to print. The name of the company was "Digital Cinema United." They're a Los Angeles-based firm that went above and beyond (and I'm not getting paid to say this) to accommodate us in every way. It's their job to make sure that the theaters get their hard drives on time. (Most movie theaters will ask for the drive a week in advance of the release). I didn't want to trust my own luck in printing and shipping CRUs to theaters and risk making a mistake, so I outsourced it to Digital Cinema United. They didn't disappoint.

Introduce Yourself to the Theater Manager

When a movie theater agrees to showcase your film, you will be responsible for sending over the appropriate marketing materials so that the theater can put your film up on display. Movie posters, cutouts, and banners are always welcome, but sometimes you have to visit the theater to make sure that everything is up as promised. Not that theaters will lie about their intentions to display your marketing materials, but sometimes employees get forgetful and you need to pop in, introduce yourself, and ask them to put your stuff on display. After our movie got accepted into AMC and we were asked to send materials to Times Square, I took the liberty of going down there and meeting the manager in person. I introduced myself, gave him a card, and spent a few minutes talking about my movie. That conversation turned *fun*, real quick. The guy was a movie buff, and we ended up spending half an hour discussing the movie and upcoming releases. He gave me a tour of the theater and promised to put my marketing materials on display. Lo and behold – a few days later, I popped into the theater and there was my banner, the size of a bus, hanging off the AMC rails in a theater I've been to many, many times. Our artwork was all over the place, and because I took the time to introduce myself, the manager went above and beyond to accommodate us.

Katie Vincent and Julia Melim, live from the Red Carpet

Steal Your Artwork, Quickly!

The day after a movie's last screening, crew members will take down its marketing materials and place them inside the theater's marketing room. And if you've ever been inside an AMC marketing room, you know that they are a cinema landfill. Packed to the brim with posters, cutouts and merch, collected over the course of the year from about 10,000 different films.

So, if your artwork lands in that room, it will most likely be lost in the shuffle and thrown away. Almost every single theater from which we did not retrieve our marketing materials lost our artwork, which ended up costing us a pretty penny. Every movie theater has its own version of a marketing room, and that's the place where old artwork goes to die. So if you want to save your artwork, I suggest you visit the theater on the film's last running day and ask the manager to put your materials aside. Otherwise, they'll be lost forever.

Marketing Materials, The Ultimate Checklist

Whether your film gets released to theaters or goes straight to VOD, you (as the film's distributor) are expected to produce and release a panoply of attractive marketing materials. These are designed to sell your movie to the public, they're an inevitable part of your distribution strategy. To make this easy for you, I'm going to divide these marketing materials into four key categories:

(1) Pre-release Materials. Artwork produced in the weeks/months leading up to the film's release. Up to thirty days before the film's release date. These include the movie's 1:30 minute teaser trailer, the film's official trailer, graphics, and social media cards.

(2) Release Materials. Artwork produced and released during the sixty-day launch period. Thirty days *before* and thirty days *after* the film is released. These include videos, *lots* of videos, 30-second ads, review spots, TV spots, and social media artwork, reviews, list of theaters, memes, movie stills, behind the scenes, etc.

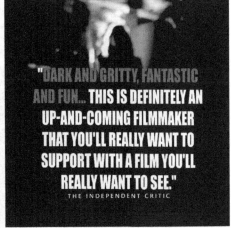

(3) Prints. Artwork produced specifically for print during a film's theatrical release, its premiere and red carpet event, the festival tour, and post release.

(4) Post-Release Materials. Artwork produced after the film's theatrical release has ended. This consists mainly of ads, featurettes, Blu-Ray promotional videos, and graphics intended to sell the film on iTunes, DVD, VOD, Blu-Ray, etc.

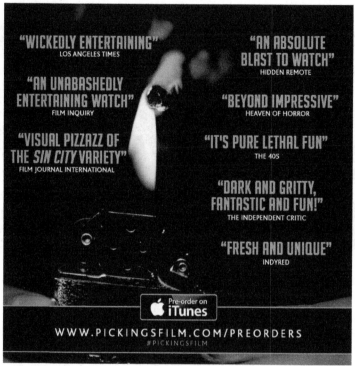

Reviews

One of the most important functions of your very first feature film (aside from education, that is) is to establish yourself as a "filmmaker to watch." You do that by getting your film reviewed in the media. Reviews lead to exposure, which leads to sales, which lead to a "public opinion" of yourself as an artist and the quality of your work. Now, regardless of what your *personal* thoughts are on the matter of film critics, the fact of the matter is that critics (love them or hate them) do serve a very important purpose. Film critics can make or break a filmmaker's career, they can create buzz around a movie or completely destroy it. Really good criticism can last for years, and even ages. Celebrated films will be watched 100 years after the passing of the people who made them because if the overall consensus is that you've made a masterpiece – then you've made a masterpiece. The *perception* of your work is what ultimately counts. Box office numbers are great, but they never last. What truly lasts a lifetime is the public's opinion about a particular film. This is why films win Oscars, get on the AFI Top 100 list, and stay in the spotlight long after their theatrical run has ended.

I get why some filmmakers hate critics, and I get why others love them. When they're nice to you, you love them, and when they're mean to you, you hate them. But my view on movie critics and reviews, in general, is different than most. I do my best to *learn* from them. When someone writes a bad review on a film that I am very happy with, I won't pay too much attention to it, because I am *personally happy* with the result I achieved. I have succeeded (in my mind) in producing the work of art I aspired to. However, when I am not satisfied, when I am critical of myself and the quality of my own work, then I'll read them all, and try not to take them too personally.

My early experiences with reviews (both from critics and audiences) were quite painful. For starters, after making my first short film, *Prego*, I received some really positive reviews in person, negative reviews online, and positive reviews in the media. It went from positive to negative to positive, and then it shifted, and the online community embraced it. It went viral and amassed over a million views on YouTube, but the results were mixed – some people hated it, some people loved it, and despite all the awards it won, there were plenty of comedy festivals that passed on it, and lots of people who were irritated by the film's message. It was the kind of movie that people either really loved or really hated; in other words – *mixed*. In my mind, *Prego* wasn't a very good film because *I* wasn't 100% happy with it, but whenever I watched it with audiences, and people were laughing out loud, I began to question my own taste, and the thought, "maybe it's not that bad" began to sink into my subconscious. Only now, almost five years after making it, can I watch it in enjoyment without being overwhelmed by self-criticism or self-doubt. CUT TO two years later and my first feature film, *Pickings*, is released to theaters. One of the first reviews to hit the web came from *Hidden Remote*, overall positive in tone, but critical of my handling of the film's characters. Next to follow were several positive reviews and a *really* positive review from the *LA Times* – you can probably guess my state of mind at that point in time. As a person who didn't like the final product, I was getting positive reinforcement from people who were doing this for a living. My confidence rose, and my feelings about the film began to shift; then came the *Village Voice* review – it was horrible. I suddenly found myself in the exact same position as *Prego*. I was marketing a movie that was getting some really mixed reviews. People either really loved it or really hated it, not a lot was in between.

It was July of 2018, and the film was playing at the Long Island International Film Festival, where it was nominated for Best Feature Film and Best Director. We did the screening, the red carpet, and the Q&A for the film, and it was there that I had an interesting conversation with an experienced film director. The man gave me a powerful piece of advice that I doubt I'll ever forget. "The only critic you need to listen to is yourself. If you're unhappy with your film, strive to improve; if you're happy with it then you need to find the people who love it because those are the people who love your taste, then make your next movie for them." That is a great way of looking at film reviews as a whole. The purpose of critics is to dissect and analyze your movie, to present its flaws as well as its strengths to their reading audiences. If you read their reviews and agree with what they have to say, that means you share the same taste, that means you need to adapt and take steps to assure that the same won't repeat on your next film. If you disagree with your critics, then there is no lesson for you to learn. Don't try and change your method just to please a critic, that's a recipe for disaster. Instead, *find your audience* and keep making the movies you want to make – the kind of stuff you're *happy* with.

Taking Advantage of Reviews

So, you have some good reviews, you have some bad reviews. The big question is – how do you use them to market and sell your film? How do you use these reviews to get an agent or a manager? How do you strike while the iron is hot and take advantage of the buzz around your film? The answer comes back to marketing. Marketing *yourself* and marketing your film:

1) Integrate quotes into social media assets, such as TV spots, 30-second spots, posters, banners, etc.
2) Add a quote to your personal biography.
3) Craft an email to agents', managers' and producers' reps seeking representation, include reviews.
4) Add a favorite quote to your resume and to your personal email signature.
5) Link reviews when pitching your film to film festivals.
6) Send recent reviews to reporters, local magazines, and newspapers where you want to be interviewed.
7) If you're working with a publicist, they can use these reviews to get you booked on radio and TV.
8) Send emails to potential foreign sales agents, distributors, and when pitching to TV and SVOD.

"When you make the kind of movies I make, you get weird letters from people." ~ David Fincher

Foreign Sales

If you sell your film to any distributor, that distributor is most like-ly working with a long list of foreign sales agents, and if you're the one distributing your film, then it is *your* responsibility to sign with one. Sales agents are tasked with selling territorial rights to your film as well as exploiting broadcast, SVOD (Subscription VOD), and TV VOD nationally. They are a terrific source of rev-enue that can sometimes be your *biggest* source of revenue, espe-cially for those of us working in genre film. Our approach to secur-ing a foreign sales agent followed the same route as our approach to securing film reviews and contacting film critics. We created an Excel file, Googled "Film Foreign Sales Agents," and called every single person on that list. We came across several companies that showed interest in the film; we received a few contracts and nego-tiated terms with all of them. We ended up signing a contract with a Canadian-based foreign sales agent, and I'm happy to say that they already sold the rights to a couple of territories.

The one thing I would say about sales agents is this: it's their job to sell your film, nationally and internationally, and, therefore, they *must* be aware of your marketing and distribution strategy. It is your responsibility to consistently keep up and follow up with their efforts. It is your job to find out who they're pitching your film to and what their pitch plan is, because any miscommunica-tion in that department can lead to you getting in each other's way. So, make sure you get a clear idea of their timeline, who they're speaking to, who said yes, and who said no to your film. That way, you can coordinate the release of your film into new territories without stepping on each other's toes. Another thing to keep in mind is that if your agent is trying to pitch your film to Netflix, that means you cannot have your film out on iTunes, Amazon, and other VOD services until Netflix gives you the "go ahead," which is why agents pitch to Netflix during the film's theatrical release. That should be your first pitch. The same rule applies to other SVOD services. If your film is available on Amazon Prime (which is free of charge), TV stations and other buyers won't be able to buy it;

therefore, you must plan out your release to each platform in accordance with your sales agent, so you don't accidentally burn any bridges prematurely.

Aggregators

There are several companies out there that serve as VOD aggregators, meaning it's their job to encode your film and make sure it complies with the technical requirements for various platforms such as iTunes, YouTube Movies, Xbox, etc. They then submit your film to these platforms on your behalf, giving you 100% of the revenue generated. Quiver Digital is one of the leaders in VOD distribution (www.quiverdigital.com). A package deal could cost you around $3K if you haggle (including iTunes, Google, YouTube, Xbox, PlayStation, etc.), but you'll have to pay extra for TV, Netflix, and Hulu pitches.

If you are short on cash and don't have the budget to pay the entire sum to an aggregator, I recommend choosing only one channel (either Google Play or iTunes), or going the Amazon route (which is free of charge) and then slowly expanding into other channels.

> *"Well, do anything. If you do something right, we'll use it, and if you do something wrong, we'll fix it, but do something and do it now."*
> ~ Louis B. Mayer

Distributing Your Film on Amazon

One of the best places to promote, market, and distribute your film is on Amazon. This is partially because of the vast array of tools that Amazon offers its filmmakers, and how easy it is for anyone to access them without a dollar in out of pocket cost. Whether you are releasing your film theatrically, going straight to VOD, or if you're dead broke and can't afford any of the other distribution channels, releasing your film on Amazon is a must (it's also free).

When I started writing this book in mid-2018, I was distributing my film to Amazon VOD via the **Amazon Video Central** Service (www.videocentral.amazon.com), while our Blu-Ray and DVDs were physically printed in New York City and shipped to Amazon via their **Amazon Advantage Program** (advantage.amazon.com). However, by the time this chapter was written, Amazon had unveiled a new program called **Amazon Media On Demand**, which allows you to print and sell your DVDs, Blu-Rays, soundtracks and audiobooks on Amazon without having to print, ship, and keep inventory. In addition, Amazon provides a powerful service called AMS (Amazon Marketing Services), which allows you to advertise and market your films on the Amazon website (advertising.amazon.com). This marketing platform is very effective, it shows you exactly how much money you spent on your ads and how many products you sold in return. It's one of the few ROI-driven ad services on the internet. You can run campaigns for as little as $5 or $10 a day and get your movie sold on the biggest platform on planet earth. In addition to Amazon, there are a few other platforms that allow you to sell your film directly to consumers without having to pay anything upfront. These platforms are listed on the checklist at the end of this chapter.

DVD & Blu-Ray

When the time came to create our DVD and Blu-Ray packages, we opted to use Adobe Encore. Although it is no longer in circulation, you can actually download it for free (if you're an Adobe

Cloud subscriber) from the Adobe website. The software allows you to create menus in Photoshop, and if you've taken my advice and gained some experience in Photoshop, this is where it pays off, *big time*! Designing my own menus gave me a lot of freedom, and it made both the Blu-Ray and DVD appear sleek and professional. A quick tutorial on YouTube, thirty minutes of training, and you know everything you need to know about that software. It is very easy to use. My DVDs are being distributed via Amazon Media On-Demand @ manufacturing.amazon.com and Amazon Advantage.

The Soundtrack

The ultimate goal of any filmmaker is to create a piece of art that lasts, something that stays inside your viewer's head for a while, possibly long after the credits crawled and the screen turned black. One great way of accomplishing that goal (aside from making a masterpiece) is by selling your film's original music (whether it's song or score) to the good folks who watched and hopefully enjoyed your film. In the case of *Pickings*, I took the opportunity to partner with the insanely talented Katie Vincent (who starred in my previous film, *Prego*), and together we created an amazing soundtrack for the film. Three of the songs were performed by the actors on camera. Another three were written and performed by Katie herself, who played the oldest daughter Scarlet in the film. Another song was performed by Bill Turner, who did such a good job that we ended up using his live recording on set as opposed to the studio-recorded version. In total, the soundtrack has eight tracks, four original songs, three bonus tracks, and one public domain song, performed by Turner. I honestly don't think there are any negatives to creating and selling an original soundtrack. In fact, with services such as DistroKid and Tunecore, anybody can upload and sell their music online with ease and for a very minimal cost. Producing a music video and distributing it on YouTube, incorporating the music in the trailer, and marketing two products (as opposed to one) will give birth to new sources of revenue.

Submitting your music to awards and sending it to blogs, radio stations, and music reviewers gives you more *exposure*, which, in turn, helps you sell your music, which helps you sell your film; it's vertical integration at its finest and a very smart business move. In the case of *Pickings*, we also created a graphic novel of the film, which is scheduled for release in 2020.

DIY International Distribution

Let's say you want to release your film in Japan, but you don't have a sales agent, how do you go about that? Well, you basically follow the same approach to releasing a film in the United States.

Step one – you dub it or subtitle it (that's your cost, you have to spend the money, there's no way around it). You could partner with a Japanese producer or a translator or just hire a company to handle the dubbing for you.

Step two – you submit it to Japanese film festivals, you take your American marketing materials (trailer, posters, key art, etc.) and translate them to Japanese (you can use Google Translate or hire someone off Craigslist or Fiverr).

Step three – you schedule a release date on Japanese streaming websites and VOD websites (such as Amazon Japan Prime @ videocentral.amazon.co.jp); you contact your film aggregator and create a new project in Japanese and submit it to iTunes Japan; Google Play and others.

Step four - Create a presence online (in Japanese), upload a Trailer to YouTube with your movie's name in Japanese (again, use Google Translator), upload materials to social media and promote the page. Spending $5 a day on Facebook Ads can bring about a great deal of exposure (especially in foreign markets where social media advertising is underpriced).

In short, if a Japanese version of your film exists, then you can release your film in Japan. Same goes for any other nation. You just
have to "do it yourself!"

*"I think cinema, movies, and magic have always
been closely associated. The very earliest people
who made film were magicians."*
~ *Francis Ford Coppola*

Distribution Checklist

So, as we're getting ready to wrap this final chapter, I wanted to take this opportunity to present to you the various platforms by which you can market, distribute, and sell your film, as well as the cost associated with each platform. There are pros and cons to each, and I will detail them here:

Amazon Advantage
advantage.amazon.com
Allows you to sell your film in various physical formats on Amazon.com as well as sign up for Amazon Vine (an Amazon network of reviewers). Advantage allows you to customize your film page on Amazon and be in the running for Amazon's Black Friday deals.

Amazon Prime Video Direct.
videocentral.amazon.com
Allows you to sell your feature (as well as short films and web series) on Amazon on-demand and Amazon Prime. You can sell in the US, the UK, as well as Japan and Germany. Make sure you keep the "Prime" option unchecked until you have exhausted all of your other distribution channels. Remember that TV and foreign sales agents won't take your film if it's available for free on Amazon Prime or any other streaming service.

Amazon Advertising
ams.amazon.com
Allows you to advertise your film on the Amazon website and monitor your ROI. For as little as $5 per day, you can advertise your film on Amazon and see for yourself whether the ad is worth the investment or not. Amazon tells you how many people who clicked your ad went on to buy your film, which makes it easier to monitor.

Amazon Media on Demand
manufacturing.amazon.com
Allows you to print and sell DVDs, Blu-Rays, audiobooks, and soundtracks via Amazon on-demand, which means you don't have to keep stock or handle shipments like you would with Amazon Advantage. Keep in mind that Amazon does not offer any UPC codes (barcodes), which you'll need to print on the back of your product. You can buy these fairly cheaply (at $5 per barcode) online.

Amazon Seller Account
sellercentral.amazon.com
The only benefit to creating an Amazon Seller Account in my opinion is so that you can make use of Amazon's pre-order function. Once you create a new listing, you can set-up a release date and select the "handle by Amazon" option, then all you have to do is ship a box of DVDs/Blu-Rays to Amazon, and they'll put your film up for pre-orders.

Walmart Marketplace
marketplace.walmart.com
Allows you to sell your DVD/Blu-Rays on the Walmart website. It's a sizable source of revenue. Requires account approval, which could take a few weeks.

Quiver Digital
www.quiverdigital.com
Allows you to sell your film on iTunes, Google Play (YouTube Movies), Vudu, xBox, Playstation Network, Steam, Hulu, TubiTV, Netflix, and some TV SVOD networks. You're paying anywhere from $200–350 per platform, so keep in mind – it adds up.

Doco Digital
www.docodigital.com/
Specializes in Netflix aggregation. Their parent company ODMedia is listed on the Netflix Studios Preferred Fulfillment Partner List.

Reelhouse
www.reelhouse.org
Allows you to upload and sell your films inside a social community of fellow filmmakers.

Vimeo on-Demand
vimeo.com/ondemand
Allows you to sell your films on the Vimeo platform. It's free of charge and not a bad source of revenue. Especially useful for selling digital pre-orders if you can't afford the other channels.

IndieFlix – A Streaming Service
www.indieflix.com
You could submit your film to stream on IndieFlix. They pay 50% of their subscription revenue which means that much like Amazon Prime and other SVOD services, you get paid every time someone watches your film on their service.

Fandor
www.fandor.com
Another streaming service where you can submit your film to play alongside hundreds of other indie films.

IndiePix Films
www.indiepixfilms.com
A website that streams award-winning indie films. They mainly focus on documentaries.

Speck
moviesonspeck.com
Speck sells movies to TV platforms and SVOD services such as Hulu and Netflix. They work on a non-exclusive basis and pay 100% of the revenue to the filmmaker. Super cheap submission fee ($50).

Mediabank.TV
Allows you to exploit foreign rights and TV rights.

RightsTrade
www.rightstrade.com
A global marketplace for exploiting TV broadcast and foreign rights for features and shorts. Costs around $200 per month.

eBay
You can sell your movie posters, DVDs, Blu-Ray, and merchandise on eBay. Printing merchandised items such as pens, mouse pads, koozies, notebooks, and USB sticks with your film's name, website and graphics is a great way to get your movie's brand out into the world-wide-web.

Baker & Taylor
www.baker-taylor.com/supplier_details.cfm
A DVD/Blu-Ray wholesale company. You'll need to submit a vendor application and keep stock of your DVD/Blu-Ray, but this could be a great source of revenue for you. Requires some understanding of wholesale/retail distribution.

Alliance Entertainment
www.aent.com/vendor
A Blu-Ray/DVD distribution company.

Trailer Distribution Platforms:

- YouTube
- Vimeo
- IMDB
(contact them to request a free Scorecard account)
- Video Detective (Rotten Tomatoes, etc.)
www.videodetective.com (scroll to Submit Content)
- Trailer Addict
www.traileraddict.com/add-your-film

DCP Makers & Distributors

Companies that make copies of your film's DCP and ship them out to theaters/festivals in time for your screening.

- Digital Cinema United
- Make DCP
- Simple DCP
- Neptune DCP
- Deluxe (1-800-423-2277)

Metadata Distribution

When the time has come to distribute your film, you want to make sure that people can find it. The first obvious choice is IMDB; however, keep in mind that AMC, Regal, and other theaters get their metadata from a company called TMDB (themoviedb.org).

Honorable Mentions

Muso
www.muso.com
Protects your film and takes down illegal copies from the web.

Fiverr
www.Fiverr.com
For $5, you can hire artists, illustrators, bloggers, and film reviewers.

Taboola
www.taboola.com
Video content advertising, ideal for trailers, 30-second spots and TV ads.

Stage 32
www.stage32.com
A community of online filmmakers, full of meetups, opportunities, and contests.

> *"I consider myself a student of cinema. It's almost like I am going for my professorship in cinema, and the day I die is the day I graduate. It is a lifelong study."* ~ Quentin Tarantino

Just Do It

At the end of the day, if you really want to be a filmmaker, then you have no other choice but to go out there and make some films. Sit your butt down and write, shoot, edit, release, and repeat. Adapt the filmmaker's mindset and keep yourself immersed in the art and craft of filmmaking. Listen to blogs, read books, spend time polishing and improving your skill, and do your best to learn about the entrepreneurial side of filmmaking. You don't need a million dollars, you don't need a fancy camera, you just need a will and a desire strong enough to crush excuses into powder and move you along the path towards your goal. Time is fleeting, and the world is not going to wait around for you to get your act together. In other words, be a filmmaker!

Final Words

There is always more you can do to market your film, there are always more people you can call, more ways to promote your work, more websites to submit it to, more territories to sell it to, more ways to keep your film alive and give people the opportunity to watch and talk about you and your craft. But eventually, the day will come when your film will have to be put aside to make room for the next one. The day will come when you have to sit down and reflect upon the things you've done right, and think about the things you've done wrong, and then begin to prepare yourself for the following challenge. Some people, those of us who call ourselves "hustlers," already have our next film in mind. Others need some time off, some time to chill, reflect, and prepare their bodies and souls before embarking on their next adventure.

Making movies is a *privilege* and a *responsibility*, and at the end of the day, the life of a filmmaker is a life filled with fun, excitement, anxiety, exhaustion, wonder, love, stress, and weirdness, lots and lots of weirdness. You need a really thick skin to make it in this game. But if you endure, if you work *really hard*, if you take the time to learn and improve, and never ever give up, you will succeed. There is just no way around it, *those who don't quit can't fail.* And in this creative world, frustration can often push you off the edge. Creative difficulties, financial challenges, bad reviews, on-set drama, miscommunications – all of that is more than tolerable when you consider the fact that you get to make dreams for a living. You get to create a legacy for yourself, and you are actively spending your time and money on bringing your dream to life. How many people can say that about themselves?

So when you find yourself on a Saturday night inside a dimly lit room with a bucket of popcorn and an oversized cup of soda in your lap, and those previews kick in, and your own movie trailer is among them, and you listen to people whisper with excitement, that smile on your face will be so fucking worth it. I can't even begin to express to you how much fun that's going to be for you. The experience of walking down the street to a movie theater you've been to a million times, only to see your poster under that banner is surreal, to say the least. To be on that red carpet, to share your vision with the world for the price of an admission ticket, to sit among them in the theater and watch them *laugh* when they're supposed to, *cry* when they're supposed to, and *feel* when they're supposed to – that experience will reinforce within you the real reason for *why* you've decided to make movies in the first place. It will give you so much energy and vigor that it will be imprinted in your DNA. It will follow you to your next production meeting, it will reflect itself in confidence, knowledge, experience, and a perpetual sense of excitement. You'll be one of the few who get to make dreams and tell stories for a living, and you get to do it *independently*.

Mere weeks after my first feature film was released to theaters, I began sifting through my notes and felt a sense of urgency, a flash of inspiration that "forced" me to take the time and write this book. I set out to produce a filmmaking guide that would contain within it all the information I wish I had at my disposal when I was first getting started. And I sincerely hope that you found some value in this book. I hope you found some good ideas, resources, and inspiration. I hope it opened your eyes and gave you an insight into the filmmaking process. I hope you take some of my own experiences to heart and use the guidelines I presented to maximize your potential and embrace the mindset of an independent filmmaker. And I *really* hope that in a few years, you'll take the time to write your own *Lessons from the Set* and pass them along to other filmmakers like yourself who share the same dreams and ambitions as you. Finally, I hope this book gave you the tools you need to take your ideas and turn them into something real, and I can't wait to watch you take your dreams and put them on the screen.

Wishing you the best of luck!

Usher Morgan
Writer, Director, Producer
WWW.USHERMORGAN.COM
INSTAGRAM.COM/USHERMORGAN